Gilded S

GILDED SUFFRAGISTS

The
NEW YORK SOCIALITES
Who Fought for
WOMEN'S RIGHT TO VOTE

Johanna Neuman

WASHINGTON MEWS BOOKS
An Imprint of
NEW YORK UNIVERSITY PRESS
New York

WASHINGTON MEWS BOOKS

An imprint of

NEW YORK UNIVERSITY PRESS

New York

www.nyupress.org

First published in paperback in 2019

References to Internet websites (URLs) were accurate at the time of writing.
Neither the author nor New York University Press is responsible for URLs
that may have expired or changed since the manuscript was prepared.

ISBN: 978-1-4798-3706-9 (hb)

ISBN: 978-1-4798-0662-1 (pb)

For Library of Congress Cataloging-in-Publication data,
please contact the Library of Congress.

New York University Press books are printed on acid-free paper, and their binding
materials are chosen for strength and durability. We strive to use environmentally
responsible suppliers and materials to the greatest extent
possible in publishing our books.

Manufactured in the United States of America

10 9 8 7 6 5 4 3 2 1

Also available as an ebook

To the memory of
EVELYN *and* SEYMOUR NEUMAN,
who nurtured the child

To
HILDIE NEUMAN LYDDAN *and* WILLIAM C. LYDDAN,
who nurtured the idea

And to
JEFFREY GLAZER,
who nurtures the woman

Contents

The illustrations appear as a group following page 87.

INTRODUCTION

I N every successful movement for social change there is a moment
when the generations cross paths, when an idea once deemed radical loses its toxins, now familiar rather than frightful, assumed rather
than threatening. In the campaign by women to win the right to vote in
America, that moment came in 1908, when an unlikely band of wealthy
socialites better known for the excesses of their Fifth Avenue balls and
the Beaux Arts luxury of their Newport mansions helped reignite a
claim for citizenship. Not since Elizabeth Cady Stanton first advocated
a woman's right to vote at the 1848 Woman's Rights Convention at Seneca Falls had the debate over the female franchise so energized the
national political landscape. Leveraging their social standing for political gain, these gilded suffragists normalized the idea that women of all
stripes—not just those of the intellectual circle who had originated the
idea—wanted the vote. No one was more astonished than the newspaper
reporters who covered them. It was as if, said one scribe, their infusion
of celebrity had taken the campaign from dowdy to fashionable.[1]

At a time when the newspaper industry was at its zenith—New York
at the turn of the century boasted twenty-nine daily papers obsessed
with the doings of society[2] and a multilingual immigrant press debat-

ing the terms of American citizenship—these women were its media darlings, chronicled for every aspect of their fashion, décor, and travel. When they embraced suffrage, they became the first celebrities to endorse a political cause in the twentieth century. Intent on demonstrating that "it is not only the masculine type of woman who wants the ballot,"[3] they dressed in the latest fashions from Paris as they lobbied legislators and addressed lunchtime crowds with press hordes following close on their high heels. Ignoring the sarcasm of anti-suffragists who accused them of "flirtation . . . on a gigantic scale,"[4] these fashion-plated activists became players in the vibrant media landscape, no doubt reassuring men that they could vote for suffrage without losing their masculinity and calming women who feared that the ballot would make them unwomanly. Joining one of the broadest coalitions for social change in U.S. history, one that combined under its tent the poorest immigrant with the wealthiest socialite, the angry radical and the mild-mannered progressive, they gave the movement a sense of moment.

In their motives, they were hardly monolithic. Their inspiration ran the gamut from progressive ideals of good governance to unabashed efforts to protect their class privilege. Some joined Heterodoxy, a women's club based in Greenwich Village that held weekly debates over such heretical topics as free love, socialism, and racial tolerance. Others balked at marching in the suffrage parades along Fifth Avenue for fear it would mark them as ladies of the night. Some went to jail for protesting in front of Woodrow Wilson's White House, choosing prison rather than paying a modest fine. Others distanced themselves from Britain's Emmeline Pankhurst, ducking the specter of militancy and violence.

What connected them was a sense of great social change. It was a time when a new century beckoned and bohemian critics in Greenwich Village were challenging every institution from capitalism to marriage, experimenting with socialism, free love, art, and birth control. For women of the gilded set, modernity meant jettisoning old social customs—the cotillion and the costumed ball, the layers of clothes and rigidity of table settings, the decorous courtship and the marriage of strangers—in favor of education, career, and independence. If they had remained on the sidelines, they would have become anachronisms, the fate of those who clung to their status as wives and daughters of America's most infamous capitalists, just as the Jazz Age was making celebrities of sports figures, musicians, and radio actors. Instead they made a bid for influence—not the moral suasion of motherhood or the indirect power of social standing, but the political influence of the men of their class, long denied them because of their gender.

Some contemporaries dismissed their participation as a fad, the indulgence of bored socialites trying on suffrage as they might the latest couture designs from Paris.[5] Historians have echoed the critique, casting the activism of these gilded suffragists as a power play to preserve what one scholar called "the prerogative of the elite to speak for the poor."[6] What has been missing in suffrage history is an understanding that when women named Astor, Belmont, Harriman, Mackay, Rockefeller, Tiffany, Vanderbilt, and Whitney exploited their social celebrity for political power, they galvanized interest among a growing urban public.[7]

In newspaper accounts of the day, their names were hidden behind the moniker of "Mrs. Somebody Else." Excavating their identities and biographies was a work of archaeology, the sense of discovery bolstered as their numbers grew to more than two hundred. Researching their religious and political affiliations, their club memberships and civic causes, the source of their wealth and the generation they were born into—all provided stunning examples of how a new century had shifted the ground beneath their feet.[8] By 1920, more than a tenth of the gilded suffragists had divorced, quite a few had ridden bicycles or attended a university, and many had become published authors, baring their souls in scandalous candor.

Comfortable with the power that wealth conferred, these women treated politics as an extension of their realm as social figures. Accustomed to running large estates, they knew how to prod and when to delegate. Conditioned to press sensationalism, they knew how to manage the media. With large budgets and a taste for luxury, they also rev eled in dressing the part. Katharine Houghton Hepburn was president of the Connecticut Woman Suffrage Association and an ally of birth control advocate Margaret Sanger. As her daughter, actress Katharine Hepburn, told biographer A. Scott Berg, "Mother's secret was in remaining extremely feminine. She dressed beautifully, she tended to her husband, she showed off her well-groomed children. And then, while she was pouring the mayor a second cup of tea, she would discuss with great intelligence some great injustice being heaped upon his female constituents. And then she'd smile and say, 'More sugar?'"[9]

The results of their intervention were consequential—and instructive. From the celebrity capital of New York, they joined a cause that had been "in the doldrums" and made it seem intoxicating to a nationwide public. Newspaper coverage surged, attendance at suffrage events swelled, and the campaign gained ground. In their footprints, they also left a roadmap of how social change is made in America—sometimes by defusing radicalism, other times by breaching political decorum, always by appealing to a public that in the case of women's suffrage had proved indifferent to the cause for more than fifty years. As one activist wrote to a friend who had been traveling in Asia, "It's now fashionable among the actresses to be a suffragette—Ethel Barrymore has come out for it and Beatrice Forbes Robertson has even abandoned the stage to lecture upon it. Oh, God, it's so good."[10]

1

A CLUB OF THEIR OWN

*In New York Society, the older families
never allow the turmoil of outside
life to enter their social scheme.*

HENRY CABOT LODGE[1]

CLAD in his gold-laced uniform, the watchman on duty at the
Spouting Rock Beach Association knew by sight every carriage
in Newport, Rhode Island. Only the elite could pass through his gates
to sunbathe at Bailey's Beach, a stretch of sand claimed by the wealthy
in 1890 after trolley service made an earlier and more desirable plot,
Easton Beach,[2] accessible to all sorts of people—"including domestics
and Negroes, some of whom one would rather prefer not to meet in the
water."[3] Unless the visitor was the guest of one of the members or bore a
note of introduction "from an unimpeachable hostess," no pleading, "no
power on earth could gain them admission."[4] As the *New York Times* put
it, "Only the swellest of the swell" could penetrate "the walls of exclu-
siveness surrounding the place."[5]

At the turn of the century, few tributes to Gilded Age excess glittered
as brightly as Newport. The mansions that dotted Bellevue Avenue were
America's answer to the grand castles of Europe—fortresses of marble
with enormous winding staircases and intricate architectural detail, filled
with the sculptures, portraits, tapestries, and paintings that the new titans
of industry had hungrily imported from France, Italy, and England. Every
summer, wealthy families descended on Newport from Boston and New

York and as far away as Charleston to reside in their "cottages," play golf, polo, and tennis, sail their boats, race their horses, indulge at the casino, and attend lavish balls. They hired or brought servants to attend to every creature comfort and famous chefs to oversee multicourse meals. Mostly, they came to claim their place in this storied fraternity.

At Bailey's Beach, women were shielded from the elements—and social offense—by enough gauze, linen, hats, bloomers, stockings, and gloves to stock a small milliner's shop. Catherine Kernochan, whose brother Pierre Lorillard developed the Tuxedo Park Country Club, once appeared at Bailey's wearing "bathing shoes, a black blouse, black pantaloons, a full black skirt, a jacket with billowing sleeves and a large Mother Hubbard bonnet."[6] Marian Fish, wife of Illinois Central Railroad president Stuyvesant Fish, may have set a beach fashion standard one day by wearing "a full dark green satin skirt with a flounce and piping of white satin. White satin and lace lined a pointed vest and there was also lace on the belt and collar and on the wrists of the sleeves. This outfit was worn with bloomers, stockings and sandals." Swimming would have been an act of acrobatics.

Modesty—and club rules—required that bathing dress cover even the ankles. Elsie Clews, a New York heiress who summered at the family home in Newport, caused something of a stir—and received "a serious warning from the house committee"—when she put her naked feet into the sea water to experience the Atlantic Ocean without stockings, incidentally exposing her well-shaped legs to admiring stares. Eager to uphold Victorian standards amid this generational assertion of immodesty, the board of directors laid down the law: stockings for women were required at all times.[7] Still, the younger set continued to test the limits of parental permissiveness by convening for nude bathing parties at midnight on Bailey's Beach. One dowager commented tolerantly, "I don't suppose the young people realized what they were doing. I understand they were all very drunk."[8]

One warm August day in 1902, five women steeped in the wealth that gilded Newport met to challenge male privilege.[9] It is unlikely that they set out to spark a nationwide debate over the contours of relations that had dictated behavior between men and women for over a century. Nor did they intend to give new spark to a political movement long given up for dead. By their own accounts, they meant only to end their exclusion from one of the great habitués of gentility—the book-lined, hushed men's clubs that catered to the urban gentry in Manhattan and London. Still, the effect was riveting. Years later Virginia Woolf would write about a woman's need for "a room of one's own." Now, five well-bred socialites from "good" families, all listed in the *Social Register*, met to plot a club of their own.

It is hard to overstate the audacity of the idea, the revolution in gender assumptions created by the very notion that women could build their own club in the city. After the land was purchased on Madison Avenue between East 30th and East 31st Streets, after the organizing committee had hired Stanford White to design the building and Elsie de Wolfe to furnish it in a way that would clear out the musty curtains of the Victorian era, still there were doubters. The Princeton Club put its own plans to build in the city on hold, "in abeyance on the ground that the [women's] club would soon fail and be for sale cheap."[10]

Even more destabilizing to men of a certain class and time was the idea that women would want their own space, separate from the home. The threat to masculinity was such that one man remarked, "Women shouldn't have clubs. They'll only use them as addresses for clandestine letters."[11] The gentleman failed to mention that this was precisely how men used their clubs, often receiving letters from paramours that "a tactful servant would always bring . . . on a silver tray, butter side down; this was, of course, on the chance that the lady might be connected, in some fashion, with another member."[12] When news of the women's club venture became public, a German newspaper decreed that it presaged "the swan-song of the American home and family." Former president Grover Cleveland took to the pages of the *Ladies Home Journal* to proclaim that woman's "best and safest club is her home. A life retired is well inspired."[13] One newspaper called the club a "Death Knell to the Home."[14]

Instead, in ways that surprised even its founders, the Colony Club became a site of debate over the controversial issues of the day, none as vexing as the heretical idea that women should cast ballots in local, state, and national elections. This unlikely outcome, the legacy of unexpected consequences, owed something to the turmoil of change swirling through turn-of-the-century New York. As one scholar put it, "The tides of modernity, which had washed over Paris in the 1870s and subsequently over Vienna, Prague, Munich, Berlin and London, had finally reached American shores."[15] It was an era of experimentation, a time when Anne Morgan, a new moneyed aristocrat whose father, J. Pierpont Morgan, was the titan of Wall Street, attended lectures on socialism, and Fanny Villard, an old-school liberal whose father was famed abolitionist William Lloyd Garrison, lectured so often about women's suffrage that she often grew hoarse.[16] Scott Joplin opened an office at 128 West 29th Street to experiment with a new form of music called ragtime, and Ida B. Wells moved to 395 Gold Street in Brooklyn to escape arsonists who had burned down her newspaper in Memphis and to create a New York chapter of her anti-lynching Women's Loyal Union.[17] By the 1910s, the Washington Square home built by Cornelius Vanderbilt at the height of the Gilded Age would be torn down for apartments and "shabby rooming houses," where artists, writers, and radicals came for cheap spaghetti dinners and abundant debates over meaning.[18]

The names of those who met in Newport that warm August day are in dispute. So auspicious was the occasion that, much as those who convince themselves they were at the scene of great history, some may have deceived their own memories, their stories repeated and embellished in years since by journalists and scholars. What is unchallenged is that Florence Jaffray Harriman, thirty-two-year-old wife of banker J. Borden Harriman, whose family called her Daisy, was the spark for this nascent experiment in female independence.

Daisy had been privately tutored, joining J. P. Morgan's children for school at their home at Madison Avenue and 36th Street, the first residence in Manhattan boasting electrical lighting.[19] Her family's home, at 615 Fifth Avenue, pulsed not with electricity but with political ambition. Her father, F. W. J. Hurst, was a shipping magnate with deep ties to the Washington establishment and an abiding pride in his tenure as president of the New York Yacht Club. Daisy was three years old when her mother, Caroline Hurst, died, leaving her to be raised by her father and maternal grandparents.[20] She had early memories of leaning over the banister to watch the 1876 presidential torchlight parade through the streets of Manhattan or listen to the conversation of visitors in the downstairs parlor, among them John Hay, James Garfield, and Chester Arthur.[21] Among those attending her 1889 wedding were Grover Cleveland and John Jacob Astor IV, reflecting her father's fascination with the bookends of New York's political and financial power.[22] She was an avid sports fan and athlete, once confessing, "which was the more glorious at Newport, yachting or polo, I could never decide."[23] Now, with a five-year-old daughter and homes in New York, Newport, and Mount Kisco, Daisy Harriman embarked on a more public role. It was a journey that would, improbably, take her to the highest ranks of the Democratic Party, and to a harrowing post as President Franklin Roosevelt's chief of mission to Norway during the Nazi invasion.[24]

As was their custom, the Harrimans were renting in Newport for the season, this year at the Yardley Cottage at 91 Rhode Island Avenue.[25] Daisy was making occasional treks back to the city, usually for a few days at a time, to oversee renovations to their townhouse at 128 East 36th Street. One evening in Newport, complaining about the dust and disruption in their home in Manhattan, she told her husband, "I can't stay in the mess. What hotel shall I go to—the Waldorf?" In 1893 William Waldorf Astor had opened an "opulent thirteen-story Waldorf Hotel," quite popular with the elite, at a Fifth Avenue corner where the Empire State Building would later rise.[26] Borden was president of a bank so decorous that in 1906 it would offer a separate branch for female customers.[27] Now he harrumphed that he did not approve of women going to large hotels unaccompanied, lest they be taken for harlots. "But Bordie, what can women do?" she asked, perhaps with a hint of coquettishness. Almost as an afterthought, she added, "There ought to be a woman's club and we go to that in the summers and have parcels sent there and do telephoning."[28]

The next day she shared her vision with Kate Brice, whose father, Calvin Brice, had been a U.S. senator from Ohio and lately a railroad president. "She had been at a ball the night before, and was only just up and rather sleepy, but she responded at once," Harriman recalled. Kate dressed and the two of them made the rounds. "Before the August day was over," they had corralled enthusiasm from Ava Willing Astor, a Philadelphia heiress and wife of the richest man in the country. Also on board was Emmeline Dore Heckscher Winthrop, an auburn-haired pixie whose husband, Egerton Winthrop, "a cultivated man," had introduced a young family friend, Edith Wharton, to the glories of Darwin, Huxley, and the great French novelists.[29] Maud Bull, whose husband, Henry, would later preside over the exclusive Turf and Field Club, was busy planning a dinner for the Newport Horse Show, but readily agreed.[30] So did Margaret Lewis Morgan Norrie, who, along with Eleanor Roosevelt, would become a fixture of reform in the Hudson Valley's Dutchess County.[31]

Once Daisy Harriman returned to the city, by her own account, the idea drooped in lethargy until one weekend when she went on a hunting expedition with her husband's family. The party included his cousin Mary Harriman and likely Mary's younger brother Averill, who in 1955 would become the forty-eighth governor of New York. While at Barnard, Mary had volunteered at a settlement house on the Lower East Side, and was so moved by what she saw there that she reached out to other debutantes to continue the work. Soon the idea of their Junior League, an educational and charitable volunteer organization, had spread nationwide.[32] Now she told Daisy that she often dreamed of having squash courts on the roof of some building in Manhattan. "I fizzed up again, quite as I had in Newport," Daisy Harriman recalled. After that, word of mouth found converts. By December 1903 she had corralled a forty-woman organizational committee, one that glittered with wealth, leavened by spunk.

Anne Tracy Morgan, youngest of J. P. Morgan's four children, "sent word she was keen, especially if we included a running track in our plans."[33] Growing up at Highland Falls, a country home overlooking the Hudson, Anne had enjoyed the outdoor life—riding, fishing, hunting, golfing.[34] Now, at 170 pounds, the twenty-eight-year-old Morgan longed for the kind of athletic facilities offered by the Union and Metropolitan Clubs, especially a swimming pool. Her father supported the venture, joining the male advisory committee.[35]

Elisabeth Marbury, known as Bessy, was all in too. One of the first women to excel as a theatrical agent, Bessy would represent, among others, George Bernard Shaw, Oscar Wilde, W. Somerset Maugham, Edith Wharton, Theodore Dreiser, and Eugene O'Neill, and was credited with all but inventing the modern American musical comedy.[36] She lived in the heart of Union Square, at 17th Street and Irving Place, with actress and later decorator Elsie de Wolfe. Describing themselves affectionately as "the bachelors," the two organized Sunday afternoon salons with a stunning array of up-and-coming talents and thinkers.[37]

Helen Hay Whitney, a published poet whose father was Abraham Lincoln's private secretary and first biographer, was on board.[38] So was her sister-in-law, Gertrude Vanderbilt Whitney, who hosted the Colony Club's first annual meeting in 1905 at her home at 871 Fifth Avenue.[39] Sarah Stillman Rockefeller, Elsie to her friends, daughter of James Stillman, president of the National City Bank, and newly wed wife of William G. Rockefeller, heir to the Standard Oil fortune, joined the founders' organizational committee, as did Helen Tracy Barney, Anne Morgan's beautiful twenty-year-old cousin, whose father, Knickerbocker Trust president Charles T. Barney, agreed to serve on the male advisory committee.[40]

Perhaps no one better exemplified the Colony Club's odd pairing of inherited wealth and social rebellion as the thirty-seven-year-old Helen Benedict Hastings. Daughter of financier E. Cornelius Benedict, Helen was a natural wit, prompting friends to call her the "feminine Sydney Smith," reference to an English humorist whose articles occasioned much comment in New York.[41] Founding the Ladies Four-in-Hand Driving Club, Helen urged women to take the driver's seat and steer four horses through the streets, as a man would.[42] Her wedding to architect Thomas Hastings on the first day of May in the first year of the new century attracted so many of New York's glitterati that two special trains were commissioned to take one thousand guests from Grand Central Terminal in New York to Greenwich, Connecticut, where two hundred coaches were waiting to get them to the church on time.[43] The groom was one of the city's leading architects, and his commissions would come to include the New York Public Library, the Manhattan Bridge, and the Standard Oil Building.[44] Biographers believe that Helen and Thomas were homosexuals, taking "a social cover marriage, a common practice for the period . . . to keep their families at bay and provide a public face."[45]

At first, the Colony Club founders thought small—or anyway, small for them. They contemplated renting the upper floors of a hotel and hiring a caterer to open a restaurant on the main level.[46] By 1903, with support from the men's advisory committee and robust fundraising of their own, organizers had managed to raise $400,000 for land and a standalone building, a number close to $11 million in contemporary terms.[47] By 1905, after sending invitations to women of prominence in the professions as well as in society, organizers had received 926 requests to join a club that would cap membership at 700.[48]

When, on January 20, 1907, the venue opened its doors at 120 Madison Avenue, the Colony Club—named in honor of the nation's founders and decorated in the blue and buff of the Continental Army—stood as a tribute to innovation. Staff uniforms made in Paris, a "parking room" for dogs (provided they weighed less than eight pounds), and a running track "suspended by brackets from the ceiling"—all suggested a new address for a new era.[49] Still, much like the men's clubs on which it was modeled, the Colony Club also became a refuge from the increasing grittiness of urban life, a haven of comfortable chairs, good food, athletic facilities, and the amiable company of like-minded members of the gilded or professional class. No Jews, Catholics, blacks, or factory workers need apply, but dues were sufficiently within reach—$100 annually, $2,600 in today's terms—to attract a few professional women of literature, business, and science.[50]

Controversy had attended nearly every aspect of the planning, especially the decision to give the decorating assignment to Elsie de Wolfe, whose only previous experience was decorating the home she shared with Bessy Marbury at 13 Sutton Place. During one planning meeting of the board of governors, one critic asked in exasperation, "Are you all out of your heads, giving an important job like this to a woman who has had no experience?"[51] Even as she worked, de Wolfe recalled having to "fend off in-house critics who kept moving the furniture" she had already put in place. Reviewers later judged her designs breathtakingly fresh, establishing her as the new star of a new profession that came to be known as interior design. Banishing the "somber, cluttered interiors" and dark Turkish tea corners of an earlier era, she used wicker furniture, garden trellises, tiled floors, and chintz, making fashionable a bit of the English country house in metropolitan New York.[52] Diana Vreeland, a former *Vogue* editor and consultant to the Metropolitan Museum's Costume Institute, said later that de Wolfe "simply cleared out the Victoriana and let in the twentieth century."[53]

If the Colony Club was a showcase of modernist décor, it also represented a startling shift in gender equilibrium. Children were banned. Male guests, allowed to attend public lectures on the main floors, were prohibited elsewhere, although a later rule change admitted clergymen and physicians to the bedroom levels.[54] Though alcohol was banned—Daisy Harriman's husband scoffed that no institution could make money without the elixir of strong drink—the club prospered, moving uptown several times with Manhattan's northward growth. To members experiencing their first taste of independence, the result was intoxicating enough, even without liquor. Mrs. Charles L. Perkins, "a mother of club presidents and governors," spoke for many when she told Harriman, "I've waited for this evening all my life. I have just telephoned the boys,

2

'Don't wait dinner; I'm dining at my club.' My dear, I've been getting that message for years—now I'm giving it!"[55]

Harriman became the club's first and longest-serving president, a tenure that lasted from 1904 to 1917. At the club's opening she delivered a speech, the first she had ever made, which she had practiced so often at home beforehand that her ten-year-old daughter Ethel memorized it "as other children of that age know about 'the boy on the burning deck'" (the opening line of a popular poem, "Casabianca").[56] In her remarks, Harriman said the critics were quite right that the home should come first in a woman's life, but argued that "the club if used in the right way should enrich the home." There would be lectures on Tuesdays—the first week of the month on literature, the second on politics, the third on art, the fourth on music. There would also be a state-of-the-art gymnasium to provide regular exercise, "most essential to health and happiness, and very hard to obtain during the winter months in New York." Mostly there would be a sisterhood of influence, "a common meeting ground for women of all interests," a place a woman might leave "with a broadened point of view, and her life enriched by contact with the best in art, literature, music and civics, and with the wish to extend her interest beyond just a small group or clique of people."[57] The Colony Club was thus opened not only as a gymnasium, but also as a school of civic engagement.

This appeal to what politicians a century later would call "a cause greater than self" resonated.[58] Born after the Civil War, many members represented a new generation, raised on the unparalleled wealth of the postwar boom but coming of age in *fin-de-siècle* America. With millionaire husbands who delegated to them the task of running large estates, they were keen to partake of the *zeitgeist* of change swirling through the city. "It is more than a coincidence that the civic awakening that is stirring in our cities . . . has come with the civic activities of women's clubs," said one clubwoman. "I have yet to hear of a town that is experiencing a civic awakening that has not had an active women's club."[59] Though the Colony Club was decidedly more of a social group than a civic club, amid the myriad reform campaigns in need of their money and time, many were eager to help reshape an expanding city.

On January 1, 1898, the four boroughs of New York—Manhattan, Queens, Staten Island, and the Bronx—had combined with the independent city of Brooklyn. By this simple gesture of legislative fiat, New York City's population increased to 3.4 million.[60] A metropolis was born, and with it issues of transportation, housing, and sanitation. Immigrants, rural workers, and African Americans streamed into the city, adding to the din of a building boom. In June 1902 the Flatiron Building opened at Fifth Avenue and Broadway, a wedge-shaped design that people said resembled more of a clothes iron than a skyscraper. "Since the removal last week of the scaffolding," reported the *Tribune,* "there is scarcely an hour when a staring wayfarer doesn't by his example collect a big crowd of other staring people—sometimes a hundred or more, with heads bent backward until a breakage of necks seems imminent."[61] With Thomas Edison battling George Westinghouse over the best currents to use in expanding the subway system, the Brooklyn Bridge rising over the East River, and tunnels burrowing toward Penn Station from beneath the Hudson River, the city was bursting with promise—and soot.[62] Matilda Gay, who had befriended Edith Wharton when both were expatriates living in Paris, wrote her after a trip back to New York in 1908, "The perpetual tearing up of the city, and the noise and the smoke, now that the omnibuses have been replaced by autobuses, is enough to drive one mad."[63]

The Colony Club came of age in this vortex of change, representing an important if unintended marker in New York feminist history, one with a long backstory. When, in 1868, a visiting Charles Dickens was honored at a banquet dinner sponsored by the New York Press Club, Jane Cunningham Croly tried to buy a ticket. Club officials refused. Three days before the event, they sent word to Croly (who often wrote newspaper columns on fashion, cooking, and the arts under the byline Jennie June) and other female writers that they could attend if they sat behind a curtain. Declining this pyrrhic offer, Croly vowed to "form a club of our own [where] we will give a banquet to ourselves, and make all the speeches ourselves and not invite a single man."[64] Twenty years later, during the citywide celebrations to mark the centennial of George Washington's inauguration, women were again excluded from the newly formed Sons of the American Revolution.[65] They formed the Daughters of the American Revolution, becoming more famous than their male counterparts. And in 1900, when Josephine St. Pierre Ruffin, daughter of a French-African father and a British mother, was refused admittance to a meeting of the General Federation of Women's Clubs, she formed her own—the National Association of Colored Women's Clubs, dedicated to "raising to the highest plane the home life, moral standards and civic life of our race."[66] The advent of clubwomen, temperance advocates, and social reformers was "one of the most important sociological phenomena of the [nineteenth] century," said social critic Charlotte Perkins Gilman, "marking as it does [the] first timid steps toward social organization."[67]

Against this backdrop of nascent female activism, the Colony Club offered a venue for women to consider the great issues of the day. Organizers drew an especially large audience for one Tuesday afternoon debate on women's suffrage in 1908. Moderated by muckraking journalist Ida Tarbell, a Colony Club member, the session quickly took on the quality of legend. Like Barnard College founder Annie Nathan Meyer, Tarbell was an anti-suffragist, an intellectual who opposed enfranchising women, fearing that they would fail as politicians.[68] She opened with a plea for comity, but the conversation quickly turned contentious.

Speaking against the idea of enfranchising women, club member Alida Blake Hazard predicted that giving the vote to women would lead to socialism, an even greater evil in her view than political empowerment. She noted the "curious alliance . . . between the Suffragists and the Socialists." And she quoted Elizabeth Cady Stanton, matriarch of women's suffrage, who had once warned that if men did not grant women the vote, suffragists "would rise up as labor, the Socialists and the Anarchists had done, and there would be a revolution like that in France."[69] On the other side was Fanny Garrison Villard, wife of railroad executive Henry Villard and daughter of abolitionist William Lloyd Garrison. Her late father had waged a failing battle for female delegates to be seated at the 1840 World's Anti-Slavery Convention in London.[70] Now his daughter said that consequences are not the purview of activists. "I was brought up in the school which considers only what is right, leaving the results to take care of themselves," she said. "We believe that if a thing is right, the results will be right."[71]

When details about the debate reached the newspapers, the club's board of governors recoiled. Candid discussions were unlikely if the implicit promise of privacy, "which the members would naturally expect in their club house," was breached. In a special notice to Colony Club members, the board decreed that in the future, "no member of the club may bring a guest to the Tuesday afternoons without first obtaining a special invitation, which may be secured by application to the Committee on Literature and Art."[72] It was one thing to debate suffrage within their circle. To risk what the board called "notoriety" would simply not do. Colony Club defenders would close the gates to all but the invited.

Throughout 1908, club members debated suffrage without word leaking to the newspapers. Harriman called them "talkfests," and recalled one evening when Katherine Duer Mackay was assigned to take the anti-suffrage position. "With her arms full of books and papers, followed by a footman carrying more," Mackay—a descendent of colonial power, married to one of the wealthiest men in New York—announced, "I've read them all in a week and I am converted." Harriman later recalled, "It ruined the debate to have her call '*Camerade*' in that fashion. But her conversion gave suffrage an ally of inestimable value."[73]

In December 1908, seated with other prominent women in a special box, Harriman attended a suffrage lecture at Carnegie Hall.[74] Like Mackay, Harriman had been galvanized to act by considering the arguments of anti-suffrage lecturers. Now, on going public with her own support, "my presence was taken up in the morning papers as proof that the Colony Club members were followers of Susan B. Anthony. A storm of protest ensued from all the 'anti' members of the Club and so, on my husband's advice, I never went to any meetings again or marched in any suffrage parades until after I had ceased to be president." Five years later, while she was still club president but commuting to Washington to serve on President Wilson's Commission on Industrial Relations, a Colony Club acquaintance told her, "I want to advise you that a clique in the club is antagonistic to you and think you should resign as president. . . . This feeling has been steadily growing since you went to the suffrage meeting."[75]

If Harriman's voice was stilled, others began to speak up. In the spring of 1909, Edith Black Bailey lent her "big red automobile" to a suffrage street rally, where it served as a rostrum for soapbox campaigning. Begun that year, "in timidity and half in doubt," the soapbox lecture usually featured one suffragist to hand out literature and another to speak on an elevated box or car seat. In New York, the effect was cacophonous. "In one district a red and white flag flanks the suffrage banner while a bohemian speaker explains the justice of equal suffrage; in another locality the same message is given in liquid Italian to swarthy laborers and their womankind, lavish as to earrings and perhaps more interest in 'bambini' than votes," wrote one enraptured witness, albeit given to stereotypes.

> Here an earnest-faced woman carries on the strain in Yiddish, there the Scandinavian tongue proclaims the new strife for right, the Fatherland tells the same tale in guttural tones and dominating all others the crisp, forceful English speech reiterates the doctrine of government of the people, by the people and for the people, and women are half the people. Is it not wonderful, this sonorous chorus of many notes blending into the one mighty chord of equal justice?[76]

Not everyone was entranced. Like Alida Hazard, antis saw in street campaigning the threat of socialism, assimilation, and a "suffrage melting pot" of "extreme methods." Worse, they assailed the unladylike behavior of climbing onto a car seat and speaking in public, surely signs of a gender upheaval in which female "economic independence . . . would depose man as the head of the home" and replace the "sacred marriage" tie with a "mere partnership contract."[77] Despite the dustup, Bailey's car returned safely to the Colony Club, where participants were feted to a luncheon by one of the speakers, Maud "Mootzie" Cabot.[78] Pearce Bailey's family had given its name to the most exclusive beach in Newport. Now the family automobile had become a prop in a political debate.

As passions intensified, the Colony Club hosted events on both sides of the issue, although there was not always a bright line between the two, making it sometimes difficult to tell condescending friend from ignorant opponent. British journalist William Thomas Stead was invited to speak at the club shortly after it opened. As a newspaper editor, he had pioneered a new concept of "government by journalism," launching investigations aimed at pressuring officials by influencing public opinion.[79] Now he argued for women's enfranchisement as a means of humanizing the political world. "In politics," he said, "the best half of American life does not count for one percent." Looking out on an audience of women gathered for a fundraiser to benefit the Collegiate Equal Suffrage League, he added, "You may be miserably inefficient, but however sentimental, weak and emotional you may be, that is no reason for handicapping you for life."[80] Conversely, at a Colony Club meeting of the National League for Civil Education, an anti-suffrage group, James Walsh, dean of the Fordham University Medical School, suggested that extending the franchise to women would change little, as science had demonstrated that while they were capable of intellectual advances, women, like children playing with fire, always retreated from the heat.[81]

The suffrage issue may have divided them—conservatives against liberals, matrons against debutantes—but at the club, they were family, a sometime catty network of intermarriages and social alliances. Whatever their views on suffrage, they were forced by dint of status to mingle and make small talk—at social teas, racetrack outings, dog show exhibitions, or luncheons for visiting royals. Interactions were inevitable, courtesy expected, fashion observed. They were connected too through the sporting activities that defined their leisure class, giving many of their wealthy husbands an occupation and many a nascent sport a solid financial footing. The Newport Golf Club, brainchild of sugar magnate Theodore Havemeyer, hosted the first U.S. Open tournament in 1895.[82] That same year, society leader Hope Goddard Iselin became the first female to participate in an America's Cup race, as the boat's timekeeper.[83]

Weddings brought *de rigueur* attendance, not so much marriages as mergers within the confines of the class, fascinating must-be-witnessed fusions of money to title (heiress Gladys Vanderbilt to Hungarian Count László Széchenyi), new money to old money (Theresa Fair, heir to Nevada's silver mines, to Herman Oelrichs, scion of Baltimore wealth), or money to fame (August Belmont Jr., who built the Belmont Racetrack, to actress Eleanor Robson). At Annah Dillon Ripley's wedding to French Count Pierre de Viel Castal in 1910, Katherine Mackay tried to convert to the suffrage cause Elizabeth Griscom, whose husband, Lloyd, had served as U.S. ambassador to Persia, Japan, Brazil, and Italy. Elizabeth Griscom's influence, noted the *Club Fellow*, "would be tremendous in its effect," but she "refused to be captured," brushing Mackay off with a promise to "think it over."[84]

At one Colony Club suffrage meeting, the *New York American* remarked on the "array of carriages, autos and cabs" that descended for the evening. "Occupants for the most part were exquisitely gowned women," said the paper, and "there was scarcely room to move in the big clubhouse."[85] Edith Black Bailey, one of the speakers, was so skillful in combining "humor with logic" that "ripples of laughter" followed her remarks. *Town & Country Magazine* noted that Bailey was "really inspiring, even to the antis in the audience, and she deserved better praise than that vouchsafed her by one of the morning papers, which announced that she won her hearers by her good looks."[86] The *Club Fellow* was biting in its report, chiding these women for wearing the finest fashions while claiming to be victims of male oppression. "The sumptuous Miss Eleanor, in diamonds and black velvet, did not fulfill my idea of a slave, even a white one," sneered the *Club Fellow's* writer. "The suffragists know enough to put their best foot forward and the best dressed women too."[87] Some three hundred women and three men heard the speech, during which Bailey crystalized the issue for women of leisure when she quipped, "Voting is only the servant question on a large scale."[88] Surely electing a candidate to public office—weighing the options, pondering the personalities—was no more difficult than employing a cook or a groundskeeper for one's estate.

There were other light moments too, many involving Marian "Mamie" Fish, whose husband, Stuyvesant Fish, was a descendant of governors, congressmen, and cabinet officers. With her sharp tongue and her husband's money, Mamie Fish redefined entertaining in Newport and New York, the more extravagant the better. She once told architect Stanford White to design a ballroom for the new Fish home on 78th Street in such over-the-top style that "a person who was not well bred would feel uncomfortable."[89] Alva Belmont, a friend, once confronted her, asking if it was true she had described the pug-faced Belmont to acquaintances as a frog. "A *toad*," Mamie corrected. "A *toad*."[90]

As talk of suffrage interrupted her parties, Fish frowned, insisting that women would not benefit "by mixing in the mire of politics. They always have moved and always should move in a higher sphere and deal with better and more lasting things than the election of this one and that one to office." She worried about the vote's effect on fashion, noting, "Can we fancy a Madame Recamier or a Madame De Stael dressed in knickerbockers with short skirts and a derby hat engaged in a hand-to-hand fight at the polls?" A brief nineteenth-century fascination with bloomers had opened the movement to ridicule.[91] Now, as the cause attracted more fashionable women, she came over, a victim of the urge to stay atop the trends. An astonished *New York Times* announced her allegiance with the headline "Mrs. Fish Gone Over to the Suffragists," attributing her conversion to the sartorial femininity of the campaign's newest advocates. "Fashion has approved it," said the *Times*. "Colony Club meeting costumes show that her dread of knickerbockers and derbies was unfounded."[92]

In its first years, the Colony Club had seen the growth of society's involvement in suffrage. Within its walls raged a debate over whether the vote would bolster or weaken their inherent social power, the step-child of privilege. Twenty years before, amid the great circulation wars between William Randolph Hearst and Joseph Pulitzer, an earlier generation of society activists had first planted the idea that women of the leisure class aspired to political rights. Married to husbands of Gilded Age infamy, such as John D. Rockefeller, Courtlandt Palmer, and Russell Sage, they had voiced their opinions from the comfort of their homes, to a circle of their social equals. In something of a prequel to the activists at the Colony Club, they became the first group of elite women to attempt to leverage their social status for political power. Before the advent of radio or television, long before the invention of the Internet, even longer before 24/7 news coverage and social media, newspapers and magazines dominated the landscape. At a time when print was ascending, these elite women of an earlier generation rode the crest of a new phenomenon called celebrity journalism.

2

THE CELEBRITY ENDORSEMENT

*The undignified methods employed by certain New York
women to attract a following [only promote] . . .
notoriety, a thing that no lady ever seeks.*

CAROLINE SCHERMERHORN ASTOR[1]

T HE Petit Chateau stood in visual contrast to nearby brownstones, a wedding cake surrounded by sand blocks. As gawkers stood on Fifth Avenue shivering on a cold March night in 1883, all was warm and aglitter inside. Hostess Alva Smith Vanderbilt wore a white satin princess gown, made in Paris, embroidered in gold, topped by a veil of velvet, a diadem of diamonds, and a strand of pearls once owned, it was said, by Catherine the Great.[2] With a guest list of 1,200, a price tag of $250,000 ($6 million in today's dollars), and silver party favors from Tiffany's, the costume ball was meant to serve notice on Knickerbocker landowners who had long dominated New York culture that the new posse of railroad, oil, steel, and financial interests had arrived.[3] It was as if a gaudy show of excess had gilded the transition from old money to new. "Dozens of Louis XVIs, a King Lear 'in his right mind,' Joan of Arc, Venetian noblewomen . . . danced and drank among the flower filled . . . third floor gymnasium that had been converted into a forest filled with palm trees and draped with bougainvillea and orchids," said one witness.[4]

Henry Clews, a Wall Street financier who had emigrated from England at the age of seventeen, attended the party with his wife, Lucy

Madison Clews, a descendant of James Madison who was dressed as fire in a "gorgeous costume of iridescent bronze over flaming yellow satin." Observing the evening's glittery nod to history, Clews saw at once that the mantle of status had passed not only from old money to new, but from Europe to America. "It may not have been quite so expensive as the feast of Alexander the Great at Babylon, some of the entertainments of Cleopatra to Augustus or Mark Antony, or a few of the magnificent banquets of Louis XIV," he remarked, but in its social significance the Vanderbilt ball was "superior to any of those historic displays of amusement and festivity."[5]

If the Vanderbilt ball in some sense heralded a new American, Gilded Age aristocracy, it also represented a new phase in the history of journalism.[6] The era of celebrity reporting had arrived, and with it a public fascination for the excesses of what the *St. Louis Post-Dispatch* called the "insolent wealth and offensive luxury" of the leisure class.[7] Resonating to Horatio Alger's gospel of rags to riches, a new generation of readers, many newly arrived in the city, hungered for details about the lives of the rich and famous.[8] Publishers were only too eager to oblige, even if it meant invading the privacy of wealthy patrons they once protected.

The invasion began in 1880, when Charles Anderson Dana, publisher of the *New York Sun*, hired an unnamed but well-connected reporter to track the latest intelligence about the "smart set." These first society columns were rather chatty, eliciting much speculation within elite circles over who the author was and which unfaithful servants or associates were feeding him information. The following year, the *Tribune* added society coverage; when Joseph Pulitzer purchased the *World* from railroad baron Jay Gould in 1883, coverage ratcheted up even further. Pulitzer "made an ostentatious display of Society's activities in the Sunday edition of the paper," noting "everything that had occurred during the past week . . . with a schedule of events to come during the current week."[9] The paper had one column about Broadway stars, "Among the Players," one about clubwomen called "Doings of Women Folk," another catchall column called "People Often Talked Of," and a gossip column about Mrs. Astor's Four Hundred entitled "In Millionaire Society."[10]

Inspired by the catty London weekly *Truth*, widely read in New York men's clubs, a new "journal of society" also joined the scene.[11] Unlike the daily newspapers, *Town Topics* was written of and for the elite. A white-haired St. Nicholas look-alike who took his lunch every day at Delmonico's, editor William d'Alton Mann is credited—or disparaged—as the "godfather of modern gossip." He delighted in "blind items" that alluded to scandalous behavior—a playboy about town seen leaving the Newport cottage of a prominent social leader—placed coincidentally next to an innocuous column in which the two lovers were mentioned as attending a charity event.[12] This wink to the reader was a code well understood by the *Town Topics* readership, which by the turn of the century reached 140,000.[13] It was just such a blind item—about President Roosevelt's eldest daughter Alice, said to have listened to dirty jokes while drinking at a 1904 Newport soiree—that provoked *Colliers* to write an editorial despairing of such methods. Mann's associate, Judge Joseph Deuel, responded by accusing *Colliers* of libel. At the ensuing trial in December 1905 and January 1906, Mann's testimony captivated New York's wealthy victims, to say nothing of a salivating public.[14]

Press coverage was intense, public interest considerable. "Women by the score stepped on each other's heels in their eagerness to gain admission to the courtroom," reported the *Times*, many "dressed as if for the theatre."[15] Mark Twain sat at the defense table to view the proceedings, while famed Spanish-American War correspondent Richard Harding Davis sat with the press. As testimony drew more heated, William Randolph Hearst sent the *American*'s drama critic to critique the legal maneuverings. He also hired the foreman, cartoonist F. T. Richards, to "an exclusive contract to sketch the principals from the jury box."[16]

The extent of Mann's larceny was stunning. In current terms, his haul topped $10 million. During a single day of testimony, Mann admitted that since the mid-1890s he had accepted "loans" totalling $187,500 from the likes of J. P. Morgan, Collis Huntington, Charles Schwab, William

K. Vanderbilt, and William Whitney. For this generosity, these titans of industry and capital were off limits to gossip columns, their names included in a list posted on the newsroom wall, a dubious fraternity of the immune, a cadre of those willing to pay to keep playing.[17] Nor did his journalism-for-blackmail scheme stop at society's celebrities.[18] *Town Topics* had so maligned Russell Alger in the late 1890s that the secretary of war was able to quiet the attacks only by giving Mann $100,000 of Alger-Sullivan Lumber Company stock and a seat on the West Point Board of Visitors.[19] The wealthy had become invested in their celebrity.

While *Town Topics* made money by bribing society figures, newspapers were not above paying their associates for gossip. Harold Seton, a producer of plays on Broadway who interacted with many of the gilded set, regularly supplied *Herald Tribune* society reporter Lucius Beebe with juicy items. Seton bristled with indignation when other papers, notably Hearst's *Journal*, got details wrong. He was pleased when Beebe used his material accurately, and grateful not to be disclosed as the source. "I have just returned to New York from another visit to Newport," he wrote in one letter, about the nouveau riche and their overindulgence in liquor. "All trace of birth and breeding seemed to have departed, temporarily, from the Socially Registered inebriates, as, with bleary eyes and drooling lips, they staggered about."[20]

No one understood better the import of this combustion of public fame and printer's ink than Alva Smith Vanderbilt. She had grown up the daughter of Alabama cotton wealth decimated by the Civil War. Schooled in Paris, she had avenged her father's financial downfall by marrying a grandson of railroad patriarch Cornelius Vanderbilt. Now, filled with the social ambition that attaches to those who have known wealth and lost it, she set out to host "the most brilliant ball ever given in New York," conspiring to force even the reluctant guardian of high society, Caroline Schermerhorn Astor, to attend. Because of Alva's deft handling of the newspapers, it was said, the Vanderbilt ball "awakened editors for the first time to a better understanding of society and its importance as news."[21]

In the weeks before the 1883 ball, Alva Vanderbilt had invited a *New York Times* reporter for an exclusive preview of the interior of 660 Fifth Avenue. Likely hiring a press agent—within a decade this would be standard operating procedure for society hostesses—she provided "the name of her florist, the precise dimensions of the grand hall, gymnasium and dining room and the types of stone and wood paneling used in the interior as well as the names that appeared on her guest list." So successful was this sophisticated turn in press handling that the *Times*, whose reporter attended as a guest, gave the ball prominent display on its first and second pages.[22] The *Sun* also placed the story on its front page, while the *Tribune* and *World* each devoted four columns to the event.[23]

Twelve years later, when her daughter Consuelo married the Duke of Marlborough, Alva Vanderbilt again played press agent, orchestrating coverage so extensive that the curious lined Fifth Avenue and lunged at the couple as they left St. Thomas Episcopalian Church, trying, the bride recalled, "to snatch flowers from my bouquet."[24] In the run up to the wedding, the *Herald* had printed what it claimed was the only authentic illustration of Consuelo's dress, provided by the family, devoting more than one column of type to the "satin bridal costume . . . in which she will be presented to Queen Victoria." And with Alva's acquiescence, *Vogue* published illustrations of Consuelo's bridal underwear, on loan for the sketch artist. "The clasps of Miss Vanderbilt's stocking supporters are of gold," reported one weekly, "her corset-covers and chemises are embroidered with rosebuds in relief."[25] Consuelo was mortified. "I read to my stupefaction that my garters had gold clasps studded with diamonds, and wondered how I should live down such vulgarities," she wrote.[26]

Later still—divorced from William Kissam Vanderbilt, remarried to Oliver Hazard Perry Belmont and then widowed—Alva Smith Vanderbilt Belmont would bring those same press management skills to her new occupation, the suffrage movement. Using the assets of these two family fortunes, in 1910 she hired a press agent for the National American Woman Suffrage Association and installed Ida Husted Harper in

New York, forcing the mainstream suffrage organization to move its headquarters from Warren, Ohio. For the first time in fifty years, in an effort to appeal to the masses, salaried staffers would run a major movement organization once headed by ideologues and fueled by volunteers.

In colluding with the press to forward her schemes, Alva Vanderbilt had entered into what one scholar called a "Faustian bargain." Upper-class American families had long patterned their estates and their social habits on those of the European aristocracy, importing the sports, architecture, fashion, and high-tea rituals of the older ruling class. Their greatest inheritance was what one scholar dubbed an "ethos of exclusion." With more men's clubs than any city in the country, elite New Yorkers barred the doors against those who did not meet their strict standards for respectability and maintained secrecy within the walls of their clubs and the confines of their private railway cars and yachts.

Now, public appetite for news about the mighty had to be fed, and the wealthy were helpless to end the feast. "Unable to control the press, and unwilling to consider life without heightened visibility," New York socialites became "America's first celebrity-martyrs."[27] Like contemporary figures famous merely for being famous, they had invited into their circle a ravenous publicity machine that would lionize them on the way up and delight in pillorying them on the way down. Privacy, once their most treasured luxury, was but a figment of memory. In his notebooks, Henry James lamented that this comity had been disturbed by "democratization of the world." He faulted newspaper reporters for their "invasion, . . . impudence and shamelessness," and blamed "the devouring *publicity*" of modern life for extinguishing "all sense between public and private."[28]

For Alva Vanderbilt Belmont, who lacked the old money credentials of some of her peers, publicity was an equalizer. What she understood, perhaps better than the press critics who derided her social excesses or the suffrage leaders who would later balk at her autocratic ways, is that when the press in the 1880s anointed the wealthy as the media stars of their day, it conferred on elite women a benefit unlike any before—the power of the celebrity endorsement. And when, in 1894, some society women better known for their charitable donations and good-government reforms instead exploited their newfound celebrity to embrace women's suffrage, society and its reporters were stunned.

"All these women are in [the] Four Hundred," exclaimed Pulitzer's *World*, barely able to contain its incredulity. Calling their involvement in suffrage an "insurrection," the paper announced, "Here were nearly two score names as widely known and honorable as any in this state—names of people of the highest social standing. The upper class of women are enlisted. Woman suffrage is the one interesting subject of discussion in the fashionable world."[29]

From the beginning, almost everything about the suffrage battle of 1894 was unexpected. As part of the state's periodic review of its constitution, first enacted in 1777, delegates were appointed to convene to consider changes. Among the proposed amendments was one removing the word "male" from voting requirements in article 1, section 2. Hoping to flood the state capitol with one million signatures, Susan B. Anthony, president of the National American Woman Suffrage Association, asked four wealthy reformers, Catherine Palmer Abbe, Dr. Mary Putnam Jacobi, Josephine Shaw Lowell, and Margaret "Olivia" Sage, for $50,000 ($1.4 million in today's terms) to fund a house-to-house canvassing drive.[30] To her surprise, they declined.

In ways subtle and obvious, all four had worked to assimilate the immigrants that had overwhelmed New York's streets and traditions. By 1900, the city's population had climbed to 3.5 million, and more than a third of them were foreign-born.[31] Society leader Catherine Palmer Abbe, whose first husband, Courtlandt Palmer, had left her vast Manhattan real estate holdings and whose second husband, Dr. Robert Abbe, was a renowned scientist who worked with Marie and Pierre Curie, was a frequent contributor to civic reforms.[32] Inspired by the centennial of George Washington's inaugural in 1887, Abbe had founded the City History Club, an organization dedicated to educating immigrants to the glories of American history—offering classes and theatrical performances, launching preservation campaigns, and planning historic excursions into the city's streets.[33] Dr. Mary Putnam Jacobi was the first woman admitted to study at the University of Paris's Ecole de Médecine and, in 1871, the second female member of the Medical Society of New York County. Active in efforts to improve sanitation conditions in tenements and provide clean milk stations for immigrant mothers, she preached that compassion was as important as science in treatment of disease.[34] Josephine Shaw Lowell, a reformer from a prominent family (her brother Robert Gould Shaw commanded the all-black 54th Massachusetts Regiment during the Civil War and her sister Sarah had married into the Minturn shipping family known for anti-slavery activities) was the first woman appointed to the New York State Board of Charities.[35] Margaret "Olivia" Sage was a graduate of the Troy Female Seminary, established by Emma Hart Willard in 1821 as the first American institution to offer women an education comparable to that of men's universities.[36] Olivia had come to believe in women's ability to improve the polity. In 1905 she penned an article, "Opportunities and Responsibilities for Leisure Women," that spoke to this new reform instinct. "An immense amount of feminine talent and energy was wasted," she charged, predicting "the reawakening of women, . . . the building her up on a new basis of self-help and work for others." Disparaging the evils of drinking, smoking, and gambling, she urged "all our rich idle women" to reform the public square. "Every woman can make her village or town better," said Sage, who thought the wealthy had a greater duty because "woman is responsible in proportion to the wealth and time at her command."[37]

Perhaps weary of being asked to give money, nurturing their own reform agendas, the four now made clear that they were not interested in affiliating with traditional leaders in women's suffrage, who in their view had been campaigning with little effect for nearly fifty years. "The women who are making this movement are rich and conscientious," one unnamed social leader explained to the *Times*. "They feel that this is a progressive step. This has nothing to do with the work of the women suffragists, although we owe them a debt of gratitude for the progress so far made."[38] As the *Times* put it, they "have taken steps to have it quietly made known that they have no official connection with the professional 'woman's rights' agitators who have been demanding the right to vote for twenty-five [*sic*] years."[39]

How they settled on their strategy is not recorded, but once they had declined to fund Anthony's petition drive, they launched their own. They would give lectures from their parlors to stir interest, and gather signatures in what the *Times* called "the dainty white-and-gold atmosphere" of Sherry's restaurant at Fifth Avenue and 37th Street.[40] Lou Sherry had "very generously placed a white mahogany round table in his salesroom . . . occupied by a monster petition."[41] As the *Sun* helpfully explained to its readers, Sherry's was "a resort of fashion," not a place "with which radicalism or eccentricity is associated."[42]

Their activism would be genteel, not the coarse wrangling of political parties but the quiet appeal of the influential. Dr. Jacobi explained that amid rising immigration, they hoped to blunt "the shifting of political power from privileged classes to masses of men."[43]

Catherine Abbe was particularly outspoken about the need for society women to leverage their social standing.[44] "It is the Lord's work," she said of the parlor meetings. "We will get over 1,000 signatures of prominent men through social influences alone."[45] They sought the vote not as a measure of universal suffrage but as a marker of educated privilege. Unlike the male criminals, mentally ill, uneducated, and immigrants who had access to the ballot, they claimed the vote as women of erudition, to counteract those of the uninformed.

The idea of elite women speaking on any political topic was intoxicating to others of their class, who attended in such numbers that rooms overflowed, and to the press, which swarmed as if to cover a fancy dress ball. In May 1894, some thirteen hundred people were turned away from a debate at Sherry's, and speakers "could scarcely push their way to the platform." In an assessment that likely stunned its readers, the *New York Times* noted, "Never in its history has Sherry's seen such a gathering of people as flocked there last evening."[46] So effective was this branding of suffrage as a new cause of the wealthy that one woman stopped at the petition desk at Sherry's to inquire whether "she might put her name down, even if she did not belong to the Four Hundred."[47]

Converting a parlor—the refuge of domesticity—into a political war room took considerable doing, as a reporter for Pulitzer's *World* noted when he described how "two-story tables of mahogany, satinwood and marquetry" were "cleared of china and silver, to leave room for suffrage literature."[48] At Olivia Sage's home in April, two hundred "women of fashion" attended a suffrage discussion with chairs crunched together and overflow seating in the hallway. As Sage stood in her own parlor, with a glittering audience that included financier Jay Gould's daughter Helen, a reporter for the *Sun* expressed surprise that this former schoolteacher "presided with dignity and a great deal of self-possession," using "no notes at all and was not the least embarrassed."[49]

Dressed in fashionable clothes, wearing violets "but no other ornaments," these "charming matrons" confounded journalists who derided suffrage activists as "masculine and vulgar."[50] Now they saw "women of much refinement, remarkable intelligence and exquisite femininity" gravitating to the cause. Of another "crowded drawing room meeting," the *Sun* observed, "The question of woman suffrage seems to have taken precedence over all others in the minds of many leading ladies of fashionable society," including one who told a reporter that someday a woman would be vice president of the United States. Acknowledging that such a sentiment "sounds ludicrous and makes men laugh," she added, "The men will see that the women will laugh last, and he who laughs last laughs best, you know."

Unlike Alva Vanderbilt, who flaunted her wealth and the position it conferred, many of these first-generation celebrity suffragists were more modest. Cettie Rockefeller was a Baptist, to whom courting publicity was a sinful indulgence. Olivia Sage was, said one biographer, "a product of an evangelical Protestant upbringing that bred a strong sense of duty."[51] Florence Clinton Sutro, wife of prominent New York lawyer Theodore Sutro, was a Universalist who worshipped at the Church of the Divine

Paternity at Central Park West and 76th Street.[52] When a *Times* reporter asked her for the names of those who had signed the suffrage petition, she demurred, expressing a reluctance to invade boundaries of privacy. "We are not like the Woman Suffrage League," she explained, eager to distance herself and her movement from the "agitators" who had been seeking the vote through publicity stunts. "We do not want advertising. We shun it. We do not want our names made public. We want to keep out of the newspapers. We want enfranchisement, not notoriety."[53]

In April, the staunchly anti-suffrage *New York Times* offered a qualified welcome, on the front page. "The society of women of New York want to vote," the paper began. "Having reached this determination, they have set about accomplishing their desire in the energetic manner characteristic of them on all occasions."[54] Still, like sports reporters in a later generation forced to cover steroid or domestic abuse, subjects far from their field of knowledge, these journalists were thrown into a tizzy of denial that would test their stereotypes about women, wealth, and gender.

After covering a parlor meeting in February 1894, a reporter for the *World* suggested that female speeches about the need for a vote are likely "to arouse the risibilities of men who have not been educated up to the standpoint of regarding a woman in any other way than as a beautiful and helpless angel, to whom they should give their seats in public conveyances, and to gratify whose lightest whim they should fight and die." To the *World*'s reporter, "it was funny to a man whose wife and sisters protest that they will 'never, never vote' to be told that he was standing between womankind and the divine gift of the franchise." And when one speaker had the audacity to point out the inequalities of salary between male tenors and female opera singers, an injustice she said could be remedied by the ballot, for the reporter "it was hard not to snicker right out in meeting."[55]

In April, Harriett Gibbs Fox hosted a parlor meeting at her home at 18 East 31st Street. This time, as "a bunch of white double tulips stood in a dull-gold vase on a small table under the arch of the handsome parlors," speaker Eleanor Sanders confronted directly the charge that society's interest was "mere fad and caprice." She described one woman "of social position and modest personality" who circulated the petition at sixteen saloons, only to discover no signers.[56] In the face of the liquor industry's known opposition to women's suffrage, such perseverance might be seen in some quarters as folly, but here it was hailed as a measure of diligence. John D. Townsend, the "fighting lawyer" who had defended Boss Tweed on corruption charges and would later write a book about city politics, captured the excitement generated by the parlor suffragists.[57] "You cannot go anywhere now but some one meets you with a woman-suffrage petition and asks you to sign it—and every one does sign," he said. "The only person I have known who would not sign was a bachelor."[58]

When Laura Rockefeller opened her home at 4 West 54th Street in May, the audience "overflowed the parlors, crowded the hall, which is larger than the parlors of an ordinary city home, and filled the broad staircase almost to the top." It was, said the *Times*, "one of the largest parlor meetings that has been held in this city since the interest in the subject of political equality began to focus itself."[59] Trying to understand what had propelled these women of the leisure class to invade the male purview of politics, the *Times* interviewed suffragists staffing the desk at Sherry's. In a piece entitled "Their Enthusiasm Growing," the paper reported that some socialites had taken a course on political economy the previous winter, and were surprised to learn of legal barriers to women in taxation, property, and marriage. Others told the *Times* that they had been turned away at the polls for trying to vote for school commissioner, though the state had enacted school suffrage for women in 1880.[60]

Sometimes these new activists faced a backlash within their own families. Lee Wood Haggin, who married into the gold-rush rich Haggin family of Turkish origin, hosted a parlor meeting at her home at 10 East 54th Street. Turnout was so enormous that, as the *Times* put it, "Mrs. Haggin's large parlors were crowded to their utmost capacity, notwithstanding the fact that the invitations sent out had been limited to the immediate friends of the hostess."[61] When a reporter for the *Herald* called for her comments, she demurred. "My family is opposed to the campaign we are waging and so I shall not express my view," she said. "I am obeying the dictates of my conscience in the part I am taking."[62]

And sometimes the meetings sparked contention between those who favored suffrage and those who did not, among women who came to hear the speeches but not necessarily to applaud. It was a tussle among equals, over the prerogatives of class. Would the ballot, so stark in its overt political power, lessen their moral influence? Would exercising the vote rob them of their authority to steer policy from above the fray?

"Excitement reached fever heat" on Thursday, April 26, 1894, at Emma Constance Perry's home on East 38th Street when Josephine Jewell Dodge rose to oppose suffrage.[63] The *Times* reported her appearance as a "little diversion."[64] Founder and first president of the Association of Day Nurseries of New York City, founder of the New York Charity Organization Society, Dodge shared with other reformers a benevolent view of philanthropy and civic duty, but thought it better to influence reform from outside the political structure, preserving femininity.[65] Later president of the National Association Opposed to Woman Suffrage, Dodge spoke for those who feared that the franchise would provoke a gendered "social revolution such as the world has never seen."[66]

It was not, as one scholar noted, that anti-suffragists were hostile to women in public life, only to women in politics.[67] Fearful that uninformed immigrants would unravel the skein of public life, worried that women would lose their moral authority if they descended into the pit of partisan politics, antis argued that it would be better for the health of the polity if universal suffrage were repealed and the vote restricted to those who could read and write in the English language. Once the voter rolls were purged of immigrants, drunks, illiterates, and onetime criminals, a vote for educated women might be appropriate. Until then, they had plenty of duties at home without adding the responsibilities of military or jury service.[68]

Until the 1894 campaign, male derision had been the movement's loudest obstacle, female indifference its silent enemy. Now, a worthy opponent had publicly entered the ring. A seminal moment, this debate within the parlors, covered by the press, brought the fight into the open and in an unexpected way girded the movement for victory. As Crystal Eastman, sister of Max Eastman, editor of the *Masses*, and like him a prominent figure in Greenwich Village literary circles, noted, "Indifference is harder to fight than hostility."[69]

Thrust into the public eye, anti-suffragists situated their campaign at the just-opened Waldorf Hotel, down the street from Sherry's at Fifth and 33rd Street. Copies of their anti-suffrage petition were also available at Cooper Union, a university-without-walls created in 1859 by industrialist Peter Cooper. Anti-suffrage rhetoric may have influenced suffrage leaders, who now turned the movement's rationale from a natural rights argument (that women were entitled to the vote as citizens) to a municipal housekeeping one (that politics would benefit from the maternal instincts of women).[70] By whatever name, the increasingly high profile of the anti-suffragists politicized both sides.

The prospect of fashionable women warring over suffrage was intoxicating to publishers, who sharpened pencils for the fight ahead. Often the subtext of newspaper copy was whether politics would harden these women, itself a proxy for the question of whether granting women the vote would enfeeble men. In this, society advocates were reassuring. Noting that "women of Society have taken up the question of woman's suffrage," the *Evening World* explained to its readers helpfully, "mannish advocates are still in the field, but they are in the background, and the gentlewomen who have been induced to go in front are working in a way to win, if not 'equal rights,' a great deal of interest in the question."[71]

Another reporter for the *World* explained it this way: "There are two kinds of women in New York politics just now—ladies and females. The ladies belong to society; the females belong to the Suffrage League." The activists "do not enjoy being patronized even a little bit," observed the reporter, while "the fashionables" were just looking for "something to do." Society women had made clear, reported the newspaper, that "unpleasant women" were not welcome. Also treated dismissively were suffrage "professionals," now having "the greatest difficulty getting admission cards to these exclusive meetings" and "biting their finger nails to the quick . . . hoping that this humiliating influence may bring about the coveted 'woman's rights.'" To the reporter, the tensions seemed "delicious."[72]

As delegates to the constitutional convention gathered in Albany, one of their first decisions was to name as presiding officer Joseph H. Choate, a prominent New York society lawyer and legislator who had his sights on the governor's mansion. His wife, Caroline Choate, called Carrie, had been "among the first in society circles to come out openly" for suffrage, becoming a leader "in the task of securing signatures for the petition." Tall and "rather slightly built," with dark brown eyes, she was described by her husband as "the most graceful of women."[73] A talented painter, she at first resisted his marriage pleas, wearing a ring inscribed "Wedded to Art."[74] Now, she convened parlor meetings, although she avoided "publicity as much as possible, probably because of her husband's position as a delegate to the convention."[75]

To the shock of movement leaders, on his first day as presiding officer, Joseph Choate stacked the convention's suffrage committee with opponents. Led by the inestimable Elihu Root, they were almost uniformly and in some cases rabidly against granting women the right to vote. "It was clear to the suffragists," concluded one scholar, "that when Mr. Choate . . . packed the Suffrage Committee with conservative anti-suffragists . . . he was counting on the popularity he would acquire from the convention to win the governor's seat."[76] Conversations between husband and wife, by then married for thirty-three years, must have tested the civility of their partnership. Choate never did serve as governor of New York, but in 1899 President McKinley appointed him U.S. ambassador to the Court of St. James, where he served until 1905. Perhaps in deference to his wife's interest in painting, he also served as one of the founders of the Metropolitan Museum of Art.

By campaign's end, Susan B. Anthony had managed to collect 600,000 signatures, a sizeable number though short of her target of one million.

No matter. Pleas went unheeded, as delegates failed to pass the women's suffrage amendment; ninety-eight delegates voted against it, and only fifty-eight voted for it.[77] Like a fleeting spring shower, the advent of the gilded suffragists might have been quickly forgotten, but for an unexpected legacy of their participation.

Convinced that the surest path to the ballot was through an informed electorate, they now created an organization to interest the public in civic issues. Headquartered at 143 West 43rd Street, the nonpartisan League for Political Education sponsored lectures and debates that attracted an audience hungry for substance. Formed in 1895 to "arouse among women practical interest in public affairs, in civic institutions and in good government,"[78] the league offered lectures on history, instruction in parliamentary procedure, and courses in social ethics.[79] One scholar described it as the first self-conscious effort to use print media and the public square to espouse policy.[80] Later, in the aftermath of the ratification of the Nineteenth Amendment, their renamed and relocated Town Hall became a staple of New York City oratory and performance. Designed by the architectural firm of McKim, Mead & White, which had created many of the mansions where parlor suffragists spoke, Town Hall would host some of the great names of twentieth-century public life. Booker T. Washington, Eleanor Roosevelt, Woodrow Wilson, and Winston Churchill spoke from the hall's podium.[81] In 1921 Margaret Sanger was arrested on stage while discussing birth control. In 1944 Langston Hughes led a town meeting on race. And in 1963 Bob Dylan played his first major concert there, unveiling his new song "Blowin' in the Wind."[82]

Suffrage leaders had hoped that the advent of society suffragists would help defuse press derision, as it seemed to have done the year before in Colorado. Iona Hanna, wife of a prominent banker and the first female director of the Denver school district, had invited wealthy clubwomen and social figures to join the Denver Equal Suffrage League, attracting "the best people." Observers noted one immediate result. Where once the press had been dismissive, now "not one paper in Denver said a word of ridicule or even mild amusement concerning suffragists."[83] With support from the Populist Party, male voters approved the state constitutional amendment allowing women to vote, 35,698 to 29,461.[84] Suffrage leaders hoped that newspapers and magazines in New York would follow suit.[85]

If New York reporters did not hide their sarcasm at the advent of gilded suffragists, they did lavish attention on an issue all but invisible before the 1894 campaign. *Harper's Bazaar* published twenty-one stories on the subject, *Vogue Magazine* twelve. Among the dailies, Pulitzer's *World* published 187 stories, the *Brooklyn Daily Eagle*, 159, and even the anti-suffrage *New York Times*, 148. For the next fourteen years, interest flagged as the cause faltered in failing state campaigns across the country. By century's end, only four states had given female citizens the right to vote in national elections—Wyoming (1890), Colorado (1893), Utah (1895), and Idaho (1896).[86]

Not until 1908 did press interest again fire, this as a new generation took to the podium. Nothing stoked media scrutiny more than the entry into the movement of two of society's most glittering celebrities, who waged a public contest for the title of preeminent suffragist that converted many within their circle and electrified many others in the public. Though Katherine Duer Mackay and Alva Vanderbilt Belmont denied that theirs was a rivalry, their contest for power was as intense as anything Samuel Tilden ever attempted against William "Boss" Tweed when Tammany Hall and the governance of New York were in the balance.

That two women of wealth and social standing were competing for the role of suffrage leader suggests a notable shift in society's view of politics. No longer content to defer to their husbands and fathers in matters of the state, these two giants of social celebrity fought not to replace Mrs. Astor as a preeminent social leader or compete with their husbands in business prowess but to assume a title new to both women and society—political kingmaker. Alva Belmont was a child of the Civil War, a veteran of wars for social dominance whose infamous divorce from William Vanderbilt and remarriage to Oliver Hazard Perry Belmont had, like all her adventures, been lived in public on the front pages of the nation's newspapers. Katherine Mackay was a Gilded Age beauty whose seemingly picture-perfect marriage and genteel activism protected her from public criticism, even as tensions in her personal life made her the first celebrity built up and then torn down by a capricious press.

Together, their involvement engendered a shift in public attitudes, as magazines and newspapers gave more coverage to the suffrage movement in the 1910s than at any time in history. Unlike the first generation of society suffragists, who spoke from their parlors to a New York audience, Mackay and Belmont were national figures, celebrities chronicled nationally for their clothes, their décor, their marriages, and now their activism. Gertrude Atherton, a San Francisco novelist then often compared to Henry James and Edith Wharton, mused that because of "the individual awakening of the women of Society," the chaperone had disappeared ("the modern American Society girl . . . is quite capable of taking care of herself") and, most notably, suffrage had replaced bridge whist as the nation's hobby. "Suffrage has arrived," she declared. "It is fashionable. It has put the would-be Mrs. Astor . . . out of business. . . . Fancy Mrs. Mackay wasting her time leading Society."[87]

3

THE BIRTH OF A RIVALRY

Woman suffrage, once the cause forlorn and rejected, has
entered the drawing room. And the women who have
invited it there are those who may lead . . .
in a cause as in a cotillion.

MABEL POTTER DAGGETT[1]

RARE is the revolution that arrives with such elegance. Invitations bearing the Tiffany hallmark were "very stunning and expensive," "as gorgeously got up as smart wedding cards." Complete with reply paper and envelope, 150 invitations summoned recipients not to a costume ball or a society wedding but to a political rebellion—a 1909 campaign by high society to win the vote for women.[2]

Katherine Duer Mackay, whose family name first appeared in the *New York Social Register* when that oracle of exclusivity began publication in 1887, was an unlikely choice to lead the suffrage charge.[3] In her lineage she counted a fourteenth-century Scottish king, a delegate to the Continental Congress and his wife, that "famous belle of Revolutionary days, Lady Kitty Duer," a Supreme Court justice, and two Columbia University presidents.[4] The Duers were, in effect, High Establishment. As one scribe put it, "The names of Duer, King, Alexander, Van Rensselaer and Travers are ones for which the historian of New York finds frequent and honorable mention, and Mrs. Mackay traces her descent to all of them."[5]

Described by *Town Topics* as "the perfect specimen of willful, wistful beauty," the dark-haired Duer was an only child of privilege. Schooled by private tutors, summering in Newport, she was raised in a Manhattan home where servants wore uniforms.[6] On a ship bound for Europe in the summer of 1896, she met Clarence Mackay, heir to a new money fortune of silver mining cable technology. On being introduced to the twenty-one-year-old belle, Mackay saw at once the source of her allure, observing, "She's as beautiful as her name."[7]

By 1909, when Katherine Mackay's embossed suffrage invitations were mailed, she and "Clarry," as the rags called him, had been married eleven years. Clarence Mackay was chairman of the Postal Telegraph and Cable Corporation and a horse breeder of international renown. His fashionable wife hosted extravagant dinners at their home at 244 Madison Avenue, and at Harbor Hill, the 628-acre estate in Roslyn, Long Island, featuring horse stables and dog kennels, gardens and garages. Atop a hill was their house, larger than the Parthenon, designed by architect-to-the-stars Stanford White.[8] One room, lined in cedar, was devoted exclusively to table linens.[9] In 1904 Katherine Mackay published a novel, *The Stone of Destiny*, in which a husband laments a wife who cares little for the world beyond personal interests. Unlike her protagonist, Mackay did.

The mother of three, Mackay ran for a seat on the Roslyn school board in 1905, taking advantage of a law enacted twenty-five years earlier granting women in New York the right to vote in local school elections.[10] The idea of a woman in government was still rare in politics, and all but unheard of in her circle. Friends, she reported, were "rather startled" that she planned to attend meetings with men.[11] The press was equally astonished. Pondering why a member of the gilded class would seek public office, the *Nation* speculated that "women of leisure and culture . . . have the time that few men have" to devote to the work. In a reaffirmation of gender stereotypes, the magazine added that unlike men, women "care very much less for political influences than they do for the proper education of children."[12]

During the campaign, her male opponent, Dr. J. H. Bogart, had belittled her for representing "petticoat rule." After she defeated him, Mackay pushed a reform agenda that included an end to corporal punishment, making her an immediate favorite with students, who scrawled on fences, sidewalks, and barns the schoolboy graffiti "Mrs. Mackay Is All Right." Showing considerable political acumen, Mackay persuaded Bogart to run for an open seat at the next election. This he did, winning the race, giving Mackay a grateful and reliable ally for her reforms. As the *New York Herald* put it, "His attitude toward the proposals that come from the woman who read him out of the school board and then read him back in again is now said to be as distinctly respectful and considerate as that clever woman could wish."[13] If she was a novice, she had proven herself an able politician, further enhancing her reputation.

When Mackay embraced suffrage, there was much excitement in movement circles, and some talk of installing her in a leadership role. "Workers in the cause have said that a leader was wanted who combined high social position and acknowledged intellectual attainments—one who would further compel serious attention to the movement and disarm ridicule," explained the *New York Irish-American*.[14] It helped that she was the epitome of femininity, projecting an air of ladylike refinement. "Mrs. Mackay, even when attending committee meetings, is always wonderfully gowned," noted *New Idea Magazine*.[15]

Soon she would vie for press attention with Alva Vanderbilt Belmont—newly widowed, spectacularly rich, and eager to leave her mark on politics as she had on society. The domineering Belmont, more of a bulldog than a kitten, was accustomed to getting her way, and now she applied the skills of publicity she had mastered as a society hostess to align herself with the forces of reform. If Mackay's ambition was cloaked in manners, Belmont's was bald with audacity. If Mackay meant to persuade men of her circle with the allure of her beauty and the polish of her speech, Belmont would appropriate the hardball tactics of male politics, turning it against the men who had betrayed her. Together, Mackay and Belmont energized a suffrage movement that had sunk into what even its friends called "the doldrums,"[16] creating the kind of buzz that only a celebrity feud can.

Harriot Stanton Blatch was the first suffrage leader to grasp the possibilities of Mackay's entry into the field. Daughter of the movement matriarch Elizabeth Cady Stanton, Blatch had recently returned to New York after living in England for twenty years as the wife of a British businessman, stunned to find the American movement launched by her mother in "a rut worn deep and ever deeper," one that "bored its adherents and repelled its opponents." For political ineptitude, or perhaps naïveté, nothing topped one activist's admission to Blatch that she did not lobby Theodore Roosevelt during the 1904 election because she did not want to "bother" him during the hectic campaign.[17]

Eager to reinvigorate the movement, Blatch in 1907 had recruited working-class supporters, borrowing a tactic from British suffragettes. Her pitch was simple: young workers toiling in New York's garment industry could win improvements in salary and workplace conditions only if they had the ballot, and the suffrage movement could win the ballot only if it demonstrated widespread support. Forming an Equality League of Self-Supporting Women, she held meetings "in a dingy little room on 4th Street off the Bowery."[18] Soon, with a membership fee of twenty-five cents and the blessing of labor leaders who rallied their troops at Cooper Union, enrollment grew "by leaps and bounds."

Within two years, the alliance between Blatch's middle-class and working-class supporters had fractured. Union leaders suspected that Blatch would drop the working class as soon as suffrage was won.[19] For her part, Blatch said she was tired of the "persistent need for funds." She was convinced that "the money lying ready for suffrage is limitless; how to tap the reservoir is the only problem."[20] When Mackay came "to tell me in her charming, spontaneous way of her newly awakened interest in suffrage," Blatch brightened.

Mackay told Blatch that she was not inclined, as a friend had suggested, to "ally herself with the orthodox suffrage forces and take office under their leaders." Instead, she was more "inclined to forming a society of her own." Blatch thought the situation clear. "Here was a young and beautiful woman, a social leader, longing for a broader stage to move upon than the usual outlet given by fashionable society. Naturally an office under a leader did not attract her in the least. She wanted to be on

top, running a show herself." Though Blatch was frustrated by the deliberate pace of Mackay's planning—months were consumed in selecting
a name for the group after "The Feminist Propaganda" was rejected—
she patiently helped Mackay assemble a stellar team of reformers for her
newly named Equal Franchise Society.[21] Rabbi Stephen M. Wise, Columbia professor John Dewey, and New York Consumers League president
Maud Nathan—along with suffrage leaders Blatch and Carrie Chapman
Catt—all gave substance to an organization that might otherwise have
been dismissed as the latest fad of bored ladies of leisure.[22] "My conviction was that she could be of immense value to the suffrage cause by
drawing into the movement valuable recruits," recalled Blatch.[23]

News that Mackay would attend an Interurban Suffrage Council lecture at Carnegie Hall in December 1908 electrified interest. "All of the
boxes in the hall have been sold at good prices, every reserved seat has
been engaged and there are now in the hands of the committee of ar-
rangements more applications for places on the platform than can be provided," reported the *Baltimore Sun*. Those claiming space, and declaring
their support for the still controversial issue, were a who's who of wealthy
socialites. There was Edith Kingdon Gould, an actress who had married
the son of Jay Gould.[24] Patriarch of family wealth, her father-in-law had
been a railroad magnate, stock manipulator, and Boss Tweed ally considered so ruthless in business tactics he had earned the sobriquet the "Me-
phistopheles of Wall Street."[25] Also in prominent attendance were Edith
Shepard Fabbri, great-granddaughter of Cornelius Vanderbilt; Ruth Sears
Baker Pratt, wife of a prominent banker who in 1925 would become the
first woman elected to the New York Board of Aldermen and in 1929 the
first woman elected to Congress from New York; Emmeline Winthrop,
a member of the Colony Club and a founder of the Girls' Branch of the
Public School Athletic League; Hope Goddard Iselin, a millionaire by
both her father and her husband and the first woman to compete as a
crew member in the America's Cup yacht race; Virginia Fair Vanderbilt,
a Nevada silver mining heiress whose mother-in-law was Alva Belmont;
and Dorothy Payne Whitney, perhaps the wealthiest woman in the room,

who with her husband, Willard Straight, later founded the New School for Social Research.[26] With their arrival, the *Sun* predicted a more "dignified" campaign, appealing to "the more influential members of society," free of that refuge of the rampant, street corner speeches.[27]

Alice Stone Blackwell, whose mother, Lucy Stone, had labored alongside Elizabeth Cady Stanton and Susan B. Anthony in the lonely vineyards of nineteenth-century activism, could barely contain her excitement. "Five dollars paid for single *seats* in the gallery merely to hear the speaking," she exclaimed. "People clamoring for tickets . . . five hundred seated at table and five hundred turned away disappointed; people cheerfully paying two dollars for seats in another room, where they could not see the speakers during the luncheon, and submitting to uncomfortable crowding in a space far too small"—it was all a marvel.[28] Blackwell knew that in the 1840s, when her mother had lectured against slavery and for women's rights, so shocking was the spectacle of a woman speaking in public that men hissed or threw eggs.[29] Now crowds were fighting for tickets to hear a female speaker. "Snobbery is a sorry thing, in a suffragist or in an anti," Blackwell wrote, "but the suffragist has for so many years been sniffed at by the anti as an unfashionable, unpopular and unwomanly creature that she may perhaps be excused for breathing a sigh of relief. . . . It is nice to have 'smart' people demanding your tickets when they would not look at them before."[30]

Six weeks after entering the arena, Mackay made her speaking debut at a suffrage luncheon in early 1909, signaling both the genesis of her activism—she aligned herself firmly with those who believed that the "mother's vote" would ensure a more moral polity—and the confusion her involvement stirred among reporters accustomed to covering her as a socialite. "Mrs. Mackay's address was followed by a great deal of applause, and Mr. Mackay leaned over to shake her hand," wrote the *New York Times*, which often inveighed against extending the vote to women.[31] Like critics trained to attend to details of an operatic ensemble, journalists reported on her attire as news. Whether they recorded these details to trivialize her activism or satisfy reader curiosity is difficult to ascertain.

What is clear is that she and her cohorts were the media celebrities of the day, chronicled for their sartorial and, now, their political attire.

Even the anti-suffrage *New York Times* took note of the luncheon, reassuring readers that the initial excitement would fade, much like the fickle whimsy of fashion these socialites represented. The advent of women "of recognized social position as leaders in the woman suffrage movement has obviously increased the public interest," the paper conceded. "Women who are supposed to be authorities on dress and manners, who are at home in the most exclusive social circles, are bound to influence others who . . . yearn for recognition." Not to worry, though, these society activists were not in it for the long haul. "Fashionable agitation for the extension of the suffrage is not to be regarded as dangerous. Its leaders will soon find agitation tedious," the *Times* added in full-throated mockery. "There are so many pleasanter things to do, when one has ample leisure and money."[32]

Mackay's Equal Franchise Society was an invitation-only organization, formed not to reach the masses but to invite the elite to experiment with a ladylike approach to the public square. It was dedicated to influencing the influential, what *Harper's Weekly* called "persons of prominence in the social, professional and financial worlds."[33] But so extensive was press coverage that suddenly, suffrage at all levels had a spring in its step. Within a month of the society's launch, five new suffrage organizations opened shop in the city.[34] Among Mackay's early converts was Charlotte Goodrich Morton, whose husband, Paul, was heir to the Morton's Salt fortune and who had once been an anti-suffragist.[35] "Mrs. Mackay and her friends have put the cachet of style upon a woman thinking for herself," noted one newspaper.[36]

Much had changed in the ten years since 1900, when Maud Wood Park and Inez Haynes Irwin had teamed up while at Radcliffe to organize the College Equal Suffrage League. Years later, Park observed that the impact of the College Equal Suffrage League had been to give suffrage "a kind of intellectual prestige," just as the entry of Mackay and other "women of acknowledged social standing" had given the cause a "new and helpful impetus."[37] Now, as Park was traveling in the Orient, Irwin wrote to her with some passion about the change: "Altogether, Maud, the movement that when we got into had about as much energy as a dying kitten, is now a big, virile, threatening, wonderful thing."[38]

Within months the Equal Franchise Society had attracted 250 members, a number that rose to 625 within the year.[39] Even for upper-class women, the prospect of rubbing shoulders with gilded power was one lure. When Mackay invited suffrage speaker Ida Harper to give a lecture at 244 Madison Avenue, "naturally a member of Society felt that she had climbed several rungs of the social ladder when she was served tea and cakes by Mrs. Mackay's . . . flunkeys in her blue and white drawing room."[40] *Vogue* was even more sarcastic about the motives of new suffragists. "There is no doubt . . . that the Woman's Suffrage cause is to be made strong by an appeal to the snobbery of the general public," said writers of *Vogue*'s "As Seen by Him" column. "Women and men will flock to its banner if they can drink tea from the same cups as the world of fashion and disport in the same drawing rooms."[41] Celebrity had changed what it meant to be a wealthy hostess. Playing to the public now meant expanding the invitation list beyond the gilded to include those who were interesting even if they were not in the *Social Register*.

For her part, Mackay credited the spike in interest to a Cornell University professor of medicine who had argued that whenever women made political advances, the birth rate declined and the number of nervous breakdowns increased. "We have enrolled twice as many members this month as we did last, and for that I think we must thank the 'antis,'" said Mackay. "Since Max G. Schlapp's lecture at the Colony Club, we have taken in an unusually large number."[42] Mackay disbanded the membership committee, seeking not to vet potential recruits but to welcome them. No longer were invitations sent to the privileged. Society was knocking at the door. "Society women . . . seemed to feel they were really exercising a civic duty in participating in the movement," marveled the *American*.[43]

If Mackay's Tiffany-embossed invitations signaled the advent of the ladylike politician, the interjection of feminine gentility into the raw masculinity of politics, Alva Belmont's entry into the field was more like a bomb, destabilizing both the society to which she once aspired and the suffrage campaign to which she now pledged herself.

Despite portraits of Alva as a figure of clawing ambition, climbing the ladders of society to enact her very own "rags to riches" story, she was, like Mackay, a child of privilege.[44] Her father, Murray Forbes Smith, moved the family from the South, where he ran a business selling and transporting cotton, to New York when Alva was six years old, joining the exclusive Union Club.[45] Becoming a successful Wall Street broker, Smith leased a house at 40 Fifth Avenue, one of the most expensive on the block, designed by architect Calvert Vaux in the 1850s for a wealthy merchant.[46] After the war, Smith relocated his business to Liverpool and his family to Paris. There Alva was schooled, and she and her sisters were "introduced to the highest levels of French Society."[47] On their return to New York, he found the business climate changed, or so it seemed to him, from a culture where a man's word was his bond to one where greed was king. "The clever arts by which big deals were put through seemed to him underhanded," recalled his daughter. Murray Smith's fortunes fell along with his health, and this decline of stature, Alva later suggested, is what propelled her to wed wealth. As she put it, marrying William Kissam Vanderbilt in 1875 seemed an answer to her predicament, a way for "my practical nature" to ease a dying man's wounded pride.

If she married to ease her father's financial quandary, the union suited her interests as well. From childhood, Alva Smith had showcased an imperious personality, plotting her own agenda. By her own account, as a child she had wrangled a bedroom of her own by swinging a towel "with an awful deliberateness" and smashing "every one of the china ornaments" in the nursery. Though she endured a whipping from her mother, nursery attendants insisted she be separated from the other children.[48] Mission accomplished.

Power was at the center of Alva's ambitions, marrying a Vanderbilt a treasured goal. The lavish costume ball that fascinated the public and forced the old money Astors to open the gates of social validation to the *arriviste* Vanderbilts in 1883, the campaign to manipulate her daughter toward a royal wedding that made Consuelo a duchess, the infamous 1895 divorce from a philandering husband with details leaked to a press hungry for celebrity misdeeds—all made her marriage a narrative of excess.

Later, in marrying Oliver Hazard Perry Belmont, the third son (some said the "wayward son") of financier August Belmont, Alva found a "quiet and companionable marriage" with a quintessential sportsman who delighted in life as a "gentleman of leisure."[49] Oliver's father, August Belmont, had served as the first New York representative for the House of Rothschild, in the records as the first upper-class New Yorker to import a French chef. Cleverly, he sought publicity for both accomplishments, ensuring his reputation for a lavish lifestyle.[50] In marrying Caroline Slidell Perry, daughter of the famous admiral, he had cemented his wealth to her American cachet.[51] The reinvented August Belmont—born in Germany as August Schonberg—thus blunted the social stigma of his Jewish heritage and ensured his children, raised as Episcopalians, entrée to society.

Perhaps it was Oliver's willingness to brace the winds of adverse public and even parental opinion—as evidenced by his refusal to pay the hush money demanded by publisher Colonel William d'Alton Mann to keep salacious articles about him out of the gossipy weekly *Town Topics*—that first drew Alva to him.[52] The two met aboard William Vanderbilt's yacht, on trips meant to mend the Vanderbilt marriage. Whispers about Oliver's attentiveness toward Alva circulated in Newport, and nine months after her divorce, they married. Given the Jewish roots of his money and Oliver's willingness to flaunt decorum, the marriage had just the whiff of danger that may have appealed to her.[53] As one writer put it, "One begins to suspect that the setting up of hurdles in order to jump them was her way of adding a bit of zest to the sameness of a social game that was already showing itself a drag to her lively spirit. And were not the Belmonts partly Jewish? Better and better."[54]

Twelve years after their wedding, Oliver Belmont died suddenly from peritonitis and Alva found herself adrift—a fifty-six-year-old socialite with homes in Manhattan, Long Island, and Newport, looking for a chal-

lenge. Feeling "worn out with social gain," she attended an Equal Franchise Society lecture, at Mackay's invitation, at Madison Garden Theatre.[55]
There she listened as suffrage activist Ida Husted Harper delivered her
appeal. Alva Belmont said that she felt "this striking at the root," an instinct that the ballot could liberate her from the tyranny of men.[56] She met
leaders of the mainstream groups, including Anna Howard Shaw, one of
the first female ordained Methodist ministers in the country. Viewed as a
brilliant orator but weak administrator, Shaw headed the National American Woman Suffrage Association from 1904 to 1915. Despite conflicts in
leadership circles and defections to Alice Paul's more radical Congressional Union, membership on her watch grew from 17,000 to 200,000.[57]

At Shaw's invitation, Belmont traveled to London in April 1908 to attend a convention of the International Suffrage Alliance. There she found
delegates "very serious, very respectable, very placid," much like their
American counterparts. But on the streets of London and in the booming
rhetoric of Hyde Park, Belmont found a cause. Captivated by the "lively
and picturesque" tactics of the militants, she was moved "to a determined
resolve that American women must not lag behind this stupendous
march of women toward the glory of liberty."[58] Back in the United States,
she sought to upend the preaching-to-the-choir insularity of the American campaign and the exclusivity of Mackay's gilded activism.

Her debut could not have been more of a spectacle. Six months after
Mackay's first speech, Belmont opened one of the jewels of Gilded Age
architecture to public view. For the first time in the fabled history of
Newport's great mansions, the public was invited inside. She and architect Richard Morris Hunt had designed Marble House as a "temple to
the arts."[59] Modeled after the Petit Trianon at Versailles, the estate was
finished in 1892 at a cost reported to exceed $11 million ($300 million in
contemporary terms).

No American interior had ever boasted so much gold on the walls and
so much marble, "meant to flaunt the wealth and power of the young
Midases of the New World."[60] For decades, museum patrons had pined
to see its treasures. Having closed the house after her divorce, Alva Bel-

mont now threw open its doors to raise funds for suffrage. The cost was $5 (about $135 today) to tour the first floor, or $1 (some $27) to walk the grounds and hear the speeches, proceeds to benefit the National American Woman Suffrage Association. Despite the steep price—Ida Husted Harper, the association's press agent, thought five dollars just the right amount to attract respectable visitors while weeding out "mere curiosity seekers"—applications came in "from points all the way from Maine to Michigan."[61] Well in advance of the event, Bellevue Avenue "was lined on both sides for a distance of over a mile with all sorts of vehicles."[62]

Newport was shaken, and tried to take the unprecedented public opening in its stride, as if the sight of hundreds of people who were not listed in the *Social Register* crawling over the private "cottages" in the sanctuary of America's wealth was but one of many festive events of a delightful, event-packed ten-week summer season.[63] "Busy Week for Newport," headlined Philadelphia's *Public Ledger*. "Tennis, Polo and Suffragette Meetings the Features."[64] Many of the Four Hundred attended, if only to avoid engendering Belmont's fury and with it the social humiliation of being dropped from her invitation list.

Belmont had persuaded several friends to show their well-known faces as a lure to the press, including Mamie Fish, the acerbic hostess who once said of her husband's holdings, "We are only moderately well off; we have but a few million dollars."[65] A month after the events at Marble House, Fish conceded that she had attended only out of loyalty. "I went to Mrs. Belmont's house because she is a friend and asked me to come. I did not go because I have any leaning toward the cause," she said. As for reports that she planned to host a suffrage lunch at her Newport mansion, Crossways, Fish added, "I am not a suffragist and I don't in the least want to be. To tell the truth, I'm altogether too busy as it is."[66]

Crowds were huge—according to the papers, more than five hundred showed up on Tuesday, August 24, and even more the following Sunday. "Bailey's Beach and the Casino were deserted," wrote one admirer. "Everybody was here—debutante and dowager and the latest divorcee. Women, the jewels at whose throats would have financed a reform, trailed carelessly over the lawn in gowns representing in the aggregate hundreds of thousands in money."[67]

As always, attuned to the glories of what modern political strategists would call the "optics," Belmont arranged for a keynote speech by one of the remaining titans of the first generation—Julia Ward Howe, author of "The Battle Hymn of the Republic," contemporary of Stanton, Anthony, and Stone, "at ninety years old . . . the last survivor who pioneered the reform." During Howe's brief and some said inaudible remarks, Belmont stood at her side, "with reverently inclined head. And in the fluttering closing gesture of the aged hands, something like a benediction seemed to fall on the other woman with the paradise-plumed hat and the necklace of priceless pearls."[68]

On the lawn meanwhile, souvenir seekers could buy photographs of the recently deceased Susan B. Anthony, at two dollars each.[69] It was an odd pairing of political cause and artistic bounty, of social hierarchy with hawked kitsch. In the eyes of the *New York World*, "It was a great day for suffrage, with such an awesome proximity to the Social Register."[70] Others were less charitable, seeing in Belmont's extravaganza a cause born not from commitment but from boredom. Cartoonist Harold Heaton captured this sentiment in the *Chicago Inter Ocean* in late August 1909. His cartoon showed Alva Belmont distributing "The Mrs. O.H.P. Belmont Woman Suffrage Tonic." Below, the caption read, "The New Cure for Newport Ennui."[71]

Despite this evident mockery, the Marble House events marked a turning point in suffrage and journalism history, leaving a pile of dated clippings on the pressroom floor. The *Herald*, an anti-suffragist paper that in 1853 first coined the term "rampant women" to describe female activists, now changed its tune.[72] Clever as always about press management, Belmont gave the paper exclusive rights to photograph the treasures at Marble House before the rallies—as long as copyrights for all the photos were taken out in her name. She also placed $200 worth of ads in the *Herald* to promote the events.[73] Perhaps as a result, on Sunday, August 22, the newspaper devoted an entire keepsake section to the rallies, headlining, "Woman's Cause Gives Public Entrance to Marble House Wonderland of Art."[74]

It was not as if publisher James Gordon Bennett Jr., a yachtsman whose father had instilled in him the prejudices of their class, had changed his view of suffrage, "particularly in this city," as he put it, "with its incessant influx of illiterate immigrant women."[75] But he conceded that the event had been conducted "on a high plane and very beautiful." And in Belmont's view, Bennett arranged for fair-minded coverage. "We are now being given courteous consideration by the press," she told the *Morning Telegraph* two months later. Bennett "instructed the men who were sent out from his paper to see that the affair was reported in its right light." Ever since, she said, "the question of woman's suffrage has been treated with serious and courteous consideration by the press . . . throughout the country."[76]

Before the Marble House events, Belmont invited Shaw to dinner. The two talked about suffrage "until nearly one o'clock," Shaw reported to her board. "We talked so late that I missed my train and had to stay over at the hotel another night, but I got her for a life member. . . . I think she will help us financially by and by."[77] It did not take long for this prediction to prove an understatement of historic and consequential proportions.

Within a year, Belmont had forced the National American Woman Suffrage Association to relocate its headquarters to New York from Warren, Ohio, where treasurer Harriet Taylor Upton lived. Paying the association's first-year rent on the seventeenth floor of 505 Fifth Avenue and underwriting the salary of Ida Husted Harper to run its press bureau, some $60,000 a year ($1.5 million in contemporary terms), Belmont headquartered her own suffrage organization down the hall.[78] A bitter Laura Clay of Kentucky tried to rewrite the organization's rules to prevent this takeover by one of society's Four Hundred. "The chief impression we are making on the uninformed public is that we are a protégé of Mrs. Belmont," she charged. "The public are amused in calculating how long she will be pleased with her toy."[79] Resentments soon broke into print. "National suffragists fear they'll lose their identity," noted the *World*.[80] Belmont, said the *Washington Times*, "is attracting so much attention by her work in the cause that others who do as much feel they get no credit."[81]

Belmont ignored the critics and launched her Political Equality Association, setting up twelve chapters that reflected the city's polyglot culture. There was the Harlem club at 260 Lenox Avenue, the Wage Earners League at 196 E. Broadway, the Bronx branch at 830 Westchester Avenue, the Physicians and Surgeons League at 1720 Broadway, the Artists League at 140 East 34th Street, and the Negro Men and Women League at 83 West 134th Street. Like Blatch, she hoped to extend the appeal of the suffrage campaign across the city. And the group's typed statement of purpose implicitly understood the controversy that still attached to the cause: "Names of members who for reasons of their own may not wish it known that they are actively identified or connected with the movement . . . will not be divulged under any circumstances. The association to this extent is a secret one."[82]

With Fanny Garrison Villard, daughter of abolitionist William Lloyd Garrison, Belmont now reached out to women of color. As Edith Wharton captured so vividly in *The Old Maids*, wealthy New Yorkers had long worried about protecting the pedigree of their white skin.[83] But Belmont's suffrage campaign was an act of rebellion. Eager to upset the strict social codes of a class that often snubbed her, in early 1910 she persuaded Irene Moorman, president of the Negro Women's Business League, that white progressives were interested in extending the female franchise to all women. Moorman dutifully organized a suffrage meeting at the Mount Olivet Baptist Church on West 53rd Street, where Belmont spoke of "that bond of humanity and equality which alone the woman suffrage movement can create." Two hundred African American women attended the meeting, and to them she promised that if more than half of them joined her Political Equality Association, she would provide them a headquarters building. "I know that unless this cause means freedom and equal rights to all women, of every race, or every creed, rich or poor, its doctrines are worthless and it must fail in its achievement," she said. Sign up they did.[84]

Her efforts to include blacks within the folds of the movement soon ran afoul of the ardent racism in suffrage circles.[85] In 1911 Belmont withdrew an invitation to black suffragists to attend a suffrage ball after white supporters—"girls uptown and downtown"—balked, announcing their unhappiness by deciding to "stop work on their dancing frocks."[86] When, later that year, eight black activists attempted to dine in a suffrage lunchroom Belmont had opened downtown, they were turned away, offered box lunches and asked to eat elsewhere.[87] This endemic racism also stymied Alice Dewey, whose husband, Columbia professor John Dewey, served on Mackay's board. After she invited black suffragists to their home at 49 St. Nicholas Place, lawyers for the St. Cecilia Apartments threatened her with eviction, prompting her to cancel the meeting.[88] Perhaps as a result, when Belmont's Political Equality Association opened its new Harlem headquarters, only twenty black suffragists showed up, leading Belmont to tell reporters "how disappointed she was."[89] Membership across the city peaked at three thousand, and by 1911 Belmont had closed chapters in the Bronx and Harlem and on East Broadway and the Upper East Side, consolidating in headquarters downtown.[90] In fact, black women had their own platforms within the temperance movement and the National Association of Colored Women Clubs, formed in 1896. An alliance of women along the lines of gender could not blunt the primacy of race, not at a time of lynching in the South and discrimination in the North.

Mackay with her exclusive circle of influence and Belmont with her inclusive attempt to supplant national organizations had joined the movement. They represented the extremes of suffrage ideology. Mackay, as a mother and school board member, reasoned that women needed the vote to protect the public health and safety, extending the maternal purview of the home to the public square. Belmont, seeking to avenge the grievance of male betrayals, sought the ballot to claim the rights of her class, denied her as a woman. In the years to come, the ladylike suffragist, earnest and patient, and the battle-scarred activist, angry and insistent, would differ over tactics. For now, the battle between them was joined.

4

A RIVALRY COLLAPSES

No cause was ever won but first was
mocked, no gate stands wide but
at one point stood locked.

LAURENCE HOUSMAN[1]

IN early 1909, with a salivating press corps close on her couture heels, Katherine Mackay traveled to Albany to lobby legislators for a constitutional amendment. That this feminine beauty would walk the halls of the state capitol, the very pit of partisan polemics and cigar-ridden corruption, was astonishing to statehouse reporters. With her air of elegance, she quickly won over two Judiciary Committee members—Republicans Henry Walters of Syracuse and Orson J. Weimert of Buffalo—and mesmerized others along the way.[2] "By golly she's a handsome woman," said one staffer on leaving the closed-door Judiciary Committee hearing room. "You ought to see her hypnotizing those hayseeds in there!"[3]

Her reception, said the gossipy *Club Fellow*, meant that suffrage had become fashionable, and would soon enable the dream that Anthony, Stanton, "and the rest of the old guard" had sought in vain. The reason was apparent in the state capitol. "The trouble is or has been in the past that none of the good women knew how to smile as Mrs. Clarence Mackay," explained the newspaper. "Why some of our noble legislators are talking about it yet—that and her eyes."[4] The *Times* expressed alarm, noting that the modern suffragist lobby was not a "deputation of short-haired, short-skirted, masculine femininity." The "shrieking sister of the old days" was gone. Though elite suffragists "are in the wrong," said the *Times*, they would have to be handled delicately, their views "combated with intelligence, candor and good humor."[5] In the end, Weimert and Walters were the only two to stand with Mackay, her genteel calling card doused by the stubborn hold of male power.

By the time Mackay walked the halls of Albany's legislative offices, militants in Britain had inflamed the issue of women's suffrage with an aggressive campaign of violent agitation for the vote. Members of Emmeline Pankhurst's Women's Social and Political Union threw rocks at 10 Downing Street, cut telegraph wires, bombed Prime Minister Lloyd George's country house, and physically assaulted members of Parliament, including Winston Churchill. Many were arrested.

All of this received a great deal of coverage in the American press. In 1909, when Emmeline Pankhurst arrived in New York on a fundraising tour, Mackay was asked to introduce her at Carnegie Hall. She declined, issuing a statement under the banner of her Equal Franchise Society that disavowed violence. "It is not necessary for us to imitate methods which are being used in other countries," she argued. "American manhood has always treated American womanhood in such a way as to make us feel that we shall ultimately achieve our aim without sensationalism." Victory required not rocks and bombs, but literature and speeches. "It has not seemed necessary in the past, and I do not think it will be necessary in the future, for us to go out to the street corners and shriek our propaganda at the passer by," she insisted. "We have but to plead our cause without raising our voices to those men and women who are not with us."[6] The *Chicago Daily Tribune* headlined her dissent: "Mrs. Mackay Says Dignity Is Best, Deplores Shrieking Methods of British Militant Suffragettes."[7] Civility, in her view, was the underlying bond between men and women in the United States, and radical tactics were not required to win political progress.

In this Mackay was not alone. Many in the mainstream movement in both America and England shunned association with British militants, fearful that their tactics would alienate the very male voters they were trying to woo. Like Mackay, Carrie Chapman Catt, president of the Empire State Campaign, was distrustful of militant tactics. "We are suffragists, not suffragettes," she explained.[8] She avoided the 1912 parade in New York, saying she was "too ill to be present."[9] And she likened Emmeline Pankhurst to abolitionist John Brown, whose raid on Harpers Ferry all but lit the fuse that started the Civil War. "My heart aches for that woman, who is either a liberator of her sex or a serious troublemaker," she said. "Time will tell which."[10] In Paris too, suffragist Hubertine Auclert explained that British tactics "would not have any success in France. We will arrive at our destination by mildness, by persuasion, by goodness." That the Republic of France did not grant women suffrage until 1944 may say something about the wisdom of this strategy, but even in the birthplace of the Rights of Man and of the Citizen, and amid a worldwide suffrage agitation, British invitations were rebuffed. When Christabel Pankhurst, suffragette daughter and firebrand speaker, fled to Paris in 1913 to escape arrest and imprisonment by British police, French suffragists paid "far less attention to her than the French police did."[11]

By contrast, Belmont was infatuated with the Pankhursts—once describing Emmeline as a "flaming torch in the night which lighted my way."[12] On entering the movement in 1909, she told the *Washington Post*, "Men will never permit us to vote of our own volition. If we cannot gain our end quietly and peaceably, we will gain it otherwise."[13] Now she told reporters in New York that she had served as the bank for the Pankhursts, keeping the money they sent to France out of the hands of British authorities. By her own account, Belmont said she deposited and disbursed "an enormous reserve fund."[14] She also helped bankroll Christabel Pankhurst's exile in France. Engaging rooms at the Ritz and renting a flat in Paris for Christabel, Belmont offered both Pankhursts sanctuary at her chateau in Deauville.[15] Belmont's role in the British campaign is somewhat murky, though American newspapers tended to exaggerate her influence. "Mrs. Belmont . . . has arrived in Paris, in daily conference with Christabel," reported one American newspaper "It is said that

Miss Pankhurst and Mrs. Belmont are hatching up schemes for reprisals against the British government for its latest drastic actions against the militant suffragettes."[16]

It was not until 1915 that New York legislators agreed to put on the ballot a state constitutional amendment enfranchising women. Family lore has it that Harriot Stanton Blatch was in her office in Albany laying groundwork for the fight when Alva Belmont walked in to talk about where things stood. When Blatch told her that the pro-suffrage forces were having trouble with one key legislator, Alva Belmont reportedly reached for her purse and said, "How much?"[17] This story is likely apocryphal, but may point to a larger truth. Where Mackay sought to flaunt her femininity to woo hard-hearted legislators, a more cynical Belmont saw power as what men waged with their wallets. The distinction— between the coy wink and the bald bribe—divided the movement between those brandishing fashionable feminine looks and others brandishing hardball male political tactics. By whatever name, these warring styles were next on display in the 1910 struggle for the 17th State Senate District.

George Bliss Agnew, a Theodore Roosevelt Republican who had represented the 27th Assembly District from 1903 to 1906 and was now serving as the 17th District's senator, was up for reelection in 1910. A graduate of Princeton and former Wall Street dealmaker, Agnew was one of the sponsors of a bill that Governor Charles Evans Hughes had pushed to end betting at New York's popular racetracks, including the Belmont Stakes, a site created by Oliver Hazard Perry Belmont's family.[18] Passions ran high. The racing industry hired expensive lobbyists to work against the bill; churches organized a spirited crusade to campaign for it; newspapers editorialized against the bill's provision that made it a crime even to report on the races; and New Yorkers of all classes who enjoyed the art of betting and sometimes winning wrote letters of angst to Senator Agnew.[19] Amid the furor over betting, Agnew's constituent mail also included a surprising number of letters about suffrage, one on faded green stationery, from Mackay.

"The woman suffrage cause has increased in strength within the past year, in such an amazing manner, that it is no longer possible for our legislators to refrain from serious consideration of this question," she wrote in December 1909. Noting that her Equal Franchise Society represented more than 350 elite women and men in Manhattan, she added, "Wherever I go, whether it is into the settlement, the shop or the drawing room, I find the one subject being discussed is that of suffrage and every man and woman who has thought through the subject is convinced that the future growth of our state depends upon the woman's active part in its political life."[20] In Agnew's papers, there is no record of a reply.

By contrast, Belmont took fire, waging a campaign to unseat this foe of women's right to vote. She opened suffrage headquarters in his district and from there dispatched into the streets anti-Agnew cars festooned with suffrage flags and waving suffragists. Though it is difficult to say whether the economy, the ban on racetrack betting, or suffrage spelled his doom, Agnew was defeated, and Alva Belmont widely credited with arranging his retirement. "Mrs. Oliver H.P. Belmont's idea of opening Broadway suffrage headquarters in Senator Agnew's district . . . helped materially to accomplish the defeat of the opponent to the equal suffrage bill," wrote the *Morning Telegraph*. "She has no thought of letting up on politicians unfavorable to the Cause."[21] Deploying the most ruthless of male schemes, Belmont illustrated the rapier skills of a politician. Iris Calderhead Walker, daughter of a Republican congressman from Kansas, recalled Alva Belmont warning politicians, "I shall consider you false to our interests and shall not hesitate to make the fact known in important places."[22]

Belmont enjoyed playing hardball, mimicking the men of her circle who had exercised control over women. Mackay, meanwhile, was playing the fashion card. Known for her expensive taste (once, after an overseas trip, Mackay declared $15,000 in gowns from Europe, about $403,000 in current dollars), she dressed for effect. "Mrs. Mackay wore a handsome gown of a soft gold-color chiffon velvet with old gold lace and a large brown hat with lace and brown plumes," said an account of one Mackay appearance.[23] After another speech, the *Times* noted that Mackay wore "a beautiful décolleté gown of turquoise blue, with a little coat of gold lace," headlining its report, "Wins Suffragists by Her Good Looks."[24]

For Mackay's circle, fashion had long been a felicitous feature of a gilded life, emblem for the hauteur of status. Flaunting the latest styles from Paris, these socialites were accustomed to imitation of their every ensemble. Rita de Acosta Lydig, the Equal Franchise Society treasurer and a close friend of Mackay's, was such a fashion icon that in 1940, some three thousand patrons crowded an exhibit of her wardrobe at the New York Museum of Costume Art (now the Costume Institute at the Metropolitan Museum).[25]

Critics might assail them for caring too much about clothes to be trusted with the serious matter of the ballot—"What an unreasonable waste of time and money they continually exemplify in their clothing!" railed a writer to the *Brooklyn Daily Eagle*—but these society activists believed in the need to clothe suffrage in the armor of fashion.[26] Even the *Club Fellow*, which billed itself as the "society journal of New York and Chicago," and which had often taken a snide attitude toward their activism, seemed to approve.[27] "Mesdames Mackay and Lydig know the value of good clothes and spectacular effects."[28]

When she opened the Equal Franchise Society headquarters at One Madison Avenue, on the twenty-ninth floor of the Metropolitan Life Insurance Building at 23rd Street, Mackay designed the interior to exude femininity. Her office walls were decorated "in a floral design of pink and green against a blue background," the furniture in pale blue and gold, her desk "an inlaid Sheraton [with] desk fittings . . . of carved silver." As the *Tribune* observed, "Women who want to vote have frequently been accused of wanting to be like men," but Mackay's offices "convey no such impression."[29] At the Colony Club one evening, one reporter divined a motive behind her sartorial selections. "In order to prove to each other, the men and any antis who chanced to be present, that participation in politics would not deprive them of feminine lure, the members arrayed themselves in their most fascinating frocks," reported the *Sun*. As Mackay rose to introduce a speaker, "outsiders gasped with admiration" at "the sweep of her blue satin Directoire, heavily embroidered in gold."[30]

The emphasis on appearance made them easy marks for mockery. Deriding their interest in suffrage as a "new amusement," the *Club Fellow* recalled that in the past, "women of fashion as a rule looked upon these suffrage agitators as short-haired, badly-dressed freaks. To be a woman suffragist pre-supposed strong mindedness, ugly clothes and steel rimmed spectacles."[31] These code words no doubt meant to belittle suffrage activists as spinsters, lesbians, or intellectuals. Ridicule aside, it is this very sensitivity to fad that made these women such an asset to the movement. For if women's suffrage was, as Max Eastman put it, "the big fight for freedom in my time," it was also a trend—one that, like fashion, was susceptible to the whims of public opinion.[32] At a time when the social contract promised a rags-to-riches journey of upward mobility, the advent of gilded suffragists was an enormous draw.

"The question of women's franchise is creating a considerable stir and commotion among the busy women of New York," wrote one paper.

> Mrs. Clarence Mackay, the well-known millionairess, and Mrs. Belmont, the mother of the Duchess of Marlborough, have joined the cause heart and soul. Mrs. Mackay held a meeting the other day at her magnificent home in Madison Avenue, where . . . the setting and background of the suffrage meeting in the drawing room of white and gold made one feel that before the ballot came women would not be crushed under the weight of life's burdens.[33]

Still Mackay understood that reporters who came "to cover her clothes" could also be enticed to take a statement on suffrage, and her secretary recalled that the journalists never left without quotes from her about the vote.[34]

For nearly four years, Ethel Gross, a young Hungarian immigrant, worked as Katherine Mackay's secretary—handling the requests of a large household staff, assisting in her suffrage activities, going abroad with the family in the summers, and wearing clothes hand-selected by the president of the Equal Franchise Society. "I had never encountered such luxury and such wealth and such a way of living," she recalled. Mackay "bought all my clothes because she wanted me to look a certain way." They lunched at Sherry's, a president and her secretary, the latter toting a handbag large enough to carry dictation notebooks. "I had very nice clothes, . . . she spoiled me for $15.95 dresses, she had excellent taste," Gross reminisced. "I was never overdressed, I looked like her secretary." Because of Mackay's instruction on how to dress appropriately, Gross believed, when she met her future husband, Harry Hopkins, an Iowa farm boy who later became adviser to Franklin Delano Roosevelt, he saw not an immigrant but a sophisticated woman of the world.[35]

Like Belmont, Mackay could be autocratic. During construction of Harbor Hill, she penned more than a hundred notes—many on orchid-colored note cards—to architect Stanford White, conveying her preference for an English country house influenced by the Renaissance.[36] Negotiating over what White called the couple's "castle on the hill of the American dream," she left a paper trail of instructions. In one letter she ordered a change of design, saying, "This is *imperative*." In another she signed herself "The Tyrant." Harbor Hill was demolished in 1947, razed for a housing development. But when the house was in its glory, Mackay made sure that photographers had access to its treasures and reporters had a narrative about the Mackays, arguably the island's original power couple. Mackay regularly visited the editor of the *Roslyn News* to inform him of the family's travel and social plans.[37]

Then, as quickly as her star had risen, Mackay's press turned sour. There were more public bouts of imperial will and flares of temper that suggested a simmering sore. In early 1911 the *Club Fellow* reported that Mackay had left Albany in a huff after suffrage leaders failed to use the headquarters she had engaged for the cause. Fleeing the scene in anger, she disappointed wives of senators and assemblymen whom she had invited to a reception. "Those wives who had counted on making that matron's acquaintance and thus climbing the social ladder were furious," reported the newspaper, quoting one matron as saying, "We could have had tea and cakes at home." At the Colony Club, wags gossiped that Mackay was getting too imperious even for their crowd, taking the best dressing room in the Maxine Elliott Theatre during a suffrage tableaux and making "everyone else as unhappy in consequence." Predicting that she would leave the movement by spring, the paper quoted unnamed sources as saying that Mackay undertook the suffrage work "for selfish purposes only . . . for the glorification of Katherine Duer Mackay."[38]

Nasty little barbs appeared in the newspapers hinting that feelings between Mackay and Belmont were hardening into a royal clash of ambition. The *World* reported that the rivalry had led to "exultant whispers among the 'antis' of disunion in the camp of the enemy."[39] In a prescient item likely planted by Belmont's camp, the *New York Press* reported that Mackay "seems to have lost much of her enthusiasm as a suffragette. She is silent now, where a few months ago she was freely expressing herself in favor of votes for women." Hinting at a "social complication," the newspaper declared that Belmont now had the limelight to herself.[40] Likely the source for this speculation was Alva Belmont, only too eager to fan the flames of press disaffection with Mackay.

In September 1909, Belmont had hosted a "harmony luncheon" for two hundred suffragists at Delmonico's, for all the activist organizations in the state aligned with the umbrella New York State Woman Suffrage Party. Reporters belittled these women for talking politics while competing in clothes. "They talked at suffrage," reported the *New York Globe*, "but they looked at gowns."[41] Mackay did not attend, sending American Beauty roses with a note regretting her absence.[42] The following week, trying to douse talk of rivalry—or maybe to stoke it—Belmont attended a children's lawn party that Mackay held in her gardens in Roslyn, managing to deprecate her host in the process of denying any tiff. Insisting that the two had not parted company, Belmont said, "Parted? The idea!

Why, I've known Mrs. Mackay since she was a child the size of those on the lawn."[43] This was hardly the portrait of two equals, but a deliberate recasting of their relationship as that of a responsible parent and miscreant child.

As the papers had hinted, the rivalry eventually collapsed in melodrama. In 1910 Dr. Joseph Blake, a renowned surgeon, had operated successfully on Clarence Mackay's throat. The doctor had also won Katherine's heart, and their subsequent affair upended her existence. First, to the shock of friends, she resigned from the Roslyn school board, springboard to her political career. "I feel that it is not fair for me to hold this office," she said. "My absences from Harbor Hill compel me to miss meetings which, as a school trustee, I should always attend."[44] Still, the Mackay family kept up appearances, traveling to Paris for their annual summer sojourn, where Katherine took solace in shopping. In July the *Club Fellow* reported that Clarence had forbidden her from doing any suffrage work while the family was abroad. "Clarry is very strict on this point," reported the gossip sheet. "When he is around President Kitty is not allowed to talk for publication."[45] The strain on the marriage took a toll, and in April 1911 Katherine Mackay, the first member of Mrs. Astor's Four Hundred to become president of a suffragist organization, became the first to resign.[46] Alva Belmont filled fifty scrapbooks with news accounts of suffrage activities. Not a single newspaper clip in any of Belmont's scrapbooks mentioned Mackay's resignation, big news at the time.[47]

In February 1914 Katherine divorced Clarence in Paris, giving up custody of their three children, signing away her rights to Harbor Hill, and turning over her portion of the estate to her husband and young son.[48] Catherine Ketchum Blake sued her for $1 million, alleging alienation of affection, charging that Mackay had lured Blake against his will and taken a good father away from their sons. "I was forced to obtain a divorce from Dr. Blake," she told one newspaper. "I feel just beaten. . . . Dr. Blake loved his sons as much as I did, but one woman's influence was forcible enough to take him miles away from them."[49] Newspapers reported every sighting of the Blakes and Mackays, whipping their comings and goings into a froth of scandal. The *New York World* bannered the divorce on its front page, noting that while custody of the children was awarded to Clarence, Katherine could visit "whenever she desires and it is convenient."[50]

Later that year, with Europe at war and Blake serving as a surgeon at a military hospital, the two were married at the district mayor's office in Paris. Katherine, working at the Red Cross, told reporters, "I am very happy to marry the man I love."[51] Fifteen years later, while Katherine was dying of cancer, Blake, by then sixty-five, divorced her to marry a twenty-four-year-old nurse. Clarence Mackay attended Katherine's funeral, placing a lily-encrusted cross on her casket. An observant Catholic, Mackay was now free to marry opera singer Anna Case in the church, which he did.[52]

Katherine Duer Mackay had lived as a creature of celebrity, cultivating attention for her décor, her clothes, and her activism. When she and Clarry divorced, a rapacious press pounced—hounding them from Roslyn to Paris, brutal in its judgments. The *Oakland Tribune* belittled her as "nothing more or less than an adventuress, breaking up the Blake home and destroying the career of her husband in the same manner that a child might topple over a house of cards."[53] As later media celebrities also learned, public notoriety was a fickle friend, the press its handmaiden, first lionizing Mackay on the ascent, then harpooning her during a messy fall on the way down. Casting herself as a woman of wealth and femininity meant marginalizing herself in politics. Her activism was forgotten by most, but not all.

"When she advocated votes for women, thousands of women throughout the country began to take up suffrage and investigate it," a sympathetic Theodora Bean wrote in the *Morning Telegraph*. "Men of affairs, society and businessmen attended the meetings, conducted as they were without sensation and characterized by good sense, good clothes and attractive environment."[54] No accolade ever sounded more like an obituary.

In the end, the rivalry was emblematic of the changing profile of elite women at a time of great change and the shifting contours of the suffrage movement. Katherine Mackay, a "parlor suffragist," thought that male voters should be approached with civility and reason and perhaps a winning smile.[55] Alva Belmont tended to a take-no-prisoners kind of activism. The middle-aged Belmont had the means and, some suggested, the mouth to demand her rights. While Mackay endorsed municipal suffrage as an "entering wedge" toward eventual rights of citizenship, Belmont brooked no half loaf—rights to vote in all elections, or none.[56] And where Mackay endeavored to convert her own circle, including men of wealth and political influence, Belmont sought the broadest possible alliance along the lines of gender, reaching out to working-class and black women. That Mackay succeeded may be a tribute to the limits of her vision; that Belmont failed, to the breadth of hers.

In years to come, Belmont would trade her mainstream credentials for the stripes of a radical. She countenanced if not violence at least violent language. Weary of newspaper cynicism that described her clothes but not her convictions, Belmont grew more belligerent.[57] "We shall not adopt the militant methods of English women," she said, "but we will adopt our own militant method and fight the men with physical force."[58] She switched her patronage from Carrie Chapman Catt's National American Woman Suffrage Association to Alice Paul's Congressional Union, later the National Woman's Party, with Belmont as president and the Equal Rights Amendment as its ultimate cause.

Mackay, meanwhile, would fade from history's memory, a victim of the trauma in her personal life and the fall from favor of her class-driven view of politics as the purview of the already influential. Despite this erasure from the record, her contribution in the early years could not have been more consequential. She had attracted to the cause a cadre of society suffragists—including Belmont—who traded their social influence for political power and at times slighted their economic interests for progressive reforms. As one Milwaukee newspaper observed, "It is remarkable how rapidly woman suffrage has risen to the rank of a prominent issue in New York since the voluntary enlistment of women like Mrs. Mackay and Mrs. Belmont contributed to enhance its social prestige."[59]

Mackay had conducted many suffrage events from her home at 244 Madison Avenue, leased by Emily Havemeyer, heir to sugar interests.[60] After the Mackay divorce, the house, by then surrounded by commercial and retail enterprises, was sold to a developer for a sixteen-story apartment house. As the *Times* noted, "The inability to rent the big Havemeyer house at anything like a reasonable rate shows very clearly the reluctance of tenants who are able to maintain a house of that size to move into the old Murray Hill zone."[61]

It was a fitting epitaph for the old era. Like so much of Gilded Age architectural brilliance, the house lost its glitter as the cityscape grew more commercial and the wealthy became less rich. The high society so lovingly guarded by Mrs. Astor in her cultivation of the Four Hundred, the social rules so chillingly depicted by Edith Wharton in her fictional commentaries on Gilded Age wealth, the web of celebrity so eagerly conferred on wealthy women by a sensationalizing media—all of these markers of status were disappearing, no longer the terra firma beneath their feet. Like abolitionists in the antebellum period who feared they would be marginalized if they did not embrace anti-slavery, the cause of their day, society suffragists saw that the vote was a lifeline that offered a rescue from social insignificance.[62] Their motives and their causes may have varied, but for all of the gilded suffragists, political influence was a necessary adjunct to reinvention. Unlike Mrs. Astor and her circle of exclusivity, they represented what Henry James later dubbed the New Woman, pursuing meaning beyond class.[63] Defying cultural stereotypes and upsetting family plans, more than two hundred women of elite social standing put a new face on modernity. In the process, they broke barriers in education and career, and made gains in birth control and pay equality.

For Theresa Fair Oelrichs, who on her wedding received a $1 million gift from her father, modernity meant that she could light up a cigarette at a café in San Francisco in 1908, in public, sending national wags into overdrive.[64] Several newspapers opined that women now had "an unquestioned precedent for smoking if they feel so inclined," though others sounded an alarm. At a time when many cities banned smoking in public by women, the *Ocala Evening Star* in Florida lamented, "Fashionable resorts will soon resemble Red Light joints."[65]

For Helen Gould Shepard, daughter of the ruthless Wall Street stock manipulator Jay Gould, modernity meant the opportunity to carve out a new legacy of compassion in his memory. In January 1901 the Brotherhood of Locomotive Engineers passed a resolution expressing gratitude for the "kind and thoughtful consideration which we have received at the hands of Miss Gould," which, they said, "has done much to influence the management of the Gould System towards a fair and generous treatment of its employees."[66] On the occasion of her wedding at the age of forty-four, in 1913, she donated lunches for a thousand men at the Bowery Mission on the Lower East Side. She invited them to attend the ceremony.[67]

And for many of their circle, including Elsie Clews, Gertrude Vanderbilt, and Alice Duer, modernity was a rebellion against conventions in marriage, parenting, education, and career. Like Edna Pontellier in Kate Chopin's popular novel *The Awakening*, perhaps they longed to experience the vitality that comes of standing "naked in the open air, at the mercy of the sun, . . . like some newborn creature, opening its eyes in a familiar world it had never known."[68]

5

THE GILDED FACE OF MODERNITY

*Never in the history of the country have
women of wealth and high social position
taken so prominent a part in the
active life of the metropolis.*

SAN FRANCISCO EXAMINER[1]

BURSTING on the scene as a new generation of Americans came
of age in the 1890s, the Gibson Girl was America's first sex symbol.
Her eyes half-closed in seductive allure, her figure slim at the waist
but full at the bosom, this magazine illustration of white beauty represented a defiant farewell to the economic dislocations of the Civil
War and a cheeky rebuttal to the sexual prudery of the Victorian era.
Sometimes she wore tennis clothes, or rode a bicycle, or played the vio-
lin, but always she flirted with an audience of men, without benefit of
chaperone. Amid a mania for the new art of advertising, the image of
her dark upswept hair and luscious lips soon adorned every consumer
product from the handkerchiefs in men's suit pockets to the wallpaper
plastered to one bon vivant's bathroom walls.[2] When famed illustrator
Charles Dana Gibson married Irene Langhorne, "fair in feature, bright
in intellect and winsome in manner," from one of the FFVs (First Families of Virginia), commentators saw in the bride the muse for the artist's
future renderings.[3]

Gibson had never envisioned his "it girl" as a figure of politics, seeing
her more as a flirt than a feminist. But when Irene Langhorne Gibson—
whose sister Lady Nancy Astor would become the first female member

of Parliament in Britain—took an interest in the causes of her day, it became clear that even the wealthy had been captivated by the swirl of social change moving through the culture.[4] In 1913 she made her maiden speech for New York reform mayoral candidate John Purroy Mitchel under the banner of the Women's Fusion League for Good Government.[5] Wearing "a trim tailor suit with a very modern skirt," Irene Gibson at first resisted Daisy Harriman's entreaties to scale a cart to address a noontime crowd on the docks. The *Times* at once saw the problem, noting that "if women are going into cart-tail oratory either the carts will have to be changed or the new skirts." But climb she did—"someone gave her a hand from the cart, someone helped from the ground and, with a brave little jump, she was there"—and from new heights she praised Mitchel, citing his campaign to preserve parks and to fund milk sanitation for immigrant and poor mothers. Whether because of her words or her skirt, by session's end, according to the *Times*, she had "won the hearts of the goodly gathering of longshoremen gathered around a big truck at the corner of South and Fulton Streets."[6]

Exploiting her new status as a public personality, she also embraced suffrage, belting out its virtues in song at an event sponsored by the Federation of Women's Clubs, affecting the look of Raphael's *Madonna* at a fundraiser for suffrage at the Maxine Elliott Theatre.[7] In 1917, for the first time, she marched for suffrage in a parade up Fifth Avenue with, as the *Sun* put it, "a lot of other women whose names are frequently seen in society columns."[8]

For a generation (and sometimes for a single individual) to move from the exclusive costume balls of the nineteenth century to the public political parades of the twentieth suggests a breathtaking change in the atmosphere. In New York, the excitement over suffrage was palpable, "unparalleled anywhere else in the country." Trade unions, the working class, racial minorities, socialists, the middle class, and now the upper class clamored for the vote, as actresses who stocked Broadway's stages openly embraced the cause and a small cadre of progressive men, some husbands of gilded suffragists, joined the battle.[9]

Amid an unprecedented influx of immigrants, conservatives talked of social Darwinism, which held that biology's natural selection was evident in mental as well as physical attributes, and liberals spoke of the great reform needs of the day, from improving sanitation for tenement residents on the Lower East Side to ending the lynching of black men in the Jim Crow South. In the Village, Max Eastman, editor of the *Masses*, advocated for socialism and free love, while Robert Henri led a rebellion against "art for art's sake" in favor of "art for life's sake," and founded the Ashcan School, painters who rejected Impressionism in favor of a gritty urban realism. With such large questions in the balance, the cocoon spun by denizens of Newport's gilded mansions seemed irrelevant. "Great movements were stirring," wrote Inez Haynes Irwin, cofounder of the College Equal Suffrage League. "Everyone was for something and everyone was sure of victory."[10]

Thanks to the railroads and the automobile, the country was on the move. Mark Twain began a popular lecture series to pay off debts.[11] Isadora Duncan toured the country to demonstrate the joys of rhythm.[12] In the West, the American cowboy first opened and then, in Frederick Jackson Turner's memorable phrase, closed the American frontier.[13] In Cuba, Teddy Roosevelt, that apostle for male vigor, led a charge of Rough Riders up San Juan Hill, prompting debate about imperialism and America's place in the world. As one student wrote to her parents, "Politics, religion, art, music, society, everything is being revolutionized."[14]

Women in the gilded set were hardly immune to this call of modernity. In politics as in fashion, they resonated to trends. Like Irene Gibson, many came to view the reforms of their times as an invitation for relevance, and they eagerly expanded the charities of noblesse oblige to the causes of the day—support for black colleges, for environmental protections, for labor union reforms. Their lives echoed with the clamor of generational ambition. They were rebels to their own class and kin, carving out new directions in education, career, marriage, and parenting.

Born after the Civil War, spared by wealth and generation from the worst of that wrenching conflict, they came of age as one century glimpsed the next, seeing not limits but opportunities. Many pursued university education, attending newly opened women's colleges at Barnard, Bryn Mawr, Smith, or Vassar. In an earlier era, privileged women had been taught by private tutors, their education refined by summers spent traveling through Europe, absorbing the art, language, and lifestyle of other cultures. Education was meant to attract a man of position, and to convey the perquisites of class to succeeding generations. For a woman of wealth to attend college risked her class status and, critics worried, might imperil her ability to extend the bloodline. Family arguments and social ostracism often ensued.

On hearing that their daughter, Elsie, wanted to pursue a university education, Lucy and Henry Clews were aghast. A southern belle eighteen years younger than her husband, Lucy Madison Worthington Clews was "Newport's best-dressed lady of her era," a fashion plate who set aside $10,000 each summer for "mistakes in her clothes." Eager to inculcate Elsie into the glories of fashion, Lucy Clews had warned her only child that shabby clothes could provoke a common cold and corsets would benefit her figure.[15] Henry Clews, a Wall Street financier, feared that college would compromise Elsie's ability to procreate and that women were unfit for intellectual endeavors, an assertion he defended by citing the Bible, the Magna Carta, and the U.S. Constitution. In a paper he wrote for the National Society of New England Women in 1910, he declared that a woman is "endowed and equipped by nature for a higher and more important sphere of action, and her activities should centre in her home life."[16]

For the headstrong Elsie Clews, who had defied the gods of Bailey's Beach by dipping her bare toes into the Atlantic Ocean, and who observed that a swim and a trek helped her cope with the "grotesqueries" of Newport society, choosing college over cotillion was but the latest sign of rebellion. "When I wanted to go to college, I was called selfish," she later recalled. "I should stay home, I was told, and be companionable to my mother. I had never noticed that my mother found me companionable. In those years we were not at all congenial."[17] On becoming an anthropologist, she advanced views on chastity, premarital sex, and planned pregnancies that provoked thunder from many a pulpit. "The idea of men and women living like animals, separating at will, and contracting new alliances, leaving the children to be nobody's children, and to be cared for by the State, is barbarous," said Morgan Dix, rector of Trinity Episcopal Church, which tethered the wealthy to religious observance.[18]

Alice Duer—a cousin of Katherine Duer Mackay and descendent of Rufus King, signatory to the U.S. Constitution, and William Alexander Duer, president of Columbia University—provoked a different kind of controversy when she vowed to attend college. The collapse of the Barings Bank of Britain in 1890 had decimated her father's New York bank, precipitating a fall in family fortunes.[19] Alice insisted on enrolling in Barnard even if she had to pay her own expenses by tutoring other students. As the news spread, it "shocked society and alienated her friends." Caroline Schermerhorn Astor, the doyen of high society, paid a call on Alice's mother to say, "What a pity, that lovely girl going to college."[20]

That Alice Duer Miller later achieved success as a writer—contributing to the social memory of two continents in two wars with a World War I poem that inspired the 1944 film *The White Cliffs of Dover*—was a rejoinder to the naysayers. Unlike her father, with his "great authority of manner without a trace of self-assertiveness," she became a nonconformist, welcomed at the Algonquin Club's Round Table, haven for wit, where Dorothy Parker traded barbs with Alexander Woollcott, and at Heterodoxy, a club for a woman "not . . . orthodox in her opinions," including pacifists, socialists, African Americans, and lesbians.[21]

Formed in 1912, Heterodoxy met every two weeks on Saturdays in Greenwich Village, except in summer, when New York's moneyed classes departed for cooler climes. Club members debated homosexuality and birth control, socialism, racism, and pacifism—subjects that would have horrified the guests at their parents' banquets. Unlike the clubwomen of the nineteenth century, who observed strict protocol in organization and agenda, these trailblazers thrived on unscripted, uncensored conversation. Grace Nail Johnson, whose husband, James Weldon Johnson, was an official with the NAACP, ensured that unlike most women's clubs, Heterodoxy held racially integrated meetings.[22] Heterodoxy held as its greatest value diversity of opinion, and as its greatest sin, conformity. Aside from Miller, Elsie Clews Parsons was a regular, as were Vira Whitehouse, a banker's wife who would later lead the New York State Woman Suffrage Party, and Fola La Follette, daughter of Wisconsin senator Robert M. La Follette, and like him a pacifist.

Like the others, Gertrude Vanderbilt was raised with a keen awareness of the notoriety that attended wealth. Born in 1875 to a Gilded Age built on her great-grandfather's railroad empire, she was "the eldest daughter of the eldest son of the richest American family." At four, she longed to be a boy, and infuriated her mother by using scissors to cut off the curls atop her head. At eleven, as she recorded in her diary, "I knew perfectly that my father was talked of all over, that his name was known throughout the world, that I, simply because I was his daughter, would be talked about when I grew up, and that there were lots of things I could not do simply because I was Miss Vanderbilt."[23] There were summers in Newport, where the family home, the Breakers, was a breathtaking example of the colossal mansions that turned Bellevue Avenue into a national landmark.[24] And there were month-long visits to the churches and art museums of Europe, where Gertrude was much taken with the monuments, though not with Rubens, whose paintings she declared "too clumsy, . . . not ideal enough."[25]

When, at the age of twenty-one, Gertrude married the "great sportsman" Harry Payne Whitney, a scion of Standard Oil, one newspaper described theirs as a "wedding of gold," explaining that the marriage "united two colossal fortunes."[26] For the bride, the union promised a partner who understood the toll of gilded fame on personal privacy, someone who promised to be candid and who assuredly did not love Miss Vanderbilt for her money or her name, as his glittered as brightly. Within a decade, after three children and a whirlwind of travel and entertainment, the marriage devolved into what one biographer described as a "trial compartmentalization of interests." There was between them a shared tolerance for "foolish flirtations," as long as they were discreet.[27] Harry was preoccupied with his horses, business affairs, and, after the death of his father, the need to protect the family's $25 million inheritance. Gertrude returned to an early interest in drawing and enrolled at the Art Students League, located two blocks from her home at 2 West 57th Street. Setting up studios in Greenwich Village and Paris, she reinvented herself from socialite to sculptor, years later founding the New York museum that bears the Whitney name.

This search for meaning in body and soul owed something to popular novels of the day. In 1899 Kate Chopin's novel *The Awakening* had shocked polite society with its depiction of Edna Pontellier, a wealthy New Orleans woman who found sexual liberation outside her marriage.[28] Banned by some libraries, the book was much read in elite circles, influencing several wealthy women to join Margaret Sanger's controversial movement to research methods of birth control.[29] Another popular book within their circle was Edith Wharton's *House of Mirth*, published in 1905, about Lily Bart, clinging to the accoutrements of wealth by searching for a husband of standing to rescue her from her impoverished lifestyle. Edith Newbold Jones Wharton grew up in a wealthy home in what she called Old New York. It was her family, in fact, that inspired the phrase "keeping up with the Joneses."[30] Chronicling the wealthy, she brought a wry wisdom to the portrait of high society.[31] And when, after the Civil War, new money replaced old gentry in the city's social hierarchy, Wharton observed with her customary irony, "The decent people fell back on sport and culture."[32]

These depictions of societal tension helped spark an interest in writing. Critics may have disdained the book boom for its "commercialization of literature," but many of the elite became published authors, confessing candid amorous feelings—or heretical beliefs—that would have felled earlier society leaders.[33] Katherine Duer Mackay, a married woman with three children, wrote in *The Stone of Destiny* (1904) about unrequited love. Gertrude Atherton, wife of a blueblood, indulged in Darwinian ruminations against religion in *Ancestors* (1907).

Amid these explorations in education and career, young women of wealth also experimented with new forms of marriage and parenting. When she agreed to wed Herbert Parsons in 1900, Elsie Clews had no intention of enduring a traditional Newport wedding. She would agree to only one fitting for the wedding gown, so a "double" had to be brought in for intricate work. Elsie's father thought that the train should be longer, but, as her mother, Lucy Clews, wrote to the groom, "Elsie gave orders." Soon she was pregnant, eager to demonstrate that she could juggle both parenthood and her academic work, without jeopardizing either.[34] Herbert, by his own admission "the pettifogger who cannot see the big side," suggested that she discontinue her teaching at Barnard during her pregnancy. Instead, she worked continuously and delivered a healthy baby, the first of four. Two others died in childhood. They negotiated a social compact in which parenting was shared—she assumed responsibility until the children were twelve years old, when he became the primary parent.[35]

The unusual understanding between them was not without political consequence. On his arrival in Washington in 1905, Herbert Parsons was asked whether he thought his wife's views would be a liability. "If my wife were to advocate such principles as does Congressman Parsons' wife," a *World* reporter explained to his readers, "she would have to choose another place to live pretty quickly."[36] There is no record of Parsons's reply, but his wife was not unmindful of political difficulties created by her unusual views. During her husband's three terms, Elsie joined the Congressional Woman's Club (likely the only member of Heterodoxy to do so) and used the pen name John Main for her sociological books, including *The Old-Fashioned Woman*, which one reviewer described as a "sharp and witty analysis of the genesis of traditional sex roles and behavior and the cultural codes that sustain them."[37]

Often these exemplars of modernity shared the suffrage campaign with their own children. Actress Katharine Hepburn recalled that her mother, Katharine Houghton Hepburn, president of the Connecticut Woman Suffrage Association, often took her along to parades and asked her to distribute pamphlets.[38] Edith Bailey, who had contributed her automobile to a soapbox speech during the 1894 parlor campaign, now lent her twin babies to a suffrage pageant in 1911. For the tableaux, Irene Langhorne Gibson was to pose as the Madonna. The effect was ruined when one of the twins let out a tear-stained cry for "Ma-a-a-a—a!" and, as the *Evening Journal* put it, "the house roared."[39]

Relations with their own mothers were often strained. Aside from summers in Newport and winters at Fifth Avenue's toniest addresses, what Elsie Clews Parsons and Gertrude Vanderbilt Whitney shared was a desire not to become their mothers. They did not run from wealth, but they did shun the ladder of social acceptance that had defined their mothers' lives. On seeing one of Gertrude's early works of sculpture, Alice Vanderbilt urged her to hide the image from her own daughter, lest the child become wild. "The fig leaf is so little!" she exclaimed. For Gertrude, by contrast, the "unprudish attitude [in working with live nude models] and the manual labor involved in shaping plaster and clay represented . . . an explosive defiance of the entirely ladylike existence she had known."[40]

Gertrude and Elsie saw that it was their mothers, not their fathers, who dictated the terms of society. "There are no kings in American Society, . . . only queens," wrote Elsie Clews Parsons. The "onerous and endless business" of social calling, the ordeal of climbing into and staying atop society, required "a kind of self-devotion which verges on asceticism."[41] As a child Gertrude "longed to be someone else, to be liked only for myself, to live quietly and happily without the burden that goes with riches."[42] She was a teenager when she concluded, "The only way to enjoy [life] most is to have other interests besides the social ones."[43]

To the earlier generation, society had been a fortress, a warren of insular exclusivity where the gates were patrolled with constant vigilance. The whole point of restricting her guest list to four hundred families deemed worthy to feast in Caroline Schermerhorn Astor's ballroom was to define those left outside the doors. As Oscar Wilde observed, to be in society was "merely a bore. But to be out of it is simply a tragedy."[44]

No longer. In 1910, on returning to New York City after a long sojourn in Paris, social critic Frederick Townsend Martin observed a new individualism among the elite, as if the rules that once bound society to rituals of etiquette were now fluid. "It is now the individual, not the list, and hostesses ask the people whom they wish," he noted in his groundbreaking book *The Passing of the Idle Rich*. The younger set seemed as interested in work as they were in play, more aligned with the reforms of their day than with the predictable philanthropies of their circle. "The fashionable young women of the day . . . follow fads madly," he wrote. "I could name a dozen young women of the finest families in New York who in the past twelve months have thrown themselves into this sort of function."

More striking still, the young seemed obsessed with sexuality, indulging "a sort of fetish . . . [to] study hygiene, biology and the mystery of life."[45] This shift in sensibility—from a Victorian ethos of separate bedrooms to a *fin-de-siècle* experimentation in sexuality, homosexuality, and birth control—had the further effect of changing standards of beauty. Women once prized for being round—to connote maternal talents—now slimmed down. Dieting, first embraced by men, became a female fetish among those who wanted to shed both pounds and the corset.[46] Opera gowns soon reflected the trend, featuring skin of the leg, arm, and neck. As one scholar noted, "Not even the rumor that Mrs. John Jacob Astor had developed a chest cold as a result of wearing deep décolleté deterred their wearers." The aptly named *Unpopular Review* saw in the new attire a cultural peril of historic dimensions. "At no time and place under Christianity, . . . certainly never before in America, has woman's form been so freely displayed in society and on the street," harrumphed the editors.[47]

When Newport was in its glory, women of society were known to change clothes eight times a day. The after-lunch parade along Ocean Drive—in the 1890s by horse-drawn carriage and in the new century by automobiles—was a sartorial highlight. Like beauties on floats at Carnival, they preened in "their lacy dresses and feathery hats," giving Newport its imprimatur as the "unrivalled playground of fashion."[48] One observer marveled, "How they swished and rustled in petticoats of satin, of lace, of taffeta . . . embellished with elaborate designs of plump cupids playing gilded lyres, true love knots interspersed with doves embroidered in seed pearls, parasols to match every dress, enormous flopping feather hats assorted to every costume, white gloves to the elbow, three or four new pairs every day."[49]

At the turn of the century, observed writer Henry Wise Miller, "to be in society meant something. The inner circle was a closed and organized entity. Money counted as it always does, but wealth alone did not let you in. You had to be well bred, but more important you had to be acceptable to a few social autocrats who would make or mar you." So clear were the rules that "a lady could call the doorman at the Knickerbocker Club to say: 'William, is there anybody in the club I'd like to have for lunch?'"[50]

Within a decade, the "strenuous life" promoted by Theodore Roosevelt, Robert Louis Stevenson, and magazines such as *Outing* had captivated quite a few of Newport's debutantes, and even some of their parents.[51] Some took up bicycling, that great craze of the day, with enthusiasm so widespread that streets had to be widened and so popular that 120,000 spectators crowded Madison Square Garden in 1896 to see the Great Bicycle Exhibition.[52] Lillian Russell had a custom bike made by Tiffany, "a gold-plated machine that displayed the jeweler's art at its most opulent and unconventional," complete with mother-of-pearl handles and "wheel spokes featuring her initials set in diamonds."[53]

With its patented Dunlop tire that rode smoothly on pavement and its implicit invitation to tour the vast country, the bicycle became a metaphor for the raw individualism of the day, seen as a triumph of the physical fitness movement over the corset. As Susan B. Anthony told journalist Nellie Bly, bicycling had "done more to emancipate women than anything else in the world."[54] So clear was the threat to the social hierarchy that *Town Topics* railed against the bicycle's pernicious ability to undercut female morals. "Woman is in a progressive mood nowadays and will not remain content with half measures," rued the weekly. "Youthful and beauteous womanhood is going to emancipate itself by means of the bicycle." Alas, said *Town Topics*, "Women bicyclists will be wearing tights within a year."[55]

They rebelled too at arranged marriages consummated for family bloodlines rather than individual happiness. Once the scourge of society, divorce became, if not common, at least familiar. In 1895, when Alva Vanderbilt announced to her lawyer that she wanted to divorce her husband for his rather public philandering, Joseph Choate urged her to reconsider, saying, "No member of [the upper class] must expose another member to criticism lest the whole foundation of wealth be undermined."[56] The subsequent orgy of titillating press coverage—as the *World* put it rather brashly, the case had something for everyone, "the rich as well as the poor who want to be rich"—proved him right.[57] News about Willie K.'s mistress in Paris, Nellie Neustretter of San Francisco, spilled out, with details of "expensive apartments [and] a retinue of servants" he kept for her in France.[58]

After the divorce, Alva Vanderbilt said she felt the sting of public reprimand most intensely at church, where fawning was replaced by ostracism. "When I walked into the Trinity Church in Newport on a Sunday soon after obtaining my divorce, not a single one of my old friends would recognize me," she recalled later. "They gathered in little groups and made it evident they were speaking of their disapprobation of my conduct."[59]

But by 1908, when Elsie French Vanderbilt divorced her husband, Alfred Gwynne Vanderbilt, another great-grandson of Cornelius Vanderbilt, society was more challenged than shocked. The divorce set off what the *Times* described as a "social war at Newport," making for "an interesting rivalry between the two sets during the Summer here and during the Winter in New York."[60] The notoriety of "the divorcing Frenches," or as one newspaper headline put it, "The Family Where Marriage Is Always a Failure," no doubt eased the feud.[61] After settlement, Elsie French Vanderbilt became one of Newport's largest taxpayers. Two years after a federal income tax was enacted, this once avid anti-suffragist endorsed municipal suffrage for women, seeking a voice in issues that affected her pocketbook.[62]

The first foray into the political world for many was the garment industry strike in 1909, so widespread that it would become known as the Uprising of the Twenty Thousand. With the invention of the shirtwaist—modeled on a man's shirt, worn tucked into a skirt, "a symbol of newfound female independence"—the industry had boomed.[63] By 1909 the city boasted more than five hundred shirtwaist shops, and at least thirty-five thousand employees.[64] Conditions were anything but liberating. Jewish and Italian immigrants, many still teenagers, worked twelve-hour days, six days a week, with poor lighting and few safety precautions. "We can't live our lives without doing something to help them," said Anne Morgan, daughter of J. P. Morgan, who with Belmont, inheritor of both Vanderbilt and Belmont family fortunes, joined the board of the Women's Trade Union League. "Of course the consumer must be protected, but when you hear of a woman who presses forty dozen skirts for $8 a week, something must be very wrong. And fifty-two hours a week seems little enough to ask."[65]

The paradox that beneficiaries of capitalism would protest its cutthroat efficiencies was lost on no one, and newspapers quickly dubbed these elite supporters the "mink brigade." Calling them "fanatical women," a lawyer for the Association of Waist and Dress Manufacturers charged that they were supporting the strike only as a tool to forward their selfish interest in suffrage, a suspicion shared too by many union leaders.[66] But when Inez Milholland, a recent Vassar graduate whose wealthy parents supported her activism, was arrested for joining the picket line, news coverage demonstrated the value of a celebrity endorsement. Daughter of John Milholland, a progressive reformer who helped form the NAACP, Inez Milholland would later become a star in suffrage circles, and later still a martyr for the cause, dying at the age of thirty while campaigning for the vote in the West. For now, she conferred her privilege and her beauty on an ugly strike scene where factory owners had hired prostitutes to beat up the strikers—because "gentlemen" did not want to be seen beating up women in public.[67] The tone of coverage shifted. As the *Chicago Daily Tribune* headline noted, "Vassar Girl Is Arrested: Suffragette and Strike Picket Meets Rude Cop."[68]

Interestingly, the *New York Times* listed the shirtwaist strike in its index for 1909–1910 not under labor but under fashion, suggesting that the product was more valued than the labor, and hinting anew at the import of feminine appearance to the campaign for political rights.[69] If gilded activists made suffrage fashionable, they seemed to have had a similar impact on this strike, evidence of the value of their endorsement. No one got more attention than Alva Belmont, who sat in the Jefferson Market Courthouse in Greenwich Village one night, waiting up until 3:00 a.m. to bail out four workers arrested on the picket line. Informed that bail was set at $100 each, Belmont said that all she had to offer as collateral was her home at 477 Madison Avenue, valued, said the *Baltimore Sun*, at $400,000.[70] Newspapers lapped it up, making the story front-page news across the country.[71] Belmont rented the Hippodrome Theater for a mass rally, attracting an audience of eight thousand, where factory workers, union organizers, college student sympathizers, and members of the mink brigade watched the proceedings in a massive hall lit by electricity and festooned with banners demanding "Votes for Women," "Equal Pay for Equal Work," and "Give Women the Protection of the Vote."[72] The capstone of society involvement came on December 15, 1909, when Anne Morgan and Bessy Marbury arranged for workers to address the Colony Club.

The event was rife with irony. Young Italian and Jewish workers invited to tell their stories would not have been eligible for membership, nor welcome as guests. Yet 150 of New York's most elite women sat and listened as the aggrieved told their stories. One Italian worker said that a priest was sent to tell her that she should not be in the same union with Jews. "I hope you will excuse me for this language, ladies, but the priest, he tell us that if we keep up the strike we all go to hell." A fifteen-year-old Jewish worker, "a round-eyed chubby little person," explained that she had to support "my sick mother and two little sisters on $3.50 a week." A third worker said, "Why just think, we lose a penny for every minute we are late and I once had to pay $8 for a machine that I broke."[73] At presentation's end, Margaret Chanler Aldrich, known as one of the "Astor orphans" for her parents' early death, asked what the strikers most needed. Mary Dreier, a labor organizer and herself a woman of means whose arrest on the picket line had galvanized protests, answered, "Money to fight with."[74] Aldrich promptly called for a collection, and de Wolfe passed a hat, as did Rita Lydig, the club's most fashionable member. They raised $1,300 (about $35,000 in contemporary terms).[75] Then tea was served.[76]

Some union officials deeply resented the society suffragists' involvement and suspected their motives, seeing their reform instincts as little more than penance for their wealth. "I shouldn't wonder their conscience pricks them a bit—they must be ashamed of being fortune's children while so many of the girls have never known what a good day means," Theresa S. Malkiel wrote in her *Diary of a Shirtwaist Striker*.[77] Socialists within the union leadership were horrified by the economic and class ironies that separated struggling speakers from an audience of capitalism's most favored. "A remarkable meeting, one that was as peculiar as it was interesting," opined the *Call*. The "bejeweled, be-furred, be-laced and be-gowned audience" were a stark contrast with the "ten wage slaves, some of them mere children," said the socialist newspaper, adding acidly, "Seldom, if ever, have [elite women] listened with such interest to the tales of the war between capital and labor, to the incidents of pain, of misery, of grief in the great struggle between the classes."[78] At a five-hour meeting to discuss whether to continue cooperating with wealthy suffragists—which ended in a "no" vote—Malkiel accused Belmont of "political crimes against the working class."[79] Some historians have also faulted the wealthy, arguing that they defused the movement's intent. In this view, the mink brigade's support for a negotiated settlement left unchanged brutal conditions that led to the Triangle Shirtwaist Factory Fire in 1911. One of the deadliest industrial accidents in New York history, the fire left 146 garment workers dead, many leaping to their deaths from a building where the exits had been sealed.[80]

Their own class was, if possible, even more biting. *Vogue*'s "As Seen by Him" column mocked their efforts as little more than the meddling of bored socialites. "In order to get into the best society in New York this season a woman should join the Shirtwaist Makers' Union, or some other striking labor organization, and thus help to gain votes for women," wrote the authors, in evident sarcasm. "The suffrage question is the fad of the hour."[81]

Pondering the question of why these women of wealth would act against their class interests, why they would work to reform the system that was the very taproot of their gilded existence, one arrives at the essence of social change. These society reformers sought not to diminish their own power but to reform industry from within, to protect their own status by easing the plight of capitalism's most exploited victims. As Daisy Harriman explained on launching one such campaign, "We will go to employers direct with such influence as we may command. All of us have influence, and some of us are the wives or sisters of employers of a large number of factory operatives or perhaps are ourselves owners and stockholders in companies. . . . There is perhaps no better antidote for radical attacks upon present institutions than intelligent, genuine and wisely directed welfare work."[82]

In 1909 Harriman stunned her husband's banking associates by hosting members of the International Brotherhood of Stationary Firemen at their summer home in Mount Kisco, New York, overlooking the Hudson River.[83] Eager to make a difference in a wider world beyond their circle, she and two hundred other wealthy women had joined the Votes for Women campaign. Much like Colony Club decorator Elsie de Wolfe as she "cleared out the Victoriana and let in the twentieth century," they were newly awakened to modernity.[84] On opening her home at Marble House in Newport to the public for suffrage, Alva Belmont was asked why she was going through the bother. Why not just donate to the cause? Sipping tea, she told a reporter for the *New York World*, "To give money is like throwing a bone to a dog." The cause needed warriors, she said. "Besides," she added, "tickets are only $5."[85]

Acknowledging years later that she got involved in civic life because it was "fun," Irene Gibson exploited her looks for the causes that moved her, none more than that of disadvantaged children. Her husband took a benevolent view of her activism, seeing her as too feminine to be sullied by political power. "If you have a canary," he was fond of saying, "you have to let it sing."[86] For other men, these changes in gender behavior were far more traumatic, if only because the newspapers kept referring to them, mockingly, as "mere men."[87]

FIGURE 1. The Colony Club was the first exclusive women's club in New York City, designed by architect Stanford White at 120–124 Madison Avenue and so controversial that one newspaper proclaimed it a "death knell to the home." The club was the brainchild of Florence Jaffray "Daisy" Harriman, married to Gilded Age financier J. Borden Harriman, whose cousin Averill Harriman later became a noted diplomat. Intended as a social gathering place for women, instead, in ways that surprised even its founders, the club became a site for debate of topical issues, none more controversial than women's suffrage.

Photo credit: Museum of the City of New York

THE COLONY CLUB—THE TRELLIS-ROOM, WHOSE VINE-CLAD WALLS, FOUNTAIN, AND GARDEN VASES GIVE IT A PLEASANT AIR OF OUTDOOR LIFE

FIGURE 2. Thanks to Elsie de Wolfe's modernist décor, the club represented a stunning advance in interior design. Banishing the "somber, cluttered interiors" and dark Turkish tea corners of an earlier era, de Wolfe, a former actress, used wicker furniture, garden trellises, tiled floors, and chintz, creating the feel of an English country house in urban New York. Diana Vreeland, a former *Vogue* editor and consultant to the Metropolitan Museum's Costume Institute, said later that de Wolfe "simply cleared out the Victoriana and let in the twentieth century."

FIGURE 3. One of the Colony Club's founders was Helen Benedict, a natural wit whose marriage to architect Thomas Hastings in 1900 attracted so many of New York's glitterati that two special trains were commissioned to take a thousand guests from Grand Central Station to Greenwich, Connecticut. Helen was president of the Ladies Four-in-Hand Driving Club, which encouraged women to take the driver's seat and steer four horses through the streets as men did. Here she is seen in front of the Colony Club as Eleanor Jay Iselin, whose family were avid sailing enthusiasts, holds the whip.

Photo credit: Library of Congress Prints and Photographs Division

FIGURE 4. Daisy Harriman, seen here overseeing a political event to reelect Woodrow Wilson in Union Square in 1916, became a major player in Democratic Party circles. She was appointed by President Wilson as the first woman to serve on a federal commission and later by President Franklin D. Roosevelt to serve as the U.S. ambassador to Norway during World War II.

Photo credit: Bain News Service, Library of Congress Prints and Photographs Division

FRANK LESLIE'S

ILLUSTRATED

WEEKLY

NEW YORK, MAY 3, 1894 [PRICE, 10 CENTS.

THE WOMAN-SUFFRAGE MOVEMENT IN NEW YORK CITY.

SOCIETY LEADERS SECURING SIGNATURES TO PETITIONS TO BE PRESENTED TO THE CONSTITUTIONAL CONVENTION—SCENE AT SHERRY'S.
DRAWN BY B. WEST CLINEDINST.—(SEE PAGE 290.)

FIGURE 5. The first known political activism of New York's elite women came in 1894, when they joined a campaign to urge lawmakers to enact women's suffrage. They gave speeches from the parlors of their homes, converting domestic domains into political venues. Here they are seen collecting petition signatures at Sherry's restaurant. So many of their circle joined the cause that one woman stopped at the petition desk at Sherry's to inquire whether "she might put her name down, even if she did not belong to the Four Hundred."

FIGURE 6. Alva Vanderbilt posed at the 1883 costume ball she hosted with her husband, William Kissam Vanderbilt, a grandson of railroad patriarch Cornelius Vanderbilt. The event, which cost $250,000 ($6 million in today's dollars), was meant to showcase their new Beaux Arts mansion at 660 Fifth Avenue and announce to the Astors and other families of old money wealth and Knickerbocker connections that a new aristocracy of industrial power had arrived. The extravagant affair also signaled the advent of celebrity journalism, which would make Alva and other society women the media celebrities of their day, power they would later leverage for suffrage.

Photo credit: Preservation Society of Newport County

FIGURE 7. Alva Belmont used Marble House, her majestic estate at Newport, Rhode Island, to promote women's suffrage, stirring much interest within her social circle and much enmity from suffrage workers such as historian Mary Ritter Beard, who feared that Belmont's fame and fortune would taint a movement of middle-class and working-class women.

Photo credit: Library of Congress Prints and Photographs Division

FIGURE 8. Alva Belmont addresses an audience seated on the lawn of her Marble House estate, likely during the first suffrage event there in 1909. Newport was shaken, but portrayed the invasion of hundreds of people not listed in the *Social Register* as but one of many festive events of an event-packed ten-week summer season. "Busy Week for Newport," headlined Philadelphia's *Public Ledger*. "Tennis, Polo and Suffragette Meetings the Features."

Photo credit: Getty Images

FIGURE 9. Katherine Duer Mackay descended from a long line of prominent New Yorkers, including a delegate to the Constitutional Convention, a
Supreme Court justice, and two presidents of Columbia University. Marrying Clarence Mackay, who inherited his father's silver mining and telegraph
cable company interests, she became a leading social figure in New York
and later, the mother of three, became one of the first women elected to a
school board.

Photo credit: Library of Congress Prints and Photographs Division

FIGURE 10. When Katherine Mackay became the first member of Mrs. Astor's Four Hundred to endorse women's suffrage, the announcement electrified public interest, and her first speech sold out. Here she is pictured in the office of her Equal Franchise Society, on the twenty-ninth floor of the Metropolitan Life Insurance Building at One Madison Avenue, designed to exude the femininity that gilded suffragists believed would help the cause. Her office walls were decorated "in a floral design of pink and green against a blue background," the furniture in pale blue and gold, her desk "an inlaid Sheraton [with] desk fittings . . . of carved silver." As the *Tribune* observed, "Women who want to vote have frequently been accused of wanting to be like men," but Mackay's offices "convey no such impression."

Photo credit: Brown Bros. Photography

FIGURE 11. Katherine Duer Mackay is seen here at a suffrage meeting hosted at her home, likely in March 1909, and attended by seventy-five prominent social figures, including Ava Willing Astor, wife of John Jacob Astor IV, and Edith Kingdon Gould, an actress and wife of financier and railroad executive George Jay Gould.

Photo credit: Library of Congress, Miller NAWSA Suffrage Scrapbooks, 1897–1911, scrapbook 7, p. 111

FIGURE 12. Marian Anthon "Mamie" Fish was the wife of Illinois Central Railroad president Stuyvesant Fish and a close confidante of Alva Belmont's. Known for her saucy tongue (she once instructed architect Stanford White to construct a ballroom so large that "a person who was not well bred would feel uncomfortable"), she attended Belmont's Newport rallies, insisting she had come as a friend only. Later she joined the campaign, conceding that a woman need not give up her femininity to vote.

FIGURE 13. Rita de Acosta Lydig was a close friend of Katherine Mackay's, and served as secretary of her Equal Franchise Society. Often seen together on the campaign trail, Mackay and Lydig made a point of dressing for feminine appeal, prompting one magazine to say of their suffrage activism, "Mesdames Mackay and Lydig know the value of good clothes and spectacular effects." On her death, Lydig donated her wardrobe to the New York Museum of Costume Art (now the Costume Institute at the Metropolitan Museum), and in 1940 some three thousand patrons crowded an exhibit of her fashion acquisitions.

Photo credit: Giovanni Boldini's 1911 portrait of Rita de Acosta Lydig

FIGURE 14. Alva Belmont is seen here on a bicycle outing with her daughter Consuelo, the Duchess of Marlborough, and Belmont's son Harold Vanderbilt. By the turn of the century, a bicycle craze had captured the nation, a triumph of the physical fitness movement over the corset. As Susan B. Anthony told journalist Nellie Bly, bicycling had "done more to emancipate women than anything else in the world."

Photo credit: Preservation Society of Newport County

FIGURE 15. A daughter of wealth, Elsie Clews Parsons jolted the guardians of the exclusive Bailey's Beach in Newport, Rhode Island, by planting her shapely and naked ankles in the Atlantic Ocean. Later she stunned her parents by eschewing the cotillion for college, enrolling in Barnard, and becoming a sociologist, folklorist, and anthropologist whose views on marriage, gender, and childrearing elicited thunderous denunciations from many a pulpit. The first president of the American Anthropological Association, she studied Pueblo and other Native American families and demonstrated that different social structures allowed for more evenly shared gender responsibilities. Here she is pictured aboard her schooner, the *Malabar V*.

Photo credit: James Parsons, *Encyclopedia Britannica*

FIGURE 16. Gertrude Vanderbilt Whitney grew up aware that she was "the eldest daughter of the eldest son of the richest American family." When, at the age of twenty-one, Gertrude married Harry Payne Whitney, a scion of Standard Oil, one newspaper described theirs as a "wedding of gold" because the marriage "united two colossal fortunes." Soon, Gertrude shocked her husband and parents by becoming a sculptor, taking art classes that included training her eyes on nude models, and eventually founding the Whitney Museum of American Art that bears her husband's name.

Photo credit: Count Jean de Strelecki photograph, part of Gertrude Vanderbilt Whitney papers, 1851–1975, Smithsonian Archives of American Art

FIGURE 17. The wealthiest man in America, John J. Astor IV died in April 1912, one of the 1,503 ill-fated passengers who went down with the ship as the R.M.S. *Titanic sank*. He had escorted his pregnant wife, Madeleine Force Astor, to a lifeboat and then returned to the deck to go down with the ship, upholding the law of the sea, "Women and children first." His death occasioned much public debate about the role of chivalry at a time when women were seeking equal rights of citizenship. Identifying himself as "Mere Man," one reader complained to the *Baltimore Sun*, "Would the suffragette have stood on that deck for women's rights or for women's privileges?"

Photo credit: *New York American*, April 16, 1912

FIGURE 18. Newlyweds Madeleine Force Astor and John J. Astor IV are seen here, walking their Airedale dog, Kitty, who also died when the *Titanic* sank. Astor had divorced his first wife, Ava Willing Astor, when he met Madeleine, twenty-eight years his junior. Society was scandalized by the divorce and the differences in their ages, and Astor had to pay a minister to perform the wedding.

FIGURE 19. Members of the Men's League for Woman Suffrage of New York, including League secretary R. C. Beadle, gather in front of the Woman Suffrage Party headquarters. The Men's League began in 1909 at the suggestion of a woman, Fanny Garrison Villard, daughter of famed abolitionist William Lloyd Garrison. The idea was propelled forward by three men—her son, crusading editor Oswald Garrison Villard, Rabbi Stephen S. Wise, a fixture of Progressive Era politics, and Max Eastman, a Greenwich Village radical who later edited the *Masses*. By 1912, thirty Men's Leagues dotted the country and twenty thousand men had signed up for a national Men's League.

Photo credit: Library of Congress Prints and Photographs Division

FIGURE 20. In 1912, three weeks after the sinking of the *Titanic*, one thousand men came out to march for women's suffrage on New York's Fifth Avenue. Rabbi Stephen Wise marched with his ten-year-old son, who carried a sign saying, "We want our mothers to vote." The men endured considerable jeers from on-lookers, who shouted, "Oh you gay deceiver," and "Oh Flossy dear, aren't they cute." Asked why they were participating, League president James Lees Laidlaw said, "We are marching to give political support to the women and moral support to the men." The next week, new male converts descended on suffrage headquarters, eager to join the parade.

Photo credit: Carrie Chapman Catt Collection, Bryn Mawr College Library

FIGURE 21. As a public debate swirled over whether women should seek the vote when men had given their lives aboard the *Titanic*, suffrage leaders responded by imposing discipline on public parades. Women were instructed to dress in white, march in choreographed groups, and conduct themselves with seriousness of purpose. Here is one group that marched on May 6, 1912, protesting taxation without representation.

Photo credit: Library of Congress Prints and Photographs Division

FIGURE 22. A white-gowned Inez Milholland, said to be the "most beautiful suffragette," sits atop a white horse at the head of the 1913 suffrage parade in Washington, D.C., evoking images of Joan of Arc and her effort to lead medieval French troops to victory over England. Suffrage leaders were keen to put beautiful women at the front of their parades, as if to quiet male fears that suffrage would emasculate men and harden women. When Milholland, a popular orator for the cause, died of pernicious anemia while campaigning for suffrage in California in 1916, Alice Paul arranged for a memorial service at the U.S. Capitol, the first time a woman was so honored, ensuring that Milholland was seen as a martyr for the cause.

Photo credit: Library of Congress Prints and Photographs Division

FIGURE 23. Irene Langhorne Gibson (*left*) and Florence Jaffray "Daisy" Harriman campaign for New York reform mayor John Purroy Mitchel in 1913, under the banner of the Women's Fusion League for Good Government. Gibson was the wife of illustrator Charles Dana Gibson, whose fictional Gibson Girl, beautiful and independent, had come to define his wife. When Irene Langhorne Gibson (whose sister Lady Nancy Astor later became the first female member of Parliament in Britain) also took an interest in the issues of her day, it caused a stir. As the *New York Times* noted, in her speech Irene Gibson "won the hearts of the goodly gathering of longshoremen gathered around a big truck at the corner of South and Fulton Streets."

Photo credit: Library of Congress Prints and Photographs Division

Why We Oppose Votes For Men

1.
Because man's place is in the army.

2.
Because no really manly man wants to settle any question otherwise than by fighting about it.

3.
Because if men should adopt peaceable methods women will no longer look up to them.

4.
Because men will lose their charm if they step put of their natural sphere and interest themselves in other matters than feats of arms, uniforms and drums.

5.
Because men are too emotional to vote. Their conduct at baseball games and political conventions shows this, while their innate tendency to appeal to force renders them particularly unfit for the task of government.

- Alice Duer Miller, 1915

FIGURE 24. A nonconformist welcomed at the Algonquin Club's Round Table and at Heterodoxy, a club for women unorthodox in their social views, Alice Duer Miller proved an enormous asset to the suffrage movement. Her columns in the *New York Tribune* from 1914 to 1917, titled "Are Women People?," often used sarcasm to prod male voters toward enfranchising women. This example of her work, accompanied by a Charles Dana Gibson illustration, demonstrates how her wit was an important weapon in the fight for the vote.

Photo credit: *New York Tribune*, 1915, reprinted in *New York Times*, August 26, 1974

FIGURE 25. Standing on an open-car platform, with the sights and sounds of New York's Columbus Circle in the background, Harriet Laidlaw delivers an impassioned argument for women's suffrage. At this event on October 29, 1915, Laidlaw, who had earlier convinced her husband to join the Men's League, kicked off a twenty-six-hour street meeting to rally supporters in advance of the November election in New York, where women's suffrage won in New York City but lost upstate.

Photo credit: Getty Images

FIGURE 26. Louisine Havemeyer was one of the wealthiest and most colorful of gilded suffrage activists. Widow of sugar trust king Henry O. Havemeyer, she was a major collector of Impressionist art, steered in her acquisitions by her childhood friend Mary Cassatt. After lending her art collection to a gallery for a suffrage fundraiser, she vowed not to indulge in radical tactics. But Alice Paul, president of the National Woman's Party, convinced her to come to Washington to light a match to an effigy of Woodrow Wilson. Arrested, Havemeyer refused to pay a fine, instead serving in jail and becoming radicalized, joining other former inmates on a "Prison Special" publicity train around the country. Here she is seen passing to New Jersey activists her famous electric torch, modeled on the Statue of Liberty, which she used as a prop during speeches.

Photo credit: Library of Congress Prints and Photographs Division

FIGURE 27. Vira Whitehouse, wife of stockbroker Norman de Rapelye Whitehouse, once said that before she marched in the 1913 suffrage parade, all she could do was "dance and go to dinner." Here she is seen giving a street speech for suffrage that year. During the 1915 campaign in New York, she pioneered some new strategies, making cold calls to male voters and promoting a Suffrage Day at the Polo Grounds. By 1917 she was head of the campaign, working to win the vote for women in New York during World War I. With Liberty Loan campaigns and Red Cross drives draining money for the cause, she vowed to put up her pearls if necessary. After New York women won the vote in November 1917, she was hailed for enfranchising one-tenth of all American women. As Consumers League president Maud Nathan put it, "Our own Whitehouse did more than the White House in Washington."

Photo credit: Library of Congress Prints and Photographs Division

FIGURE 28. Katrina Tiffany, wife of the vice president of the legendary jewelry store that anchors Fifth Avenue to luxury, carries the flag at the October 1917 parade in New York as her husband looks down disapprovingly from the windows. That year's parade, which came as American men joined combat in Europe during World War I, urged women's suffrage as a war measure. Demonstrating female patriotism, one contingent consisted of women whose sons, husbands, or brothers were serving in the military; another consisted of nurses and Red Cross workers. Still another contingent carried a signed poster attesting that said suffragists had raised more than $7 million for the Liberty Loan campaign. The next month, a referendum granting women the right to vote in New York was approved with a nearly 100,000-vote margin, giving New York the largest pro-suffrage delegation in Congress and a clear path to a constitutional amendment.

Photo credit: Library of Congress Prints and Photographs Division

JONATHAN MAY BE IN MORE DANGER THAN JOHN

FIGURE 29. Titled "The Smooch versus the Harangue," this 1910 illustration suggested that American suffragists, who shunned violence, would be more successful in winning the vote than their British counterparts, who embraced it. John Bull, the portly personification of Britain, is seen hiding a ballot box behind his back, surrounded by female activists in wool jackets and skirts, armed with umbrellas going for his head. In the other corner is Uncle Sam, in early New England known as Brother Jonathan, hoisting the ballot box overhead, encircled by beautifully dressed *femmes fatales* in flowing gowns and feathered hats, cooing in his ears. The caption, by William Allen Rogers, read, "Jonathan may be in more danger than John." The illustration proved prescient. Universal female suffrage was ratified in the United States in 1920, as the Nineteenth Amendment to the Constitution. The same right of citizenship was extended to all adult women in Britain eight years later, as an act of Parliament.

Photo Credit: William Allen Rogers, *Van Norden Magazine*, February 1910, reprinted in *New York Herald*

ANOTHER DECLARATION OF INDEPENDENCE

DRAWN BY PAUL STAHR

© 2000 HARPWEEK®

FIGURE 30. In the original John Trumbull painting of the presentation of the Declaration of Independence, which hangs like a foreshadowing from the top left corner of this one, a committee of five—John Adams, Benjamin Franklin, Thomas Jefferson, Robert Livingston, and Roger Sherman—is seen presenting the draft to the Continental Congress on June 28, 1776. Here, cartoonist Paul Stahr depicts "A Second Declaration of Independence," in which Katherine Duer Mackay, one of the most glamorous of the New York society suffragists, is positioned in Thomas Jefferson's place wearing a black sleeveless gown. To her right is Harriot Stanton Blatch, who first recruited Mackay to the cause. Mackay is seen talking to a seated Carrie Chapman Catt, leader of the mainstream suffrage organization (in John Hancock's position). Two others—Alva Belmont (in the front row on the left, where Richard Henry Lee sat in the Trumbull version) and possibly Florence Jaffray Harriman (in mid-row on the right)—look on from their seats. That Stahr chose to feature these society suffragists so prominently speaks to their importance to the movement.

Photo credit: Paul Stahr, *Harper's Weekly*, May 14, 1910

6

MERE MEN

A great many people fear that giving a woman her honest
equal rights in the world's work is bound to make
her act mannish. . . . My experience is that so
far as it has been tried out it merely makes
her act a little more like a gentleman.

RAYMOND BROWN[1]

BUSINESS stopped in Rhinebeck, New York, the day Jack Astor was
buried. The quaint town in Dutchess County, home of Ferncliff,
the Astor estate, lowered its flags to half-mast. Bells tolled at noon, and
residents crowded the train station as his body was placed on board
for the trip to Manhattan. There, at Trinity Church Cemetery in Upper
Manhattan, the forty-seven-year-old scion of real estate wealth and
social prominence was laid to rest in the family vault next to his mother,
the indomitable Caroline Schermerhorn Astor.[2] Outside the cemetery,
thousands perched near walls and on the fence and "on either side of
Broadway and 155th Street, while others sought the roofs of adjoining
apartment houses, and the viaduct along the river overlooking the burial
ground," to catch a glimpse of this man of gallantry, who "went to his
death nobly," a man who had "died to let woman live."[3]

When the R.M.S. *Titanic* went down on April 12, 1912, it took more
than fifteen hundred passengers to their frigid death, many victims of
hypothermia in thirty-one-degree water that shut down their organs and
rendered them unconscious in minutes.[4] It made a hero of John Jacob
Astor IV, a sportsman who had hardly been that in life. And it sparked
a nationwide debate over chivalry, that unwritten law of the sea—the

call of "women and children first" that prompted Astor and other men to forfeit seats on lifeboats for female passengers. If men had protected women from death, should women enjoy rights of citizenship in life? Critics said no, chiding suffragists for their audacity—some said hypocrisy—in seeking equality at the ballot box when men had just made the ultimate sacrifice at sea.

"Let the suffragists remember this," argued one letter writer to the *Baltimore Sun*. "When the Lord created woman and placed her under the protection of man, he had her well provided for. The *Titanic* disaster proved it very plainly." In an editorial, the *Sun*'s editors agreed, arguing that women did not need the ballot. As the *Titanic* episode demonstrated, "women can appeal to a higher law than that of the ballot for justice, consideration and protection." Identifying himself as "Mere Man," another wrote in telling sarcasm, "Would the suffragette have stood on that deck for women's rights or for women's privileges?"[5]

The question hung over the movement in New York as suffrage leaders planned a street parade "the like of which New York never knew before."[6] Moved by the nobility of the men who perished, some urged a postponement. "After the superb unselfishness and heroism of the men on the *Titanic*, your march is untimely and pathetically unwise," antisuffragist Annie Nathan Meyer, founder of Barnard College for Women, wrote to organizers. Even some who planned to march wished men had not forfeited their lives for the lofty code of chivalry. "The women should have insisted that the boats be filled with an equal number of men," observed suffragist Lida Stokes Adams.[7]

For others, the tragedy only bolstered the case for giving women a vote, and a voice, in politics and commerce. Had women been involved in planning, they argued, the *Titanic*, driven by male ego and a conviction that the ship was unsinkable, might have been equipped with a sufficient number of lifeboats for all the passengers, negating the need for chivalry. "There was no need that a single life should have been lost upon the *Titanic*," wrote Alice Stone Blackwell. "There will be far fewer lost by preventable accidents, either on land or sea, when the mothers of men have the right to vote." Invoking the cloak of motherhood, Blackwell and others lobbied for the vote on grounds of moral probity, sure that a female presence in the political world would "bring humaneness, the valuation of human life, into the commerce and transportation and business of the world." As for chivalry, muckraker Rheta Childe Dorr expressed the cynicism of many when she wrote of conditions at one Brooklyn sweatshop, where locked doors and bad odors imprisoned workers. "The law of the sea, women and children first," she said. "The law of the land—that's different."[8]

Only hours after Jack Astor was buried, an estimated twenty thousand suffragists marched down Fifth Avenue in an exuberant affirmation of their rights as citizens. In response to the male chivalry represented by the *Titanic*'s fateful ending, suffragists offered female discipline. Parade organizer Harriot Stanton Blatch banned automobiles, believing that they shielded wealthy or lazy activists from the chore of actually walking—or of having been seen walking—for suffrage. "Riding in a car did not demonstrate courage. It did not show discipline," Blatch wrote later. "Women were to march on their own two feet out on the streets of America's greatest city; they were to march year by year, better and better."[9]

They were to dress in white—Macy's was the official headquarters for suffrage paraphernalia—and march in step with one another, column after column of women, "a mass of gleaming white," declaring their interest in the ballot.[10] Eager to defuse criticism that women had dallied the previous year, evidence of their unsuitability for the ballot, Blatch insisted that the 1912 parade begin promptly at 5:00 p.m. "Eyes to the front," read her orders, "head erect and shoulders back," and above all, remember that "the public will judge, illogically of course, but no less strictly, your qualification as a voter by your promptness."[11] Vowing to feminize the concept of the street parade—with its male overtones of military combat—she concluded, "Men and women are moved by seeing marching groups of people and by hearing music far more than by listening to the most careful argument."[12]

But what most fascinated press and public was the decision of an estimated one thousand men to join in the parade. The previous year, eighty-seven men had shown up for a women's suffrage parade, enduring great derision from sidewalk hecklers. Now, three weeks after the sinking of the *Titanic* that had revealed silenced resentments over chivalry, they marched in rows of four across, under the windswept blue banner of the new Men's League for Woman Suffrage. "As if to give courage to the less courageous of the mere men marchers," reported the *Times*, a band "broke into a lusty marching tune as the men swung from Thirteenth Street into Fifth Avenue." Perhaps they could still hear the jeers through the drumbeat: "Tramp, tramp, tramp, the girls are marching."[13]

Rabbi Stephen Wise marched with his ten-year-old son James, who carried a sign saying, "We want our mothers to vote."[14] A popular progressive speaker in the city, Wise once commented on the subway companies that allowed anti-suffragists to advertise, but would not accept ads from suffrage forces. "That's just the way the anti-suffrage party works—underground," he quipped.[15] Now he wrote in his diary of the derision he encountered along the parade route. "We had to laugh nearly all the way on account of the things that were shouted at us," he said in bemused recollection. "For a few moments, I was very warm and took off my hat, whereupon someone shouted, 'Look at the long-haired Susan.' Some of the other delightful exclamations that greeted us were: 'Who's taking care of the baby? . . . Oh, Flossy dear, aren't they cute? Look at the Mollycoddles.'" Still, Wise found the event uplifting, because while both male and female "rowdies" shouted insults, "the most hopeful thing" was the "respect [shown] by the intelligent class of people."[16]

Playwright George Middleton, whose wife, Fola La Follette, was a suffragist, took pride that none of the men had "deserted the ranks." He recalled hecklers crying, "'Take that handkerchief out of your cuff,' 'Oh you gay deceiver' and 'You forgot to shave this morning.'"[17] Raymond Brown, whose wife, Gertrude Foster Brown, worked for the New York State Woman Suffrage Party, was less buoyant, saying that the men felt isolated. "Tagging after the girls—that's what we were doing; and nobody would let us forget it," he wrote. In an article titled "How It Feels to Be the Husband of a Suffragette," written under the pen name "One," he addressed "the over 11,863 of you [who] requested me to go home and wash" dishes. Reassuring detractors that neither he nor his wife did the dishes, he suggested that they both had busy professional careers and could afford household help. "She values the dishes too highly," he wrote. "They are safer in the hands of a well-trained maid."[18]

League president James Lees Laidlaw, a banker whose wife, Harriet, was a leader of the New York State Woman Suffrage Party, was asked why the men were marching. He offered a succinct reply that resonated with meaning. "We are marching to give political support to the women," he said, "and moral support to the men."[19] As he had anticipated, the week after the 1912 parade, male converts descended on suffrage headquarters, including quite a few men "moved by the guying their brethren got in the parade."[20] And a few years later, when the Union League Club voted to oppose women's suffrage, William Benedict became one of the first of his fellow members to resign, donating his dues instead to the New York State Woman Suffrage Party.[21] The specter of male suffragists being heckled in the 1912 parade also touched marchers of both genders, who credited the men for giving them strength.

"It took so much more courage for a man to come out for woman's suffrage than it did for a woman," recalled Laura Ellsworth Seiler, a junior at Cornell University marching in her first parade.[22] Many singled out Laidlaw, an outdoorsman equally at home in the men's clubs of Manhattan and in the Sierra Nevada mountains of California, for making them braver.[23] "It meant much for him to do this, for he was in the very forefront and faced the derision of the men in his own clubs, as they sat in their windows and watched us go by," Charles Strong wrote in a book of remembrances issued on Laidlaw's death in 1932. In the same volume, Harriet Laidlaw confirmed the assessment, noting that "all Mr. Laidlaw's banking firm were against him in it."[24] Frances Perkins, a social worker who later became Franklin Roosevelt's secretary of labor, the first female cabinet officer in American history, agreed. "I recall him so plainly and am heartened by it still, as he joked and encouraged us on East 10th Street as we waited to 'fall in' in the great suffrage parade," she recalled. "I can never be thankful enough for the courage he gave to many of us—young and doubtful—when he took up the suffrage movement on his own."[25]

Some historians have dismissed these male suffragists as insincere, driven more by quixotic political or sexual adventure than commitment to the cause.[26] Others have ascribed the behavior of the male suffragists to a sense of chivalry, as if the vote were a courtesy, to be bestowed on delicate creatures.[27] In fact, their motives were diverse. In its early years, the Men's League for Woman Suffrage attracted Greenwich Village bohemians, radicals for whom capitalism was corrupt because it encouraged wives and children to be dependent on men for support. Feminism, armed with the vote, argued Floyd Dell, "would make it possible for the first time for men to be free."[28]

By the time of the 1912 parade, some socialists had left the Men's League, replaced by a legion of good-government reformers. In their campaigns to rid the city of Tammany Hall corruption, these male suffragists had pushed for electoral reforms, including secret ballots and separation of municipal elections from state and national ones. They saw the enfranchisement of women not as a concession of male turf or as an assault on their manhood, but a welcome boost to their anti-corruption efforts. Like Laidlaw, many were married to suffragists whose passion for the cause became theirs. And like gilded suffragists, they understood that their prominence could excite public interest and bolster the movement's profile. In their eyes, the fight for women's suffrage was not a contest between men and women, but, as is often the case in campaigns for social change, between progressives and the rest.[29]

In the face of the vibrant, celebratory parade of 1912, the reliably anti-suffrage *New York Times* tried to warn its readers that the tide was turning. In an editorial titled "The Uprising of the Women," the *Times* assailed "the refusal of woman to recognize his manhood as a title of supremacy in the world's affairs." The problem was not the "very small minority" of women who "have a natural inclination to usurp the social and civic functions of men." Nor was the problem the men who marched for suffrage. Though they were in the wrong, of course, the *Times* opined that they were "certainly more admirable and entitled to respect" than those men who seem "not to care much whether or not the women get the right to vote," and ignore "the social revolution which would re-sult." Conceding that the marchers were "young and personable, all . . . healthy and presumably intelligent," the editorial sought to shake men out of their complacency by questioning their manhood. "The situation is dangerous. We often hear the remark nowadays that women will get the vote if they try hard enough and persistently, and it is true that they will get it, and play havoc with it for themselves and society, if the men are not firm and wise enough and, it may as well be said, masculine enough to prevent them."[30] The *Titanic* tragedy was fresh in memory, but female intrusion on the male ballot threatened to eviscerate those warm chivalrous feelings.

The attempt by *Times* editorial writers to awaken men from their pas-sivity may have been too late, for 1912 proved a pivotal marker for the entry of women into national politics. As the *Washington Post* put it, "With a suddenness and force that have left observers gasping, women have injected themselves into the national campaign this year in a man-ner never before dreamed of in American politics."[31] Six states had granted women voting rights—Wyoming, Colorado, Utah, Idaho, Wash-ington, and California. The passage of women's suffrage in California had been close—the referendum won by a margin of 3,587 votes, one per precinct—but the effect was dramatic, increasing to 1.3 million the num-ber of female voters eligible to cast ballots in the presidential election.[32] No less remarkable was the impact on local elections. In 1911 Hiram Gill, mayor of Seattle, a colorful character given to wearing a "broad-brimmed Stetson hat" and sporting a "corn-cob pipe," was recalled over his "open city" tolerance of drinking and gambling.[33] His undoing came at the hands of an electorate that included nearly twenty-two thousand female voters enfranchised only the year before.[34] In New York, Yiddish papers "sold out in half the usual time," as Russian immigrant women rushed to savor the moment, asking their menfolk, "Well what do you think of the women now?"[35]

The Men's League for Woman Suffrage was actually the brainchild of a woman, Fanny Garrison Villard.[36] In 1908 Villard had urged her son, a crusading editor of the *New York Evening Post* and the *Nation*, to contact Anna Howard Shaw, the National American Woman Suffrage Association president, about forming "a men's club favoring equal suffrage." The subject had been much discussed in suffrage circles, and Shaw was mindful that some female activists were wary of a male takeover. In conferring her blessings, Shaw encouraged Oswald Garrison Villard to focus on men who might be too busy to campaign but "would be willing to *give their names* and the *influence* [emphasis hers] which goes with them."[37] In Shaw's formulation, the Men's League would give social cover by its very presence, but like a cadre of silent soldiers would not threaten female leadership. In the crossroads of unintended consequences, an organic political organization once unloosed is rarely contained. Within a year the Men's League became a loud, active suffrage organization, often garnering more attention than women's groups.

Villard reached out to Rabbi Wise, the son and grandson of rabbis and an early advocate for women's suffrage. Offered the position of rabbi at the city's most influential synagogue, Emanu-El, Wise declined, arguing that he did not want to preside over the status quo but to change it.[38] Forming a Free Synagogue, he used his Sunday lectures at Carnegie Hall to address a more secular audience. Once, he admonished wealthy Jews for holding too narrow a view of charity, funding orphan asylums while ignoring the causes of the children's abandonment. "Some think that to send a child to an orphan asylum is everything that should be done," Wise intoned. "If mothers and fathers were treated more like human beings than machines, there would not be so many orphans to be taken care of."[39] About suffrage, Wise was outspoken. "As long as women are shut out from citizenship and the exercise of the ballot, which is the symbol of citizenship, ours is no democracy," he thundered. The country was a "manocracy," where men use "brute power to shut women out from the right of equal citizenship."[40]

Villard and Wise agreed to found a Men's League. They would "share the ignominy, provided someone turned up who would do the work."[41] That someone turned out to be Max Eastman, an intellectual, socialist, poet, and later editor of the radical magazine the *Masses*. Influenced by his sister, suffragist Crystal Eastman, and by the "general mood of America," seizing on what he saw as an opportunity to "demolish traditional monogamous marriage," he agreed to take on the task of organizing men around the idea of women's liberation.[42]

For his part, Eastman, an advocate of free love and red politics, thought that the ballot would improve women's intellectual skills, the better for both socialism and sex. He reached out to other radicals in Greenwich Village.[43] But Villard, descendent of political fame, told Eastman to recruit men of prominence, the better to "impress the public and legislators," an outreach that communicated power to power, within the class.[44] Villard had given Eastman letters of introduction to twelve men of "civic importance," along with two dollars in dues, which Eastman said "sealed my responsibility" and "weighed me down. . . . I was the organizer now for certain. I held the funds. There was nothing to do but go ahead and organize."

In contacting men of prominence—he called them "civic wonders"—Eastman encountered some resistance. Hector S. Tyndale, claiming to be a suffrage supporter, practically threw Eastman out of his office, saying he'd "be damned if he'd see [the cause] made ridiculous." Insulted by this "severe blow," Eastman avoided anyone on the list for weeks. His next visit was more successful. Charles Culp Burlingham, president of the New York Bar Association, a reformer sometimes called the "first citizen of New York," was all in.[45] Burlingham, whose wife was an anti-suffragist, told Eastman he believed that "women ought to try to be more intelligent than they are, if only for the sake of their husbands." To all, Eastman made two promises, "the importance of which I had learned in my visits to the original twelve." One was that there would be no public announcement until one hundred men had signed up, offering the comfort of a crowd even as it suggested the likelihood of social ostracism. "The other was that no member would be called upon to do anything," Eastman recalled. "The main function of the league would be to exist."[46]

But when the Men's League held its first meeting at the City Club in late November 1909, press interest was considerable, and all thoughts of a silent brigade of compliant men symbolically bolstering the cause vanished. The City Club, founded in 1892 to "aid in securing permanent good government for the City of New York," was a fitting site from which to announce a new progressive cause.[47] Richard Welling, a lawyer and Harvard classmate of Theodore Roosevelt's, had been instrumental in the club's growth, and from there had launched many a campaign to improve the city's water supply and end police graft and election bribery.[48] With Burlingham and fellow lawyer Charles H. Strong, he now joined the Men's League. So did other professionals of their acquaintance, men they had met during the City Club's reform efforts, including the league's first president, banker George Foster Peabody, Metropolitan Museum of Art curator William Ivins, Republican congressman Herbert Parsons, businessman William Jay Schieffelin, and muckraker Lincoln Steffens.[49]

By 1912, the idea of men's leagues had spread to thirty chapters around the country—the Harvard Men's League for Woman Suffrage was formed by John Reed, whom Eastman had converted to the cause— and twenty thousand men had signed up for a national Men's League for Woman Suffrage.[50] The New York league's letterhead, which listed twenty-seven names at its inception in 1910, by 1915 featured sixty-seven men willing to publicly declare their support.[51] With the numbers came a sense of excitement. After witnessing the New York suffrage parade in 1915, Henry Allen, the former governor of Kansas who had been panned by suffragists for a speech he gave in Brooklyn, stomped into Carrie Chapman Catt's office to ask for a second chance. "I never got the spirit of this thing till I saw that parade yesterday," he told her. "This is not a movement, it is not a campaign—This is a crusade."[52]

Many who now joined the league saw themselves as husbands supporting their wives' causes. In their eyes, manhood was less about defending the barricade of exclusive access to the political process than expanding the definition of citizenship. Whether they were drawn to the campaign because of their wives' activism or attracted to their wives because of their support for progressive ideals is difficult to say. Either way, their gaze brought dividends, as their endorsement conferred male political power on a female cause. As Ida Husted Harper, press agent for the National American Woman Suffrage Association, observed, "Behind many a woman who worked there was a man aiding and sustaining her with money and personal sacrifice." A suffragist with a man at her side had more credence with male voters. The moniker of "suffrage husband" became a "title of distinction."[53]

Fola La Follette, a suffragist, a member of Heterodoxy, and the daughter of Robert "Fighting Bob" La Follette, the Wisconsin progressive, had married playwright George Middleton. On their marriage she opted to keep her given name, and he readily acceded. "When I defended Fola's right to do as she wished, a teapot tempest spilled over," he recalled. "Editorials, interviews, and what not followed, for we were accused of starting another of those 'feminists' demands' which were 'breaking up the home.'"[54] So devoted was he to suffrage that one columnist suggested that the playwright "be added to the list of Prominent Feminists—because he not only stands for his wife's visiting cards, but because he constitutes so large a portion of the masculine element at feminist meetings." He was often called on to give his own speeches "at street corners and 'store' meetings on Fifth Avenue during the lunch hour." Some suffragists remembered Middleton's speeches for their pithy phrases, such as "feminism is not an assault on trousers" and "marriage is a link and not a handcuff" (the latter quote more likely attributable to Crystal Eastman). No matter their provenance, these bon mots suggest the asset of the male suffragist—to take the fangs out of a social change that is destabilizing, to make the notion of sexual equality, once radical, now laughably familiar. For his own part, Middleton preferred to make appearances with his wife, who drew crowds. Her verbal gifts, her training as an actress, and her background as the daughter of a prominent politician gave her a presence that delighted him. Once, preceding her at an event in Catskill, New York, he recalled, "I died on my feet. Never have I felt so lifeless an audience." He turned the stage over to his wife, who melted "all the ice I left."[55]

Henry Wise Miller was likewise awed by his wife's orations. Alice Duer Miller was the daughter of privilege who had excelled at college. Studying mathematics and astronomy, she wrote a prize-winning thesis that experts believe anticipated the solution for the riddle of the irrational number.[56] But it was her facility on her feet that most impressed her husband. "There was a perfection in what she said from the platform and in the press," he wrote. "Coming from one of her background, [she] contributed an authority to the campaign, and did much to silence the venom and ridicule of the opponents of women's rights." Like Middleton, he too was called on to share the podium as a suffrage husband. "One of the stunts of the suffrage campaign was a husband and wife speaking as a team," he recalled. He often began his remarks with a line he had read in the *Saturday Evening Post*: "I am not a politician, and my other habits are good." And like Middleton, he saluted the justice of the cause. "The conduct of the campaign—as good as anything we have had since the Boston Tea Party—may well be taken as a model of propaganda, combining in nice proportion premeditated violence with an appeal to reason," he wrote.[57]

George Creel was not a suffrage husband. Far from it—he had to negotiate an arrangement with his wife, Blanche Bates, to devote time to the cause. "My wife and I worked out a financial arrangement," he recalled. "When—and if—I made enough money to take care of my share of household expenses for the year, the rest of the time would be mine" to spend on progressive reform campaigns, including suffrage. Although he described his wife as a "vociferous anti," he admired greatly her independent career as an actress. More, he ascribed his enthusiasm for the cause to the "deep conviction that my mother outweighed any man when it came to brains and character," although she too had "held firmly to the Southern insistence that woman's place was in the home." Despite this domestic indifference, Creel enunciated a passionate appeal for the vote, becoming the Men's League's publicity director and recruiting a committee of men to rebut editorials and letters in anti-suffrage newspapers.[58] "Equal Suffrage is part and parcel of the great big struggle for equal justice and real democracy," he wrote to prospective members. "It is as much the man's fight as the woman's."[59]

Of all the suffrage husbands who joined the Men's League, none was as notorious as Dudley Field Malone. A lawyer and fiery campaign speaker, Malone first joined the movement in 1908, when he was seated next to Anna Howard Shaw at a dinner. When it was suggested to her that she try to recruit the charming Malone, Shaw replied, "I am too good a suffragist to try to convert any man to anything before he has had his dinner." Shaw never mentioned suffrage during their conversation. "I was converted then and there by this exhibit of good sense and insight into human nature," he recounted.[60]

During the pivotal 1912 presidential election, Malone stumped for Woodrow Wilson, and was rewarded with appointment to the lucrative position of Collector of the New York Port, with a salary of $12,000 a year (roughly $300,000 in contemporary terms). Throughout his first term, Wilson clung to a southerner's view that women's suffrage was a state rather than federal issue. Four years later, when Wilson ran for reelection against former New York governor Charles Evans Hughes, who had endorsed suffrage, the White House sent Malone west, to win over California's female voters. According to an account in the *New York Times*, Malone told crowds that Wilson was "sympathetic toward equal suffrage and that if the women of California would support the Democratic National ticket he would do all he could to help them obtain a national vote." Doris Stevens, a leading figure in Alice Paul's Congressional Union, was also on the campaign trail. Rebutting Malone, she told female voters that Wilson "was not sympathetic and that the cause of universal suffrage could expect little aid from his Administration."[61]

Safely reelected, Wilson treated suffrage as an intrusion on his time, now taken up with preparing the nation for war in Europe. When suffrage leader Alice Paul staged pickets at the White House, he ordered the arrest of protesters on charges of obstructing sidewalk traffic. After the protesters were sentenced to sixty days in the notorious Occoquan Workhouse, several members of the Men's League, lawyers who had witnessed the trial, expressed their outrage. At the White House, Malone convinced Wilson to pardon the picketers. Then he resigned in protest after a fiery exchange in the Oval Office in which he upbraided the president. Wilson saw Malone as a friend, and was deeply wounded, telling his aide Colonel Edward House, "I know of nothing that has gone more to the quick with me or that has seemed to me more tragical [*sic*] than Dudley's conduct, which came upon me like a bolt out of the blue. I was stricken by it as I have been by few things in my life."[62]

On hearing of Malone's grand gesture, suffragists were ecstatic, seeing chivalry and personal sacrifice in the action. "Although we disagree with you on the question of picketing, every suffragist must be grateful to you for the gallant support you are giving our cause and the great sacrifice you are making for it," Vira Whitehouse telegraphed. Harriet Laidlaw agreed, telling a reporter, "I was thrilled. I didn't know the suffragists had such a knightly friend. I didn't dream any man would do such a chivalrous thing for us. It can't fail to have a splendid effect on the voting men in our referendum this fall."[63]

Male suffragists were more suspicious of Malone's motives. Newton Gilbert, an Indiana official and briefly governor-general of the Philippines, argued that the resignation wouldn't help suffrage because the picketing had hurt the cause. "Mr. Malone is too closely connected with the pickets," he observed. "And the pickets have hurt suffrage, which is too bad, for it's too good a cause to be hurt. I did not support Woodrow Wilson, but he is my President, and I object to having him called 'Kaiser Wilson.'" As league president James Lees Laidlaw told the *New York Sun*, the results of Malone's action "would depend somewhat on whether he got out and rolled up his sleeves for Votes for Women."[64] In fact, aside from his membership in the Men's League, there is no record that Malone ever did.

Four years later, Malone and Doris Stevens married, a stealth wedding officiated by a justice of the peace in the back of a hardware store in Peekskill, New York, and then quickly left for Paris, where Malone worked his trade as a divorce lawyer and Stevens suffered the insults of his public humiliations.[65] Some reported that Malone was "given to drunkenly insulting Stevens in public," flaunting his extramarital affairs and once hitting her.[66] Others suggest that Alva Belmont, who had hired Stevens to promote her international suffrage activism, put additional strains on the marriage by insisting that Stevens tend to Belmont's needs.[67] On their divorce in 1929, all commentary about Malone as a feminist withered.

As the women's suffrage campaign gained steam in New York, the Men's League's initial reticence to do anything more than stand guard gave way to a more public activism. By 1912 Laidlaw was also president of the National Men's League for Woman Suffrage, and he often involved the New York league in local issues elsewhere, particularly the fight for ratification of a women's suffrage amendment in West Virginia in 1916. Opponents had threatened to defeat Raymond Dodson, of the Spencer area, if he did not abandon his support for the amendment. Dodson's day job was attorney for the United Fuel Gas Company, where his boss, Harry Wallace, objected to the idea of women in politics. Word reached James Lees Laidlaw, who rallied male supporters in New York and elsewhere to save the senator. The Men's League issued a press release meant to "arouse indignation." Dodson served out his term.[68]

The fraught issue of chivalry was never far from the surface. In 1913 Laidlaw suggested that Men's League members wear a blue button of courtesy, signaling to anti-suffrage women on streetcars that, as one newspaper put it, "the days of chivalry were not over when it came to giving a woman a seat in a crowded car."[69]

The anti-suffrage *Brooklyn Life* pounced at this contortion of gender messages. In an article titled "Ostentatious Gallantry," the magazine pierced the hypocrisy of preaching equality while offering privilege. Calling the Men's League "that knightly organization," *Brooklyn Life* noted that true "gentlemen never make a special feature of courtesy and consideration for women. They do not have to. It is second nature with them and the last thing they would think of bragging about." Instead the magazine suggested that male suffragists ask women for help carrying their luggage. "It seems to us that this would be much more consonant with the aim and purpose of the league," said the magazine, "which is to drag women into politics before a majority of them has signified the slightest desire for political equality."[70] Ever eager to emasculate male suffragists, *Brooklyn Life* often ran notices and summaries of their meetings under the heading "Women's Clubs."[71]

In November 1912, when Harriet Laidlaw planned a Woman Suffrage Party torchlight parade to celebrate recent victories in California and Washington, men took a prominent role, none more than her husband, who led the march. Anti-suffrage sentiment soared. Mocking the parade as the "most pretentious celebration ever attempted," the *New York Telegram* reserved its greatest sarcasm for the men. "Don't think that Mere Man will be left standing on the sidewalk, balancing himself on one foot and then on the other, while lovely women go marching by," jived the paper. "Any man is at liberty to enter the ranks, provided he obtains an ordinary chrysanthemum for the buttonhole of his coat. They cost only five cents and what up to date man, with red blood in his veins and with a discerning eye for the beautiful, can resist the captivating glances of a suffragette?"[72]

That was the question suffrage leaders were now eager to test. Giving speeches from atop soapboxes and ox carts from Wall Street to the East River docks, they challenged male terrain. Adopting the tactics of Madison Avenue and a burgeoning new advertising industry, they sold women's suffrage as a commodity. Mostly, they privileged femininity, ensuring that coming contests would not lack for drama, or media coverage. In short, they created buzz.

7

THE TACTICAL TURN

Militant political action . . . had broken down
hitherto unimaginable taboos. . . . An emotional
earthquake had shattered the intangible yet
suffocating prison of decorum.

WINIFRED HOLTBY[1]

I T was a day of presidential firsts for William Howard Taft. After lunch on Thursday, April 14, 1910, he left the White House for the Arlington Hotel, where he became the first president to address a suffrage group, welcoming to Washington members of the National American Woman Suffrage Association. Then he traveled to Griffith Stadium, where he became the first president to throw out the ceremonial first pitch on opening day of the season. Taft is much remembered for his baseball achievement—even now honored as one of the Washington Nationals' "racing presidents." But it was his speech to the suffrage group that reverberated through political circles, exposing a tactical warfare over decorum.

Worried that Taft's appearance would rouse Democratic enmity against Republicans, Senator Elihu Root of New York had beseeched the president to make clear that his welcome was not an endorsement.[2] Taft agreed. He would be polite, even decorous, but would spell out the rationale for his opposition to suffrage. And so he told the audience that it was dangerous to extend the ballot to "Hottentots," a slang word for South Africans, "or any other uneducated, altogether unintelligent class." Since the rest of the female citizenry didn't really want the vote, he reasoned, the ballot would be exercised only "by that part of the class less desirable as political constituents and be neglected by many of those who are intelligent and patriotic and would be most desirable as members of the electorate."

Reaction was immediate. As the *Syracuse Post-Standard* put it, "When these words fell from the President's lips, the walls of the convention hall echoed a chorus of feminine hisses. It was no feeble demonstration of protest. The combined hisses sounded as if a valve on a steam engine had broken."[3] It had. Female hissing heralded the end of gender deference in politics, nurtured since the Revolution, challenged during the Civil War, and reinvigorated during the cult of manhood embodied by the century's new president, Theodore Roosevelt.[4] Women who had "grown up with Victorian standards of modesty" now felt empowered enough to raise their voices.[5]

Suffrage leaders tried to hush the hecklers, and later wrote a letter of apology to the president, but they could not silence the movement's newfound freedom of expression.[6] Like chivalry, challenged by gender equality, decorum loomed as the next great test for female advocates as they crossed from domestic concerns to the public square. In an editorial entitled "The Sowing of Bad Seed," *Vogue Magazine* warned that "the urgent calls to throw off the alleged tyranny of man have seen so many seeds of discontent sown upon all kinds of soil." The result, thought *Vogue*, was "a large crop of shouters for rights who have no real conception of just what rights they are shouting for." The magazine, usually an arbiter of fashion trends, now blamed the "reckless" tendency of suffrage leaders to attack "fathers, husbands and brothers," and pit "class against class," leading inevitably to "embarrassing situations" such as hissing at the president.[7] What had become of manners?

In England, under the banner of "Deeds, Not Words," supporters of Emmeline Pankhurst's Women's Social and Political Union answered the question by embracing militancy. As Pankhurst explained, "We threw away all our conventional methods of what was 'ladylike' and 'good form' and we applied to our methods the one test question, will it help?"[8]

In a remarkable run at power beginning in 1905, these militants for the vote threw rocks at 10 Downing Street, set fire to pillar boxes, smashed windows in Knightsbridge's luxurious shops, treated golf courses with acid, and cut telegraph wires. They heckled and attacked members of Parliament, including Winston Churchill.[9] They set off a bomb at the Theatre Royal in Dublin, started a fire at the Orchid House in Kew Gardens, and bombed Lloyd George's country house.[10] Imprisoned at the infamous Holloway Prison, many protested their incarceration with hunger strikes. The brutality of forcing liquids down their throats by tube, and a medical protest against the practice, sparked continued militancy and renewed publicity.[11] In 1913 suffrage activist Emily Davison threw herself at King George V's horse at the Epsom Derby, whether an attempt to die for the cause or to attach a suffrage banner to the horse's bridle never determined. What is clear is that her funeral, funded by the party, cemented her reputation as a martyr for the cause.[12]

Labeling them troublemakers, British journalist Charles Hands in 1906 dismissed the militants as mere suffragettes.[13] Activists in London embraced the label, eager to distinguish themselves from the constitutionalists of the National Union of Women's Suffrage Societies, and to turn derision into a badge of honor.[14] In New York, by contrast, American activists, the wealthy among them, distanced themselves from the title and the violence, eager to reassure men that if granted the vote, they would not threaten the political order. They would be suffragists, not suffragettes. In short, they would behave like ladies.

In years to come, American suffragists had many tussles over tactics—a division over whether peaceful appeals or boisterous challenges would prove more effective, a discussion of whether adopting the male tactics of the political art would empower them or sully them, even a debate over Alice Paul's decision to embrace civil disobedience and hardball politics. But nowhere is there any record of an American advocate for the vote throwing a bomb.

The difference is a function of history, and of political culture. The U.S. record of extending the vote to previously disenfranchised groups may have influenced American suffragists to embrace the system. Though it is not widely known, propertied women were eligible to vote in New Jersey from the adoption of the state constitution in 1776 until 1807. Apparently they voted en masse for John Adams in 1800, and Jeffersonians in the state capitol took their revenge by disenfranchising them seven years later.[15] Most white American men—the nonpropertied, the working-class—did not get the vote until the 1830s, when Andrew Jackson sought to expand his Democratic Party electorate. African American men got the vote—at least on paper—after the Civil War, although black men and women had to fight for it again a hundred years later during the civil rights movement. Because of this history, American suffragists may have had a view of the Constitution as amendable and the polity as expandable.

Culturally too, differences were instructive. Militant suffragists in Britain sought to frighten lawmakers in the political class, while constitutional suffragists in both countries worked to persuade or pressure them. Unlike activists in London, who fought in a political capital, suffrage leaders in New York parried foes in a city of wealth and aspiration. Theirs was not the political mission of forcing the hand of politicians, but the more commercial art of persuading the public. As a result, they now embraced the ploys of the private sector, entering into what one scholar has called "a period of stunning political experimentation as innovative as anything they had attempted in the nineteenth century."[16]

Suffrage would be sold as a commodity, and the branding would be as important as the product.[17] The range of tactics was breathtaking— sometimes silly—and always in keeping with a vibrant consumer culture that hawked products on streetcar walls and magazine pages, often using the lure of female beauty to bolster demand. Pageants, concerts, canal boat speeches, sandwich boards, organ grinder concerts, suffrage shops, whistle-stop tours from trains, "Votes for Women" signs on children and pets, pamphlets dropped from airplanes onto President Wilson's yacht—no spectacle was too outrageous, as long as a sensationalizing press would give publicity to the cause, a current of public interest rising with the attention.[18]

For many activists, their first experience defying class and gender expectations in the public square was the soapbox speech, as intoxicating as it was nerve-wracking. "You took your box—a good strong grocery box of some sort, because they had wooden boxes . . . in those days," recalled Frances Perkins, then a New York social worker. "You didn't have any loudspeakers . . . you had to do it all with your own voice." Traveling in pairs—one suffragist to speak, the other to distribute literature—suffragists often stood in front of a saloon because there, "you were always sure of a crowd." Reaction was rough. "You would get jeered at. You would get heckled. You would get asked impertinent questions, but I don't recall ever having been insulted or treated to obscene language," she said.[19]

Belle Fligelman Winestine worked for suffrage in Montana with Jeannette Rankin, who would later become the first woman elected to the U.S. Congress. "Up to that time, no one in Montana . . . had heard of a respectable young woman making a public street corner speech," she wrote. Winestine recalls being "terrified as I took my place on what was supposed to be a busy Helena street corner. Suddenly, it seemed, there was not a soul in sight. But I had something to say, so I just started talking to the world." One person stopped to listen, and then another, "and soon I had a big audience, all listening attentively—partly, I suppose, because they had never heard a woman speaking on the street." Her mother was horrified, admonishing her, "No respectable lady would speak on a street corner."[20]

The novelty of it, the shock value of the new—these were the hallmarks of a modern suffrage movement in an America teeming with newspapers, advertisements, and a public forced to confront the cause. "We believed that you had to get the people who weren't in the least interested in suffrage," recalled Laura Ellsworth Seiler, who worked for Blatch's Women's Political Union. The "whole idea was that you must keep suffrage every minute before the public so that it gets used to the idea and talks about it, whether they agree or disagree." In fact reaction was often hostile. "Sometimes, depending on the neighborhood, stones would be thrown into the crowd, . . . things would be thrown from the roof."

Seiler recalled one ploy that did not win the movement a lot of friends. "Once we hired a motorboat and ran up and down shoreline yelling through a megaphone, 'Suffrage, Votes for Women.'" Men loading cargoes were beyond dismissive. "There was lots of cussing from men loading cargo. I acquired a good many four-letter words on that boat trip." While the women hurled their suffrage slogans at the docks, "a group of men on a fishing trip circled their boat to make tremendous waves, almost swamping us." Despite the fact that the suffragists had almost capsized, news coverage was minimal. When Seiler complained to a reporter, he replied that the next time, "if I did drown, he would write it up."[21]

Male derision was a stubborn thing. One writer, signing "J.J.," complained to the *Times* that the focus on publicity had turned the cause into a "circus." Parades that featured "their prettiest girls," pageants where suffragists dressed in "flowing draperies," statements by Alva Belmont that "arson and crime" would result if voters rejected suffrage at the polls—all seemed designed not for emancipation of women but for publicity.[22] Still, they persisted.

In 1906, twenty-eight-year-old Maud Malone, who had founded the Harlem Equal Rights League the previous year, set up a polling place on Fifth Avenue. As male voters went inside to select the state's next governor, a contest between Charles Evans Hughes and William Randolph Hearst, more than five hundred women stopped by outside to cast their votes—actresses, writers, librarians, teachers, and social workers. The results of their faux election were not recorded, but mockery at their attempt surely was. The *Times* belittled Malone and her band of election clerks, and suggested that some voted for Hearst because of the beauty of his eyes. "They came very gravely," said the newspaper, "but once they got together . . . the women yielded to a natural propensity to talk a lot."[23]

Amid these adventurous ploys, New York became a national center of "dramatic suffrage activity." The city's mix of ethnic groups and seasoned reformers, its remarkable cross-class coalition of working class and leisure class, its actresses rallying Broadway audiences to the cause had, said one scholar, "created an excitement that was unparalleled anywhere else in the country."[24] By the 1910s, most major suffrage organizations had their national headquarters in New York, and often anti-suffrage groups did too. In New York, if nowhere else, the campaign grew so heated that anti-suffragists were accused, as one scholar put it, of "dumping lemons, wet sponges, rolls of ticker tape, bags of water and garbage pails on innocent suffrage supporters parading outside the anti-suffrage offices."[25] For their part, activists responded by plastering pro-suffrage posters on the walls of buildings where anti-suffragists gathered.[26] Violence may have been off the boards, but public decorum was on trial.

Of all the tactics women now employed in winning the vote, few were as controversial—or as upsetting to the mannered civility that had settled on relations between American men and women for more than a century—as the public parade. To Katherine Mackay and others in her Equal Franchise Society, the parades challenged the very heart of their ladylike activism. Worried that their first steps onto the grubby streets of New York City would mark them as radicals—or worse, as streetwalkers—they retreated. Elizabeth Callender Stevens, whom Mackay had recruited to lead the New Jersey Equal Franchise Society, resigned her position rather than participate in the 1911 parade. Over the protests of her husband, Richard Stevens, who begged her to reconsider, she insisted, "Men . . . do not have respect for women who will walk through the public streets in this manner. . . . It is so undignified and so unwomanly. . . . It will do no end of harm."[27]

Mackay herself was said to be "greatly shocked" by the specter of women marching in the streets; Alva Belmont was likewise "furious and retiring to Long Island." In a meeting of the Equal Franchise Society board of directors to discuss the 1911 parade, a "voluble" Mackay was said to have "pounded her fists on the table" in protest at this departure from ladylike activism. Once outvoted, Mackay directed the board's discussion about "banners and regalia," eager for her organization, as Blatch put it, "to make a good appearance even though she highly disapproved of the occasion and would not attend."[28] Mackay may have had qualms about parading, but she was resolved that her organization's flag—"a beautiful affair of blue satin and gold"—be prominently displayed.[29] So it was. Marching behind the Equal Franchise Society standard was Elizabeth Burchenal, one of Mackay's lieutenants, bearing a sign that no doubt made Mackay smile. It said, "All This Is a Natural Consequence of Teaching Girls to Read."[30] Despite Mackay's misgivings about the parade as a tactic, she was aware that her celebrity, and that of her suffrage organization, required showing the flag, with a bit of artistry and a lot of pizzazz.

For two years, as the parades gained in popularity and strategic effect, Belmont feigned illness, looking on from behind an office window or motoring alongside the marchers. She was said to own thirteen cars, and was perhaps the first American to import an automobile from Europe, a leading figure in what the papers called the "autonobility."[31] As she hesitated, women whose wealth was far more pedigreed than hers proudly if quietly marched for suffrage. *Town Topics* wondered what "the exclusive and precise Egerton Winthrop Sr." thought of seeing his daughter-in-law Emmeline join the parade, or the late William C. Whitney would have surmised on seeing his daughter Dorothy "in the same gallery." These women represented the "old and distinctive social elements of the very best in the Metropolis," observed the weekly, and "their presence was worth more to the leaders of the Suffragettes than a hundred Mrs. Belmonts, Thompson Setons or Inez Milhollands, who either have ceased to have social influence or never possessed any."[32]

By 1912, perhaps stung at this assertion that she was no longer socially influential, and as the campaign gathered steam, Belmont decided to risk marching at the head of her Political Equality Association, prompting one newspaper to hail "this epic in the history of womanhood."[33] The association's Harlem chapter also joined the parade, the first time a unit of black suffragists was formally welcomed, turning out "in all its strength."[34]

Belmont's demeanor, both before and afterward, suggested the gravity of the decision. "She had the appearance of a brave soldier facing fire, looking straight ahead," reported the *Times*.[35] Her friend Mamie Fish told her she doubted she could walk the whole of the route from 59th Street to the Washington Arch. "My dear Alva, you'll never be able to do it," she warned. "It must be three miles and you have scarcely walked a step in your life." To which Belmont replied, "All the more reason why I should begin now. After all, my dear, I must have something to interest me in my old age. . . . I shall walk the whole way."[36] Alva Smith Vanderbilt Belmont had been raised into the ways of the gentility, expected to respect the formalities of polite society. Though flippant with Mamie Fish, she may have been more candid with her daughter Consuelo, telling her, "To a woman brought up as I was, it was a terrible ordeal." Journalist Marie Manning saw great moment in Belmont's walk, as it forced politicians to pay mind. "The greatest shove ever given to the . . . movement will always be that lady's appearance at the head of a suffrage parade in New York City," she wrote.[37]

Later Belmont opened a suffrage lunchroom in Manhattan serving "good wholesome food, all home cooked and prepared by competent cooks . . . at reasonable prices for the working men and women of the District and visitors who come to town daily." So popular did the venue become among male patrons—it was said that the very idea was "inspired by a man who lamented that once women got the vote, there would be no one to make his lunch"—that tables were reserved for men only, whether to protect women from unwanted male attention or men from too much suffrage lobbying is unclear.[38] Perhaps no stunt challenged the gender landscape more than when activist Mary Morgan Brewer climbed into a Staten Island boxing ring in 1915 to deliver a pre-fight lecture on suffrage. Receiving a chorus of "howls, stamping and cat-calls by 1,500 fight fans" outraged at the very idea of a woman at a temple of raw male power—to say nothing of her audacity at delaying the boxing match—she spoke, then "calmly sat down and watched the ten-round bout" as Ted Lewis "whipped Charley White of Chicago."[39]

The viper's pen was another favorite weapon of suffragists, combining as it did evidence of erudition and intelligence, said to be lacking in the aspiring female voter. In a series of columns published in the *New York*

Tribune from 1914 to 1917 titled "Are Women People?," Alice Duer Miller exposed the hypocrisy of male resistance to female emancipation. Commenting on the Board of Education's decision to fire a woman engineer with an exemplary record of overseeing pressure boilers, or the National Education Association speaker who claimed that girls who study algebra lose their souls, or U.S. laws that required women to renounce their American citizenship on marrying foreigners, she was as knowing as she was amusing. She was at her most biting in defense of suffrage. In one column, in the form of a verse, "Why We Oppose Votes for Men," Miller observed, "Men are too emotional to vote. Their conduct at baseball games and political conventions shows this, while their innate tendency to appeal to force renders them peculiarly unfit for the task of government."[40] It was reminiscent of a tactic used by Britain's Mary Cholmondeley, who in 1909 published the play *Votes for Men*, set two hundred years in the future. In the work, the British prime minister, a woman, is approached to speak to the Men's Reinfranchisement League, and despairs, "I wish they would not pester me so. The government has other things to attend to than Male Suffrage at times like this."[41]

When, in May 1915, the New York legislature agreed to put women's suffrage on the November ballot, tactical imaginations soared, along with New York's summer temperatures. From her home on East 56th Street, Vira Whitehouse, wife of New York stockbroker Norman de Rapelye Whitehouse and a member of Heterodoxy, made cold calls to potential voters to ask their views on suffrage, an early instance of telephone polling.[42] Anti-suffragists protested, saying that suffragists were "disturbing men on a hot day."[43] At a "Votes for Women" restaurant at 70 Wall Street, Harriet Laidlaw delivered a speech as supporters distributed five hundred suffrage fans. "Suffrage sundaes, cooling beverages made principally of peaches were handed right and left," reported the *Sun*.[44] At the Polo Grounds in May, the campaign arranged a Suffrage Day. The New York Giants cooperated by draping yellow banners in front of the boxes and providing yellow dandelions for the lapels of male ushers. Suffragists distributed a flyer, inserted into each score card, with the exhortation "Fans, Fair Play . . . Vote Yes Nov. 2, 1915." Other trinkets said, "We'd Like Our Innings," and "Make a Home Run for Suffrage." After the game, Laidlaw, Milholland, and Portia Willis spoke from their automobiles.[45] As sportswriter Heywood Broun wrote in explaining the Cubs' 1–0 shutout victory, "Having a certain social position to retain, the Giants always feel a bit nervous when Mrs. John Jacob Astor and others are in the stands."[46]

Public attention to movement tactics gave courage to some who had been on the sidelines. For the first time now, they joined the great cause of their day. Rita Lydig had been treasurer of Mackay's Equal Franchise Society since it began in 1909, but her sister Mercedes de Acosta, a poet, had not found her voice until the war. During the First World War, she wrote, "I worked for Women's Suffrage as if it were the only thing that mattered in my life." She canvassed homes, ringing doorbells, engaging in debate. "But always, and under every situation, I left a shower of leaflets and pamphlets strewn behind me. Hounds would not have been necessary to trace me by my scent in those days. Anyone could have found me by following up the stream of literature on Women's Rights I left in my wake."[47]

To some commentators, these newfound strategies seemed to be working. The *New York Herald* published a cartoon in 1910 that captured the differences in the women's suffrage campaigns in Britain and the United States. Called "The Smooch versus the Harangue," the illustration featured John Bull, the portly personification of Britain, hiding a ballot box behind his back, surrounded by female activists in wool jackets and skirts, armed with umbrellas going for his head. In the other corner is Uncle Sam, in early New England known as Brother Jonathan, hoisting the ballot box overhead, encircled by beautifully dressed *femmes fatales* in flowing gowns and feathered hats, whispering in his ears. The caption, by William Allen Rogers, read, "Jonathan may be in more danger than John."[48]

Several scholars have argued that these new tactics—so unexpected because they violated "standards of respectable femininity"—assured the movement's progress.[49] Less noticed is that these departures also privileged activists of social standing. The wealthier the suffragist, "the more ladylike she was supposed to be, the greater the effect of her subversion of the norm."[50] Seeking to counteract negative publicity about boorish behavior and broad hints about lesbian intentions, suffrage leaders had favored femininity. When critics shuddered at the idea of suffragists marching in the streets, likening them to streetwalkers, activists put forward their most fashionable suffragists and kept marching. As always, male derision was the last temple to fall. "This method of propaganda is somewhat different from that of the English suffragettes who go to jail for their principles," explained one journalist, "but why break into jail when one can break into society?"[51]

How suffragists looked and dressed was a long-standing concern among activists. When Isabella Beecher Hooker convened a suffrage convention in Washington, D.C., in 1871, she pointedly asked Elizabeth Cady Stanton not to attend, fearful that she and Susan B. Anthony would not act and dress "like ladies."[52] By the mid-1890s, the tendency to apply Darwinian principles of scientific inquiry to everything from public relations to business efficiency persuaded even diehard allies that, like other commodities, suffrage had to be sold. On the eve of their annual festival in 1894, activist Mary Livermore, an early editor of the *Woman's Journal*, urged suffragists in Massachusetts to wear yellow flowers in their lapels.[53] "We have cultivated a severe plainness long enough," she said. "It may be classic and it may be artistic but it is desperately ugly. Let's have a change, and show our colors."[54]

Gabrielle Stewart Mulliner, a lawyer, an officer in the New York State Federation of Women's Clubs, and an early member of Mackay's Equal Franchise Society, stirred controversy in 1910 when she suggested that some suffragists—she called them "prize packages of frumps"—were so dated in their attire that "a few judicial deaths would be a salubrious thing for the suffragist cause."[55] Protests were many, and loud. Mrs. Clarence Burns, described by one newspaper as "a well-dressed clubwoman," responded, "If the male 'frumps' in the matter of clothes had been eliminated from history, I fear we would have had to get along without our Abraham Lincolns, our Grants and a few other of our heroes. I can hardly believe the cause of women will be settled through the aid of Fifth Avenue hatters and *modistes*."[56] But logic held no sway over fashion. Within a year, the mainstream movement had taken the admonition to heart. In an item placed in the *Washington Post* and other newspapers early the next year, New York leaders urged that any woman marching in the upcoming "Votes for Women" parade "be neat and as modishly gowned as her purse will permit." Noting that Belmont and Mackay "always keep up with the fashions," publicists reasoned, "The well-groomed, attractive matron or maid . . . has more influence over both sexes on the speakers' platform or in personal conversation than her out-at-elbows sister."[57]

Anecdotal reports of many women, and a few men, suggest that the tactic was working. Florence Nightingale Graham, a Canadian who muscled her way into the American beauty industry, understood intuitively that the issue of women's suffrage had acquired social cachet. One day in 1912, the woman who had renamed herself and her company Elizabeth Arden stunned her staff by leaving her desk to join the suffrage parade on Fifth Avenue.[58] She had rarely shown interest in the campaign, and her biographers speculate that she merely wanted to cultivate the women it was now attracting. "It was not so much the cause that Elizabeth admired as those who espoused it," they wrote. "Such a prestigious social aegis could only lend distinction to anybody who walked in its shadow." Glamor rubbed off on suffrage politics. For years to come, Arden cast herself as an activist, noting, "I've always felt strongly about women's issues. I went on one of the key marches, you know, dear."[59]

As suffragists grew more adroit at using female beauty to convert male voters, antis objected. Josephine Jewell Dodge, head of the National Association Opposed to Woman Suffrage, complained that suffragists were flaunting their sexuality. A leader in the nursery school movement, Dodge had once disparaged suffragists as "flat-chested," implying that they were lacking in maternal instincts.[60] By 1913, after the biggest suffrage parade in New York history, she saw a new face of the movement. Criticizing the "sex appeal of the parade," she dubbed the campaign "a mighty coquetry, a flirtation planned on a gigantic scale," and accused suffragists of trying to lure men with clothes that "conduce to immorality."[61]

This controversy over tactics, a meditation on decorum, also took a toll on families. Lee de Forest, one of the inventors of wireless telegraphy and self-described father of radio, supported women's suffrage. But when he married Harriot Stanton Blatch's daughter Nora, he found himself overwhelmed by his wife's preoccupation with the campaign. When the two divorced in 1911, de Forest brought suit in court for custody of their two-year-old daughter on grounds that his ex-wife was brainwashing the child with suffrage propaganda. In his court filing, he complained that Nora Blatch de Forest was completely ignoring young Harriet's education except to teach her to say, "Votes for Women" and "Hurrah for Woman Suffrage."[62]

Like de Forest, Medill McCormick, part owner of the *Chicago Tribune* and a successful Illinois politician, supported suffrage for women, and was particularly helpful to the campaign during his first term in Congress, when the federal amendment was drafted. He had encouraged his wife, Ruth—daughter of Ohio senator and famed McKinley presidential manager Mark Hanna—to accept the chairmanship of the National American Woman Suffrage Association's congressional committee in 1913. But when he happened on the suffrage shop in Chicago in 1914 and saw for sale a postcard of his wife and his baby daughter Katrina, he demanded that the item be withdrawn from the shelves. Apparently, as Ruth's biographer put it, he "drew the line at marketing his family life."[63] Ruth Hanna McCormick left her position in 1914, saying she had only planned to stay for a year, but newspapers twisted the story into a morality play, a reassertion of maternal priorities and male authority. "Mrs. M'Cormick to Quit Cause . . . He Puts Foot Down," headlined one paper.[64] Another claimed that the baby "does not recognize her mother," and the *Bismarck Tribune* asked, "Are there no other 'Katrinas' feeling the neglect imposed by the 'cause'?"[65]

Parents and children warred over the issue too, usually in the privacy of their home. One of the first students admitted to Barnard, Iphigene Ochs attended an anti-suffrage speech on campus. After hearing Barnard founder Annie Nathan Meyer speak against women's franchise, "I immediately espoused the suffragette cause. From then on I delighted in bringing up the subject at dinner." She and her father, Adolph Ochs, publisher of the most anti-suffrage newspaper in New York, had "heated discussions about *Times* editorials . . . and both of us held fast to our opinions." The two were close, going for a walk together most Sundays in Central Park. In her memoir, Iphigene Ochs Sulzberger recalls that she never went "so far as to embarrass my father by marching in suffragette parades, but I used to sneak my allowance to the women's suffrage committee at school."[66] House Speaker Champ Clark announced in 1914 that he would support a federal constitutional amendment for women's suffrage, though preferring a state solution. His daughter Genevieve Clark remarked, "He would not have dared to come home if he had not" declared his support.[67]

Marriages strained over the issue, sometimes resolving in a shared support for the cause. When he married Olivia Langdon in 1870, Mark Twain argued that the day when women cast their votes would be a good "time for all good men to tremble for their country." The idea of "women voting and babbling about politics and electioneering," the image of "one of our blessed earthly angels peddling election tickets among a mob of shabby scoundrels," was, to the Twain of 1867, "revolting." By the 1880s he was speaking for suffrage, convinced by Livy, a good friend of Julia Ward Beecher.[68] Years later, their mutual friend William Dean Howells introduced Twain to Rabbi Stephen Wise. Howells reminded Twain that he had heard Wise speak about suffrage at Carnegie Hall. "Yes, I remember," Twain quipped. "I heard him speak for equal suffrage, and I am still for it!"[69]

Even more poignant was the chasm over suffrage between sisters. Annie Nathan Meyer, who in 1887 organized a committee to raise funds toward a women's college at Columbia, was a playwright and essayist and one of the first women of her circle to take up the bicycle. Despite these feminist instincts, she was also an anti-suffragist, believing that the "new duties" of citizenship would be a "disintegrating influence" on family life.[70] Meanwhile Meyer's sister, Maud Nathan, was president of the Consumers League, dedicated to improving conditions for working women, and a member of the board of directors of Katherine Mackay's Equal Franchise Society. During a debate in which she reportedly routed a male anti-suffragist, Nathan asked rhetorically, "Is woman ready to vote? Can a fish swim?"[71] The two sisters also differed on Jewish religious tradition—Meyer was ambivalent about Jews who were "not of the desirable sort," while for Nathan Judaism was the source of her philanthropy. The story of these two sisters was well known in reading circles, as editors at the *New York Times*, the *New Republic*, and other publications often commissioned a written debate between them. After the Nineteenth Amendment was ratified in 1920, the two reunited. One of their shared delights was in successfully applying to join the Daughters of the American Revolution, honoring their great-grandfather, Gershome Mendes Seixas, a patriot who refused to fly the British flag over his New York synagogue.[72]

Unlike the Nathan sisters, the Hay sisters did not debate their differences in public. Their father, John Hay, had been Abraham Lincoln's private secretary and secretary of state to two presidents. Perhaps his daughters had learned to settle their political differences without rancor, from a man credited with exuding diplomacy.[73] Like her father, Helen Hay Whitney was a poet. She was also a wealthy racehorse breeder, member of the Colony Club, and philanthropist. In 1916 she gave a breakfast at what was then called the Hotel Plaza for women setting off on a nationwide whistle-stop train tour in support of Republican presidential candidate and former New York governor Charles Evans Hughes.[74] Her sister Alice Hay Wadsworth was married to New York's U.S. senator James Wadsworth Jr., outspoken suffrage foe. President of the National Association Opposed to Woman Suffrage, Alice called for repeal of suffrage after its enactment in New York in 1917.[75] "If Congress will give us a fair chance, if the press will give us the opportunity," she wrote in a letter to the *Times*, "we anti-suffrage women of America . . . can segregate this menace in the States where it exists until its repeal is eventually demanded."[76]

Whatever the politics inside family homes, it was the debate on the public streets that captivated attention, often with the elixir of a feminine appearance. Though she was the toast of the fiercest suffragists, with a constituency that preferred defiance to deference, Alice Paul, head of the Congressional Union, had a keen appreciation for image. In 1913 she positioned Inez Milholland, said to be the "most beautiful suffragette," atop a white horse to steer a suffrage parade in Washington, D.C., evoking images of Joan of Arc and her quixotic effort to lead medieval French troops to victory over England.[77]

"We were creating our own mythology of women on the march, women active, and dramatic," recalled suffragist Rebecca Hourwich Reyher. "Alice Paul insisted on it."[78] With her eyes "a deep hue of the jewel called aquamarine," and her spirit like "lightning," Milholland proved a magnificent messenger who complicated gender expectations of brains and beauty.[79] As a speaker, she thrilled audiences with a "modern type of oratory," not the thunderbolts of Anna Howard Shaw but the persuasion of soft-spoken logic.[80] A lawyer as well as a suffragist, an advocate of free love as well as a loving wife, a member of Heterodoxy as well as the Colony Club, a socialite as well as a socialist, she was a great draw on the stump, especially among the young—and among men.

Curtis Campaigne later wrote that his wife had dragged him to a speech that Milholland gave in 1912. "My attitude toward the movement has always been instinctively hostile mainly for the reason that, by giving women the vote, it would necessarily force them into a life which would tend to depreciate those womanly qualities and attributes which, in the present social system, wield a potent influence," he wrote. On hearing Milholland's argument that women need not "play the game of politics" as men do, he had experienced a "new open-minded surge of thoughts," no longer seeing the ballot as a bar to femininity.[81]

Once, while making a speech at Belmont's Political Equality Association headquarters on Broadway, Milholland wore suffrage buttons on her lapel. One besotted man offered to buy a button if she would shake his hand. Inez agreed. He asked if she would shake his hand again if he bought another, and so it went, this charade of intimacy, until all the buttons were sold.[82] Did his infatuation convert him to the cause? Did her beauty convince him that women could participate in political discourse without losing their femininity?

Maud Wood Park, who helped lobby the suffrage amendment through Congress, thought it likely. With a keen feel for human nature—she kept records on which senators preferred which appeals—Park saw that femininity was an asset. "People can resist logic," she said, "but can they resist laughter, with youth and beauty to drive it home? Not often."[83]

Some said it was not beautiful celebrities or novel tactics that won the vote, nor the bravery of a few mere men or a parade of unladylike women. What they said—and this conviction later hardened into conventional wisdom—was that the war had won the vote. The Great War, that war of needless slaughter and imperial ambition, that War to End All Wars, had lifted suffrage on its back and carried it over the finish line. In truth, the triumph came not as the spoils of war but as the honest victory of suffrage leaders who navigated the twin shoals of politics and patriotism at a time when the world was on fire.

8

THE GREAT WARS

*Let no one say that a war year is not the time to extend
suffrage to women. It is the time of all times.*

NEW YORK STATE WOMAN SUFFRAGE PARTY[1]

As an estimated twenty-five thousand suffragists gathered on New
York's Fifth Avenue in October 1917, "under the most delicate of
blue skies." Katrina Ely Tiffany stood at the head of the parade, carrying the American flag.[2] When she passed by Tiffany's, said a friend
from Bryn Mawr, she could look up and see "her unconverted husband,"
Charles L. Tiffany II, "looking sorrowfully down from the window."[3]
Vice president of that great emporium of jewels and luxury, Tiffany was
no fan of Katrina's activism. This despite the fact that one of his execu-
tives, George Kunz, was a member of the Men's League and that the
business had filled a special order from a wealthy client to design a Votes
for Women lapel pin in the purple, green, and white colors of the cause's
most ardent supporters.[4]

By now the spectacle of the suffrage parade had become an exuberant feature of Progressive Era New York. Thousands of women—along
with a few "mere men" willing to withstand jeers from onlookers—had
joined the procession. They marched to lobby Albany to put the issue
on the ballot. They marched to demonstrate solidarity, against the grain
of class, at a time of growing income disparity between wealth and
labor. Mostly, they marched and waved and rallied because a ferment

for change, social as well as political, was in the air. "All my girlhood Mother had repeated that a lady should never allow herself to be conspicuous," recalled one marcher in an anonymous account she wrote for *Outlook* magazine. "To march up Fifth Avenue had promised to flout directly one's early training." Instead, she found, "embarrassment is left at the street corner and one is just a part, a singing, swinging part of a great stream, all flowing in the same direction toward the same goal."[5]

But in 1917 the nation was at war, Europe in trenches and the public in no mood to entertain the demands of women for their rights when men were fighting, and dying, "over there." As anti-suffragist Marjorie Dorman observed when Europe first went to war in 1914, "Attempts to divert Congress from the grave and solemn business before it are unworthy of any citizen who has accepted the protection of our flag." Calling suffragists "traitors to democracy," she accused them of putting "personal aims and ambitions" above those of the nation.[6] On the streets, reaction was angrier still. When she caught sight of suffragists picketing the White House, Dee Richardson, a soldier's mother, was so enraged that she lunged at picketer Hazel Hunkins, spitting on her banner and sending her scrambling up a fence ledge while shrieking, "You are a dirty yellow traitor."[7]

Amid this fevered jingoism, many suffragists bowed to the nation's mood. If citizenship required supporting the nation at war, they would salute. If patriotism required abandoning principles of pacifism, they would defer their dreams of peace until after the vote was won. Carrie Chapman Catt, head of the largest suffrage organization in the country, had joined Jane Addams in 1915 to form a Women's Peace Party.[8] Theodore Roosevelt had derided them as "hysterical pacifists," unsuited for the rough-and-tumble of the male polity.[9] Now, to the chagrin of her friends, Catt turned her back on pacifism, embracing volunteerism as a suffrage tactic.

The themes of patriotism that suffused that year's parade suggest the lengths to which movement leaders went to counter any impression that women were too soft for citizenship, and to parlay a deadly conflict among men into an electoral victory for women. Two years earlier, a ballot initiative in New York to grant women the right to vote had been defeated. Now organizers were careful to dub the event not a suffrage but a woman's parade, where everyone, "be she suffragist or anti, young or old, white or black, rich or poor, is invited to join its ranks."[10] They would sell suffrage as a war measure, marching not as suffragists but as patriots. And if the sacrifice of soldiers overseas required a parade of less exuberance at home, they would march with sobriety.

"There was none of the dash and color of the banner parade two years before," recalled Gertrude Foster Brown. "The mood was serious. . . . Dark clothes were worn instead of white."[11] One delegation featured women whose sons, husbands, or brothers were serving in the military, and the sight of sacrifice in motion "stirred the people to greatest applause." Another contingent included nurses and Red Cross workers in uniform, women serving in war. A slogan committee ensured that the messaging was rigorous, with the effect that "from first banner to last sigh," the parade had all the appearance of a "walking speech."[12] At the sight of a banner stating that suffragists had raised more than $7 million for the Liberty Loan campaign, the staunchly anti-suffrage *New York Times* hailed the "patriotic contributions of women." Long a critic of women's suffrage, the *Times* placed the story on the front page, giving it the same gravitas as news that U.S. troops had entered the trenches in France.[13]

The Great War had sparked great suffrage wars and required wrenching tactical choices—between pacifism and war volunteer work, between picketing the White House and marching in flag-waving parades, between protesting war and wrapping bandages. All of these conflicts of citizenship forced activists to embrace the controversies of public life, hardening them as political actors, steeling them for the final push for victory. Of all the contests between principle and politics, none was as poignant as that of Jeannette Rankin, a pacifist Republican from Montana who had just been elected as the first female member of the U.S. Congress.

When she set out from Missoula, Montana, in early 1917 to claim her seat, Rankin's first stop was New York, where she and her brother, Wellington, her campaign manager and financial guardian, stayed with Harriet and James Lees Laidlaw.[14] Seven years earlier, the couple had hired her, fresh from a successful suffrage campaign in the state of Washington, to help organize efforts in New York. Rankin proved more adept at grassroots speeches than city organization, and soon returned to Montana to organize a suffrage campaign there. By then the three had become close friends, and the Laidlaws traveled to Montana to stump for the cause in 1914. With temperatures well below zero, the couple arrived in "their own private railroad car," and as one observer put it, "the shivering Laidlaws spoke at meetings all along the way."[15]

Now, Harriet Laidlaw took Jeannette Rankin shopping for clothes in Manhattan, paying $200 for an "afternoon dress to wear at the opening of Congress." The Laidlaws also introduced the Rankins to the city's political and social elite, and among those they met was another freshman congressman, Fiorello La Guardia.[16] Days later, arriving in Washington, Rankin was courted, and claimed, by both sides in the suffrage wars. Carrie Chapman Catt, now president of the National American Woman Suffrage Association, was privately appalled that an "unlettered" woman had been elected as the first female member of Congress. Publicly, she was celebratory, calling Rankin the "savior of suffrage" and hosting a breakfast in her honor at the Shoreham Hotel, sitting to her right.[17] On Rankin's left sat Alice Paul, the darling of militants, many of them pacifists, who put cause above all else.[18] Paul gave Rankin a bouquet of purple, white, and yellow flowers, color scheme of her National Woman's Party, and urged her to vote against war. Caught between her allegiance to suffrage and her belief that war was wrong, sandwiched between the pragmatic Catt and the fiery Paul, Rankin was positioned quite literally between the two. Conversation was no doubt strained.

That evening Woodrow Wilson, who campaigned in 1916 on the slogan "He kept us out of war," asked Congress to join the fight. His opening line was, "Gentlemen of the Congress."[19] But in fact all eyes were on the "Gentlelady from Montana." Attention fell on Rankin not because her vote would make the difference—the Senate acceded quickly, 82–6, and the House tally four days later was 373–50—but because her decision in the first vote ever cast by a woman in the U.S. Congress was rife with gendered politics. Could a woman, not qualified to serve in the military, send others to die? Did she have a right to say no?

Wellington urged his sister to "vote a man's vote," warning that otherwise she risked backlash from male voters who would see in her opposition what they most feared: the feminization of politics.[20] Like Jeanette, Harriet Laidlaw was a member of the Women's Peace Party. But she had come to believe that voting for war was an act of citizenship, that without women's support for war, men would dismiss females as too weak to fight and too unpatriotic to vote. Urged on by Wellington, she and James pressured Jeannette—hard.

"Jeannette felt very close to them and very much in their debt," wrote congressional aide Belle Fligelman Winestine. "They pleaded with her to put aside her own feelings and vote for entry into the war. It was a very difficult and emotional time for her. I could not imagine her voting for war; neither could I imagine her letting her friends down."[21] The Laidlaws "pleaded with her not to betray the cause of suffrage." As Rankin noted afterward, "The hardest part of the vote was the fact that the suffragists were divided and many of my beloved friends said that you will ruin the suffrage movement if you vote against war."[22]

Descriptions of her demeanor during the roll call vote—no doubt exaggerated and of dubious accuracy—were devastating, buttressing a belief that women were too emotional for the task at hand. "The clerk again called her name. She started slightly, passed her hand over her eyes and seemed overcome with emotion," reported the *Chicago Tribune*. When the clerk circled the roll call for the second time, she "hesitated, finally staggered to her feet, and in a choking voice gasped out, 'I want to stand by my country, but I cannot vote for war.'"[23] In the nation's 140-year history, no one had defied the ban on speeches during a roll call. To a chorus of "Vote! Vote!" she said (gasping, in some accounts), "I vote no."[24]

Reaction was fierce. The president of the New York Aero Club, formed in 1905 to promote aviation, pointed to Rankin's antics as proof that women in office would lead to "semi-emasculation of the electorate." The *Louisville Courier Journal* opined that her vote would "not strengthen the cause of . . . suffrage."[25] There were defenders too, voices to remind a gender-hysterical public that crying while voting for war was a natural emotion. Asked whether Rankin had cried, her colleague Fiorello La Guardia replied, "I could not see because of the tears in my own eyes."[26]

Harriet Laidlaw, who was in the gallery for the 3:00 a.m. vote, was equally gracious. "While I should have liked for her to vote differently," she told the *Times*, "she did her duty as she saw it after one of the most terrible mental struggles any woman ever had." Laidlaw was emphatic about one thing. "It is not true that Miss Rankin wept, fainted or had to be carried from her seat. She was perfectly composed." Later she reminded the reporter, "Please don't forget to say that Miss Rankin did not weep and did not faint."[27] For suffragists, it was bad enough for women to be seen as pacifists, far worse if they were perceived to have fainted while voting their convictions. Rankin did not seek reelection in 1918, instead campaigning for the Republican nomination for the Senate, which she lost. In 1940 she was again elected to Congress from Montana, and this time she cast the lone vote against U.S. participation in World War II. She did not seek reelection.[28]

Before Rankin's arrival in Washington, before the nation was officially at war, Alice Paul and a small group of protesters had risked public indignation by picketing the White House. Beginning in January 1917, these silent sentinels for suffrage, said to be vexing to First Lady Edith Galt Wilson but otherwise making little imprint, walked mutely in front of the gates at 1600 Pennsylvania Avenue with signs saying, "Mr. President, How Long Must Women Wait for Liberty?"[29] They picketed in shifts of three hours, every day of the week except Sundays, "in all kinds of weather, in rain and in sleet, in hail and in snow" for nearly a year.[30] At first authorities looked the other way, eager not to turn them into martyrs for a cause. President Wilson, the ever-chivalrous southerner, routinely raised his hat to them as he passed through the gates, and, amid "a cruel winter," urged guards to invite them in for a hot coffee, an offer they declined.[31]

Once the nation entered the war in April, sailors ripped at their signs, unimpeded by police, as onlookers shouted, "Send them over to the Kaiser!"[32] Authorities began arrests, on charges of obstructing sidewalk traffic. Sent to Occoquan Workhouse, "a notoriously filthy Virginia prison where the women were fed vermin-infested food and suffered beatings," many went on a hunger strike, enduring tube feeding.[33] Others paid a fine and left jail; still others were released after appeals from family members on medical grounds. By the time all were released in November, by one estimate 2,000 American women had joined the protest line, 500 had been arrested, and 170 had been jailed for demanding their right to vote.[34]

At year's end, with Alva Belmont presiding at the Belasco Theatre in New York, Paul awarded silver lapel pins depicting a prison cell door—complete with dangling lock—to all who had done time in prison.[35] In January 1919, these American prisoners of suffrage would embark on a tour of the country telling their stories, dressed in jailhouse garb, and tailed by FBI agents looking for subversive socialist speech or militant British suffragette influence.[36] For now, they stood in silence, mocking Wilson's call for consent of the governed abroad while women remained disenfranchised at home.

Theirs was the first political protest ever conducted at the gates of the White House, troubling to a Washington establishment that held sacred the address of 1600 Pennsylvania Avenue as a symbol of national identity.[37] According to the *Baltimore Sun*, the picketing demonstrated "the unfitness of those who take part in it to participate in public affairs. Why should the nation call to its aid such selfish and unpatriotic counselors as these? When they seek to harass and embarrass the President in the face of national dangers and duties such as he confronts at present, with what patience can their claims to citizenship be considered?"[38] Even the *Boston Globe*, a pro-suffrage paper, feared that they had "harmed the cause."[39]

So controversial was the tactic that one member of Paul's board of directors resigned in protest. "Have greatest respect for your judgment but feel present methods are not my methods and therefore I cannot honestly stay on the board," Elizabeth Kent telegraphed from California.[40] Lucy Maynard Salmon, a Vassar professor and the first woman to serve on the American Historical Association board, also left the organization in protest of the picketing.[41] Several readers canceled their subscriptions to the party's newspaper, the *Suffragist*.[42] And when, in June, Paul sent out a fundraising letter to supporters, Myrtle Price wrote from Kansas that she was a supporter no more, outraged by the "foolish, childish methods you have used trying to harass our overburdened president."[43]

In New York, suffrage leaders were so alarmed by Paul's breach of wartime patriotism that they urged newspaper editors not to confuse their efforts with those of the protesters. "We have a distinct feeling of shame that the only notable record of . . . disloyalty in this heterogeneous melting pot of nation . . . should emanate from the suffragists," said Harriet Laidlaw.[44] She observed wryly that if Alice Paul had truly "transplanted" British tactics to the United States, she would have signed up for war service.[45]

For Paul, the brickbats were welcome news. Formed by her Quaker roots, schooled by British suffragettes, Alice Paul was an American intellectual—she had earned her bachelor's degree at Swarthmore, and master's and doctoral degrees from the University of Pennsylvania—and she believed not in coddling but in challenging power. She adopted the Pankhursts' battle cry of "Deeds, not words," and with it their tactic of holding the party in power accountable for failure to enact suffrage. Harriot Stanton Blatch, who had joined Paul after the failed 1915 New York referendum, perhaps put it best when she said, "We are hammering the Democrats simply because they are the dominant Party, and we will keep hammering whoever is in the Capitol until we win."[46]

Coercion was the *lingua franca* of politics, rejection by voters the only language most lawmakers understood. And, at the penultimate moment, with the nation at war, Paul had no hesitancy in tightening the screws, recruiting the wealthiest women of New York society to stand at her side. The controversy that greeted their arrests, the perceived impertinence of jailing ladies of leisure, the shock to public expectation that even some well-bred ladies of Mrs. Astor's Four Hundred might storm the American Bastille, validated her decision. Their social celebrity—and their political imprimatur—kept the Votes for Women campaign in the newspapers for months. None drew more headlines than Louisine Elder Havemeyer.

Havemeyer was, one biographer noted, "an odd combination of self-assurance and naiveté." She conversed in Italian and "married in a pink gingham dress"—whims, it was said, that "charmed her husband."[47] She was "a great deal of fun," said another chronicler, her speeches "salty."[48] As a bride during the 1894 New York state suffrage campaign, she had signed a suffrage petition. Naively, she recalled, "I thought I would have my franchise by return mail." After she was widowed, one of her first actions was to lend her art collection to a gallery for a suffrage fundraiser. Eager to display her considerable collections of El Greco and Goya, and to establish a future relationship with her, M. Knoedler's Gallery on Fifth Avenue volunteered in 1912 to host a nineteen-day show, a rare mixing of art and politics.[49] "Some of our best-known and important collectors not only refused to attend the exhibition, but threatened to withdraw their patronage from the dealer who had kindly loaned me his gallery for the exhibition," she recalled years later.[50] Some members of her own family boycotted the event.[51]

She had come to the campaign as a grieving widow who adored her husband. Henry O. Havemeyer, president of the country's sugar trust, was "chubby," ruddy-cheeked, and as "Teutonic" as any German general.[52] In 1897 he had been charged with contempt for refusing to disclose how much money his interests donated to national and state political campaigns. Though he was acquitted, corruption rumors swirled, and later the U.S. government sued American Sugar Refining for underpaying import duties by rigging weighing machines. In 1907 U.S. Treasury agents raided the firm's Brooklyn plant. Soon after, Henry died suddenly of kidney failure. Battling the lawsuits and resulting bad press, suffering in quick succession the deaths of her mother, her husband, and, in 1908, her twin grandchildren, a depressed Louisine Havemeyer attempted suicide.[53]

It was artist Mary Cassatt who suggested a new cause. The two had become friends as schoolgirls growing up in Paris. During Louisine's marriage, Cassatt advised the Havemeyers on purchases that turned their three-story mansion at Fifth Avenue and East 66th Street into a renowned gallery, decorated by Louis Comfort Tiffany, visited by New York schoolchildren on field trips, and used as a backdrop for Sunday afternoon musical concerts.[54] With Cassatt's guidance, the Havemeyers amassed a stellar collection of Impressionist art, along with Rembrandts and other classics now housed in the Metropolitan Museum. Once, according to family lore, Mary convinced a teenage Louisine not to buy a Pissarro and a Monet, for which she had been saving her allowance, but to purchase instead a pastel painting of a ballet rehearsal by Edgar Degas. Though she was not much impressed by the "confused" painting, she learned later that her "500 francs rescued the poverty stricken Degas from a decision to abandon art."[55] Now, in 1908, Cassatt wrote, "Go in for the Suffrage, that means great things for the future."[56] In August 1914, as the drumbeat of war began in Europe, Mary wrote again, urging Louisine to join suffrage, "for it is the women who will decide the question of life or death for a nation."[57]

By then, Louisine Havemeyer had already thrown herself into the cause with characteristic zeal. To her children's dismay, she marched in one of the New York suffrage parades. On George Washington's birthday, she decorated a window at the Women's Political Union shop on Fifth Avenue with a "huge bronze" eagle carrying a streaming sign—in the purple, green, and white colors of her party—that read, "Votes for Women." She toured the state in her landaulet, stumping for Liberty Loans, food conservation, and suffrage. Once she brought her young grandson to one of her speeches and placed him on a chair. "Friends," she said, pointing in his direction, "if the men of your generation will not grant us justice now, you may be sure this generation will!"—at which point her grandson began to clap, prompting "much amusement" from the audience.[58]

She had told Paul that militancy was beyond her purview. "No picketing and no prison for me," she quipped. "I don't like the thought of either one." But when Paul asked her to travel to Lafayette Square in Washington, D.C., to burn a cardboard likeness of Woodrow Wilson in effigy, Havemeyer felt she could not refuse, "for how could I do less with such examples before me?" She gave a cover story to her relatives, saying she was going to Washington for a few days. By her own account, and despite lighting several matches, she never succeeded in firing up the paper figure, musing later that perhaps if she had, she would have received a life sentence. Instead, and in the face of obvious reluctance on the part of the police to cuff the sweet-faced sixty-three-year-old activist, she and thirty-nine others were arrested. Placed in a prison "discarded ten years before as unfit to hold a human being," she planted her feet as "sparks of indignation snapped within. Where was my Uncle Sam? Where was the liberty my fathers fought for? Where the democracy our boys were fighting for?"[59]

The day after Havemeyer's arrest, the Senate defeated the proposed constitutional amendment by one vote. Senator John Williams, a Mississippi Democrat lobbied by Wilson in cables from Paris, told friends that "not even the president himself could persuade him to support a cause advocated by such outrageous methods."[60] Havemeyer's participation also raised eyebrows in New York, sparking a new round of publicity. Her son-in-law was said to be horrified and her sister became ill, according to Louisine's daughter Electra, although one grandson pronounced her a "real sport." While in jail she received their telegrams. "Oh those telegrams!" she wrote, looking back from the post-suffrage comfort of 1922. "From them I gleaned I had stripped the family tree, I had broken its branches, I had torn up its roots and laid it prostrate in the sorrowing dust. What had the whole treeful of innocents ever done that I should treat them thus? Did I realize I had lost my citizenship?" Worse, they were aghast that she might be ostracized, displayed "as on an oyster shell in Society," threatening their own hold on social power.

After five days, she was released from prison and returned to New York. She reassured her sister by reminding her that John Bunyan had gone to jail. She cuddled her young grandson in her lap to assuage his fears that prison had changed her. And then she told them she was leaving town again for a few days. This time she joined the Prison Special, Paul's attempt to deflect charges of disloyalty, a train of former suffrage inmates on the road—first stop Charleston, South Carolina, perhaps with sights on starting a new civil war—in their muslin prison garb, looking sympathetic, telling incarceration tales, stoking interest.[61]

If Louisine Havemeyer was the most unlikely of the radical gilded suffragists, she was not alone. Eunice Dana Brannan, daughter of *New York Sun* publisher Charles A. Dana and wife of a prominent New York doctor, was imprisoned during what suffragists called the "Night of Terror." On November 14, 1917, guards at the Occoquan Workhouse brutalized and attacked suffrage prisoners. Lucy Burns, who met Alice Paul while both were involved in the British suffragette movement in London, was manacled to her cell door all night long in a standing position, with her hands above her head. The gray-haired Emily Butterworth was locked in a cell in the men's division.[62] When Brannan, a member of Katherine Mackay's Equal Franchise Society, called out to one woman who was collapsed on the floor to see whether she was all right, Superintendent W. H. Walker shouted, "Not another word from your mouth or I will handcuff you, gag you and put you in a straitjacket."[63]

Her husband, John Brannan, president of the Bellevue and Allied Hospitals, traveled from New York three times in one week to see his wife, a request prison authorities refused. When he finally saw Eunice, the superintendent sat in on the interview. He won her release from the court, citing a weakened medical condition as a result of the "shocking treatment" she received in prison.[64] Eunice Brannan saw in the protest—and in the administration's retaliation—an echo of the themes of the war. "We will not sit in silence," she told the court, "while the president presents himself to the people of Europe as the representative of a free people when the American people are not free and he is chiefly responsible for it."[65]

Vida Milholland, younger sister of the martyred Inez Milholland in whose name the picketing began in January, was arrested in front of the White House gates on July 4, 1917, and spent three days in jail. A singer by training, Vida sang every night to prisoners and by one account "thrilled" passersby who stopped to listen as she led a chorus of the Marseillaise.[66] Elizabeth Selden Rogers was another pedigreed New Yorker with roots to colonial founders who joined the pickets. Married to a prominent New York doctor, sister-in-law of Secretary of War Henry Stimson, she had been arrested and jailed on Bastille Day outside the White House.[67] In October 1917, she watched the New York parade from the sidelines, appalled, as the *Masses* had recently put it, by "the spectacle of women anxious to assist a military bureaucracy . . . in order to gain a political privilege."[68] She distributed copies of a broadside, "The Pickets at the White House Gates, Have They Helped Suffrage? Yes."[69] She no doubt heard the din of public opinion disagreeing. Marchers displayed a huge sign proclaiming, "We are opposed to picketing the White House. We stand by the President." Applause, said one paper, was "thunderous."[70]

The ultimate battle was still to be won at home. In 1915, after the New York ballot initiative was roundly defeated, a disconsolate Harriot Stanton Blatch withdrew from her leadership role in the suffrage campaign. The daughter of Seneca Falls pioneer Elizabeth Cady Stanton, the spark in a movement that had been left for dead in the first years of the twentieth century, Blatch had been expecting victory. Now, she angrily rejected as unworthy the very methods of soapbox campaigning and exuberant parades she had pioneered and proclaimed her "disgust at the conditions which forced women to campaign in the streets."[71] Dismissing as "suicidal" another New York try, she eschewed state campaigns and instead joined Paul's Congressional Union, later the National Woman's Party.[72]

While the ballot measure failed by 200,000 votes, the 1915 campaign was viewed within movement circles as a model of future success. Weary of the infighting and administrative lapses of Anna Howard Shaw, a contingent now lobbied for Catt to resume her tenure as head of the National American Woman Suffrage Association, which she had left in 1904 after her husband's death.[73] When she did, leadership of the

New York State Woman Suffrage Party for the first time in history fell into the hands of "women of large means, used to spending big sums of money."[74] Harriet Laidlaw chaired the legislative effort. Gertrude Foster Brown was in charge of district organization. Helen Rogers Reid, married to the owner and publisher of the *Tribune*, served as treasurer. And taking Blatch's place atop the legion of New York suffragists was Vira Boarman Whitehouse.

A southern beauty from New Orleans who had married New York stockbroker Norman de Rapelye Whitehouse, Vira had been a fixture on the social circuit. She often said that before she marched in the suffrage parade of 1913, "she could only dance and go to dinner." Once she joined the cause, she thrived on the campaign's combination of camaraderie and public expression, declaring her first soapbox speech "the proudest moment in my life."[75]

Together with her team of wealthy socialites, Whitehouse now devised a plan that entailed raising a considerable sum of money—$300,000 ($5.5 million in contemporary terms)—for the campaign. This time, Whitehouse declared, the party would "lay aside the tactics of amateurs and work henceforth like professionals." They would canvass voters by precinct, recruit Tammany Hall wives to the campaign, and campaign against anti-suffrage candidates.[76] Two years earlier, labor activist Mary Heaton Vorse had worked for Whitehouse in the suffrage party's publicity office. In letters home, she told her family about the "uptown rich ladies mingling with us poor wage slaves of the slums." Impressed by their drive, she wrote, "Believe me I have never seen any slave driver able to crack the whip louder than that languorous southern beauty, Mrs. Whitehouse."[77]

In February 1917, after German submarines targeted passenger ships in the Atlantic, Wilson broke off diplomatic relations with Germany, and fundraising for suffrage became a dead letter. "Liberty Loan campaigns, Red Cross and YMCA drives succeeded each other; high income and enormous war taxes drained pocket books," Gertrude Foster Brown recalled. "Suffragists were bitterly reproached for introducing their claims when the future of the country was at stake."[78] Money woes were exacerbated by the loss of free newspaper coverage that had attended the cause since the first parade in 1910. Now war news crowded out domestic issues, and Whitehouse and Reid decided they would need an additional $200,000 for paid advertisements ($3.7 million in current terms). "Their realistic thinking about finance would have stunned the pioneer suffragists who counted on nickel and dime contributions," said one historian.[79] Narcissa Cox Vanderlip, wife of the president of National City Bank and chairman of the party's Ninth District outreach efforts, urged a pragmatic appeal to male donors—"Let's get through with it now." Sometimes they were forced to sign advertising contracts without having funds to cover them. One of them once joked that if necessary, "we could put up our pearls."[80]

Within days of Wilson's decision to end diplomatic relations with Germany in early 1917, the thirty-seven-member executive committee voted to offer the New York State Woman Suffrage Party's five hundred thousand suffragists to Governor Charles Whitman for war service—presaging by a few weeks a similar decision by its parent organization, the National American Woman Suffrage Association. Anti-war members were furious, insisting that Vira Whitehouse had exceeded her authority, calling the board's action "high-handed, undemocratic and misrepresentative."[81] As the election neared, the party adopted a resolution reaffirming "its condemnation of the picketing of the White House, which tends to harass the government in this time of great strength" and urging "the press and public to discriminate between the small group of picketers and the great body of loyal, patriotic women in New York State who while devotedly serving their Government are working for their enfranchisement."[82]

Aside from the conflicts the war posed for suffragists in navigating public opinion, the toxic mix of suffrage and patriotism also rattled marriages at home. When, in August 1917, Herbert Parsons signed up to serve as an Army intelligence officer, Elsie Clews Parsons was furious. "Today I pity you, tomorrow you enrage, intellectually one loses interest

& that's the devil," she wrote on learning the news. By return mail her husband replied, "The trouble with you is . . . this is not the day of talk but the day of deeds."[83] Fighting "a lonely battle against wartime jingoism," even among her colleagues at Heterodoxy, Elsie clung to an anthropologist's instinct that war was "something left over from a primitive culture." Throughout the war, she refused to admit to her home anyone in a uniform, including her husband.[84]

The war took its toll on anti-suffragists as well. As early as 1915, when German submarines sank the R.M.S. *Lusitania*, Josephine Jewell Dodge had called on suffragists to accept a truce, explaining that she wanted to spend the entire $15,000 budget of the National Association Opposed to Woman Suffrage on war service. Suffragists accused her of grandstanding.[85] Following suit, Alice Chittenden, president of the New York branch, committed her organization to Wilson's preparedness campaign, raising $46,000 for the Red Cross.[86] Described as the "most dynamic of the antis,"[87] Chittenden had inherited a gift for politics from her grandfather, a New York congressman, and her mother, who in the 1890s brought Alice to anti-suffrage rallies. Now she protested the movement's attempt to conflate suffrage with patriotism. "A truly patriotic woman wants no reward for her work," she said. "The suggestion that [the state] shall offer women the political payment of a vote for war services is a direct slur on woman's patriotism."[88] Later it would be said that this all-or-nothing view of patriotism cost antis the 1917 election, as they left the public stage to suffragists.[89]

Ten days after the woman's parade, male voters in New York for the second time in three years would go to the polls to decide whether to enfranchise their wives, their mothers, their sisters, and their daughters. By this time, women had won suffrage in twelve states, and were said to have provided the margin of victory in President Woodrow Wilson's reelection campaign against former New York governor Charles Evans Hughes. Without the women's vote in California, Kansas, Washington, and elsewhere, observed one commentator, "Mr. Wilson would not have been continued in the White House."[90]

When, in October, Vira Whitehouse led a New York State Woman Suffrage Party delegation to the White House, the president sounded like any politician in thrall to a special interest. "The whole country has appreciated the way in which the women have risen to this great occasion," he said, urging New Yorkers "to show the world . . . that they are fighting for democracy because they believe in it."[91] Soon Wilson, a southerner who considered women's rights a state issue, would endorse a federal amendment on women's suffrage.

As the election neared, the *New York Times* again editorialized against the referendum, as it had in 1915, but this time its rationale suggested that suffrage forces were gaining momentum. "The amendment should be rejected this year by a majority sufficiently emphatic to put an end to the agitation at least during the period when the minds of the people are preoccupied with the grave concerns of war," concluded the paper.[92] This argument—one of timing—was echoed by men who worried about the feminization of politics in a time of combat. "First let us finish the war and rid the world of its tyrant nations," said Henry Wise Wood in a letter to the *Times*. "Then will it be safe for us to consider the effeminization [*sic*] of our electorate."[93]

On election night, "the streets felt a new election thrill." Newsboys hawked late-night editions with the clatter of favorable headlines. "Each woman felt that the victory belonged to her," wrote Gertrude Foster Brown. "The next day women were seen everywhere, wearing suffrage buttons," greeting one another with "Ain't it just grand that we won?" In the end, the city had won the day, the measure losing upstate by 1,519 votes but carrying New York City by 103,863. In a celebration, Catt opened her remarks with the salutation "Fellow citizens." The audience exploded in cheers. "For a long time she could go no further," recalled Brown. "The packed auditorium was in a tumult of joy. Women cheered themselves hoarse and men cheered with them."[94]

Suffrage had come not as a gift from male voters or as a reward for war service. It came because women had learned to frame their war service—or their pacifism—as an act of citizenship that merited equality.

Choosing to position suffrage as a war measure was a brilliant stroke that undercut anti-suffragists. Distancing themselves from pacifists and picketers proved popular with the public, valuable for mainstreaming the issue. But other tactics—protesting in the face of such patriotic winds, speaking out for peace to avoid another "war to end all wars," protesting Washington's lip service attitude toward their voluntarism— all helped force the issue too. In short, suffragists gained the vote not by the good graces of male politicos but by becoming politicians themselves, mastering both the new science of public relations and the hard choices of *realpolitik*. Some, such as Catt, played the inside game, working the establishment, disavowing their pacifist principles, while others, like Paul, picketed power, playing the outside game. For all, the war had stiffened their spines and honed their skills at manipulating that fickle creature known as public opinion. And in that transition—from private philanthropists to public figures, from social celebrities to practiced politicians—they won the right to vote.

The fight would continue at the federal level until 1920, when the Nineteenth Amendment to the U.S. Constitution was ratified. Almost immediately, a new war commenced over winners and losers. As memoirs were drafted and biographies commissioned, activists burned papers, deleted names, and skewed descriptions of events to favor one side over the other. It was a war over memory that left the record littered with falsifications. In these early accounts, women of the gilded class were largely, sometimes deliberately, forgotten. Catherine Abbe, Daisy Harriman, Louisine Havemeyer, Harriet Laidlaw, Katherine Mackay, Olivia Sage, and Vira Whitehouse are rarely mentioned in books on the cause. Alva Belmont is more frequently remembered, with derision. Their contributions—defusing male and press ridicule, leading state campaigns to victory, popularizing a movement said to be "in the doldrums" with their financial contributions and their fashionable celebrity—are largely missing from the narrative of women's suffrage. Why they were excised, and with what effect, is a story about historical memory and the costs of forgetting.

9

WHO WON SUFFRAGE?

*The remembered past is a much larger
category than the recorded past.*

JOHN LUKACS[1]

WHEN New York's male voters granted women the power of the ballot on November 6, 1917, Vira Boarman Whitehouse was widely credited with the win.[2] Orchestrating a disciplined statewide campaign, she rolled up huge majorities in the city and almost reached majority in the more rural counties upstate. New York would now send to Washington, D.C., the largest pro-suffrage delegation in Congress, forty-three men whose voters had opted to include women in politics, improving chances for a federal amendment. Commentators gushed. "No state political organization in the American Union contains half the political ability and intelligence of the group of suffrage workers who under the leadership of Mrs. Norman Whitehouse have succeeded in enfranchising at one stroke a tenth of all American women," said the *New Republic*.[3] At a celebratory dinner at the Hotel Biltmore, the women who had worked with her, who championed her as "the brilliant field-general of the New York State suffrage army," issued a full-throated "Three Cheers for Mrs. Whitehouse!" and placed a crown of "gold beads in the form of an olive crown" on her dark curls.[4] As Maud Nathan, president of the New York Consumers League, put it, "Our own White-house did more than the White House in Washington."[5]

Wary of the tiara's haughty image, Whitehouse said that she would accept the gift only as a wreath, not as a crown, that she understood it not as a "royal honor," as critics would later allege, but as a gift to one worker "from other workers as a remembrance of our common victory."[6] No matter. Like so many fallen Stalinist figures cropped from a Kremlin photograph, Vira Boarman Whitehouse and two hundred other gilded suffragists were methodically airbrushed from the metanarrative of women's suffrage.

Movement leaders had relied on gilded suffragists for their money and exploited them for their celebrity, but as memoirs rolled off printing presses without any mention of their contribution, it become clear that resentments had festered. Grievances were many. Labor's rank and file, an important contingent of support, distrusted these beneficiaries of capitalist wealth, suspecting them of using the working class to promote their own dominance. Leaders of suffrage organizations were furious about defections to rival associations, and retaliated by omitting deserters from history's memory.

Middle-class and upper-class women seethed at the attention showered on society suffragists, buckets of media publicity that ignored their own less glamorous toiling for the cause. The star power of the elite may have brought the movement publicity, solvency, and popularity, but their celebrity left wounded feelings among those without a press agent or a staff entourage. Lashing out, the movement's volunteers dismissed these gilded activists as proxies for a fad. This has been the conventional wisdom since, a consensus that the activism of socialites was mere froth, masking the painstaking work of serious suffragists.

Carrie Chapman Catt gave no credit to Vira Whitehouse for the statewide victory in New York, either in her 1923 memoir, *Woman Suffrage and Politics*,[7] or in a biography she authorized decades later. Instead, she credited Mary Garrett Hay, who headed the campaign in New York City, for providing the majority that overcame an upstate deficit of 1,519 votes.[8] That Hay had been living with Catt since the latter became a widow for the second time was well known within suffrage circles. They were companions for twenty years (one biographer wrote of the "sudden bereavement [that] shook Mrs. Catt to the soul" when Hay died suddenly of a brain hemorrhage in 1928)—and are buried next to one another in Woodlawn Cemetery.[9] Was Hay miffed at all the accolades that came Whitehouse's way for the New York victory? Was Catt embedding her companion's resentment as historic truth? Can history ever be remembered as it happened, or is memory as fickle, and personal, as any human chronicler?

Alva Belmont's contributions, financial and political, were robust. She paid the rent and salaries of the National American Woman Suffrage Association and then spent $146,000 ($1.7 million in today's dollars) for the purchase of a mansion in Washington, D.C., as the permanent headquarters of the rival National Woman's Party.[10] Defying the movement's southern strategy, meant to defuse fears that women's suffrage would enlarge the black voting bloc, she reached out to black suffragists. Attempting to forge an alliance based on gender, she funded the 1908 strike in New York's garment industry. Playing hardball, she campaigned against, and defeated, lawmakers blocking a woman's right to vote. When Emmeline Pankhurst was detained at Ellis Island in 1913 by authorities concerned she might import her violent tactics from Britain, Belmont paid for a lawyer.[11] When Pankhurst's daughter Christabel escaped to Paris to avoid imprisonment in Britain's Holloway Prison, Belmont helped defray her living expenses.[12]

Still, in the face of this activism, Belmont's contemporaries in the movement did their best to ignore her. In her memoirs, Catt mentions Belmont not once—neither as NAWSA's financial benefactor nor as a much-publicized advocate whose name was once suggested as a candidate for president of the association. One scholar speculated that Catt failed to credit Belmont because by then Belmont had defected to Alice Paul's Congressional Union.[13] In a sentiment no doubt sanctioned by Catt, biographer Mary Gray Peck wrote twenty years later that Belmont "was militant by temperament and, knowing nothing about the past history of the movement, was inclined to think that it began in the summer of 1909 with her own advent." Belmont had underwritten the National American Woman Suffrage Association. Now Peck wrote that Belmont "was generous but she was arbitrary and hard to work with."[14]

Likewise, labor activist Rose Schneiderman was so keen to expunge Belmont from the record that in her memoirs she never once mentioned Belmont's role in the garment strike of 1909. Belmont's contribution to that uprising was far-reaching—she joined the Women's Trade Union League board of directors, sat up in night court to bail out the strikers, and hosted a mass rally for striking workers at the Hippodrome, one that featured NAWSA president Anna Howard Shaw, the Women's Trade Union League's Leonora O'Reilly, and the Socialist Party's Rose Pastor Stokes. Most conspicuously, Belmont put the strike on the media's radar, leading a mink brigade of socialites to join its ranks, inspiring female college students to walk the picket lines, and hosting lectures at the Colony Club. One scholar called it a "purposeful erasure of Belmont and her activities on behalf of working women."[15] Schneiderman did mention others of wealth who helped, including Josephine Sykes Morgenthau. The wife of Henry Morgenthau, U.S. ambassador to the Ottoman Empire during the First World War, Josephine had quietly deeded property to "furnish bail also for the hundreds of women who were arrested on flimsy charges and herded into police cells with prostitutes, drunks and hardened criminals." In Schneiderman's account, she did so without the self-promotional publicity that Belmont indulged in.[16]

Such deliberate blinders toward Belmont suggest a special animus, shared by many in the movement. Historian Mary Ritter Beard, a member of Alice Paul's Congressional Union, refused to "do the Newport stunt" and attend the organization's meetings at Belmont's Marble House on Bellevue Avenue, wary that ties to "plutocratic" women such as Alva Belmont and Louisine Havemeyer would damage her reputation with labor activists.[17]

During the 1915 campaign, the Women's Trade Union League distributed a flyer asserting that "women of the leisure class" merited the vote because "they need every opportunity to devote their leisure to the welfare of the State and the public."[18] It was a sign of enormous cross-class cooperation, recognition that social change required coalitions between classes. Now, working-class suffragists kept their distance. As one scholar put it, Belmont "had a reputation for badgering maids, was blacklisted by women in domestic service," and weighed all packages delivered to Marble House to avert theft by servants.[19] For union activists, this mistreatment of her own staff was confirmation that Belmont was a hypocritical ally. In a raucous four-hour meeting to discuss whether to continue working with the uptown ladies of the mink brigade, Theresa Malkiel accused Belmont of "political crimes against working women."[20] In the end, they voted to end their cross-class coalition, concluding that women who benefitted from the sweat of exploited laborers could hardly be trusted in a campaign seeking better conditions from capitalist owners. "I have no personal feeling against Mrs. Belmont or Miss Morgan, but their contributions will not harmonize capital and labor," said socialist and firebrand speaker Emma Goldman. A successful labor movement, she added, "must be entirely independent."[21]

Middle-class women too shunned Belmont. Katharine Houghton Hepburn, president of the Connecticut Woman Suffrage Association whose young daughter Katharine, later an actress, often accompanied her to suffrage events, was so alarmed when the Congressional Union solicited Belmont's support that she tried to head off the effort.[22] Arguing that Belmont was "in the habit of running things absolutely," Hepburn warned that the diva of Newport society would try to control the organization. She feared that Belmont had "none of the idealism that would make her give in large amounts either in money or personal devotion."[23] Though Belmont proved dedicated to the cause, this notion that she was not a serious activist was the nub of the case against her. Doris Stevens, who understood Belmont better than nearly any suffragist other than Paul, thought the fear well-founded, noting that Belmont "never took part in anything she did not want to direct" and her "desire to run things" often created "antagonism" within the ranks of any organization she joined.[24]

For her part, Alva Belmont was aggrieved at this excising of her involvement, blaming Catt and Anna Howard Shaw, current and past presidents of the National American Woman Suffrage Association. Calling a press conference, Belmont charged that the two NAWSA presidents must have "forgotten who is responsible for this victory. But I don't care. I shall go down in history." Donating her Political Equality Association headquarters to the Salvation Army, she left for Europe.[25]

Two years before her death in 1933, Alva Belmont explained the legacy she felt her activism merited: a statue depicting her, cemented to the ground in the nation's capital. "She described exactly what she wanted," recalled Doris Stevens:

> A heroic figure of herself in the open air in Washington, the space to be set aside by the government, the base of the monument to contain a bas relief depicting various scenes which occurred in Washington—riots by the police and by the mob, women being loaded into patrol wagons, women arrested for petitioning President Wilson—in short, she wanted cut in stone the sacrifices which so many women had made in going to prison for this idea.[26]

Nothing came of this request, nor did it come to pass, as she had instructed in her will, that a female minister officiate at her funeral.[27] Otherwise the send-off was everything this great puppeteer of public opinion had requested—twenty honorary pallbearers including Christabel Pankhurst, Harriot Stanton Blatch, and Margaret Sanger, fifteen hundred mourners watching as the purple, gold, and white flag of the National Woman's Party, of which she was both president and financial savior, proceeded down the aisle of St. Thomas Episcopal Church. Another banner, which had been carried by picketers in front of the White House during the war, featured Susan B. Anthony's quote "Failure Is Impossible."

The faithful carried the banner to Woodlawn Cemetery, placing it in a mausoleum that Belmont had designed to mimic the Chapel of

Saint-Hubert in France's Loire Valley.²⁸ Leonardo da Vinci had designed the original in the early sixteenth century in a style described as "gothic flamboyant."²⁹ By one account, Alva Belmont requested that photos from her society years be destroyed so that she would be remembered not as the hostess of balls but as an activist for women's rights.³⁰ Whether that is true or not—so many such photographs remain from the gilded years as to cast doubt on this assertion—there is no doubt she was always savvy about the power of image. For the ages, she is buried amid this attempt to gild her reputation as an activist. To this day, the worn suffragist banner remains at her side.³¹

There is much historical precedent for excising the unpopular. In 1881 Elizabeth Cady Stanton and Susan B. Anthony published the first of their three-volume *History of Woman Suffrage*. In what one scholar has called an "origins myth," they positioned the movement's start at Seneca Falls in 1848 with the two of them portrayed as its lead players—even though Anthony was not present and Lucretia Mott was. They made no mention of Angelina and Sarah Moore Grimké, sisters from slave-country South Carolina who spoke often on woman's right to the vote, or of black women who resisted slavery, or of Lucy Stone, the abolitionist from Boston whose lectures on women's suffrage in the 1840s were so controversial that men hurled rotten fruit and verbal insult at podiums where she spoke.³²

The story of the movement's birth might begin here, with women raising their voices in the public square for their rights as citizens. Or the starting point might be placed earlier, with Abigail Adams's 1776 admonition to her husband, John Adams, to "remember the ladies" at the Continental Congress. If women were not accorded rights, Abigail Adams had warned her husband, "We are determined to foment a Rebelion [*sic*], and will not hold ourselves bound by any Laws in which we have no voice, or Representation."³³

By minimizing or ignoring these events, Stanton and Anthony shaped their own legacy as the founders. After the Civil War, they had campaigned against the Fifteenth Amendment, arguing that if women could not also gain the vote, as Stanton put it, and "avail ourselves of the strong arm and blue uniform of the black soldier to walk in by his side," they would fight his right to the franchise.[34] Infuriating Lucy Stone and other abolitionists who had given the women's suffrage movement its ideological foundation, they created a new organization that would splinter the campaign for women's rights into two camps, and impede its progress for decades to come. Reminding historians of their seminal place as heirs of Seneca Falls, they may have hoped to remove some of the tarnish.

By the time of her death in 1906 at the age of eighty-four, Anthony had successfully outflanked Stanton, Lucy Stone, and other nineteenth-century activists as the movement's prime architect, at least in the public imagination. When Stanton's more controversial writings on the misogyny of the Bible, the need for birth control, and the logic of divorce emerged in the 1890s, recalled her daughter, "leaders began to bury her alive, and to re-vivify Miss Anthony."[35] Now, in the twentieth century, the tradition of internecine rivalry was revived, as debate erupted over the rightful heir to Anthony's legacy and scholars joined the debate.

This time the argument revolved around whether Carrie Chapman Catt or Alice Paul was the real heroine of the story. Catt was the movement's titular head, president of NAWSA in two separate eras (1900–1904, 1916–1920). Throughout the campaign, she had insisted on organizational rigor and a strategic alliance with President Wilson. The wind at her back was an army, at its peak, of two million members. In June 1916, after neither Republicans nor Democrats endorsed a constitutional amendment in their party platforms, she convened a meeting of her executive committee to unveil a "Winning Plan." Designed to pressure Congress to enact a constitutional amendment, it focused on winning suffrage victories in the thirty-eight states that had not yet enfranchised women. When the states ratified the Seventeenth Amendment in 1913, requiring the direct election of U.S. senators instead of their appointment by state legislatures, it planted the notion that women were constituents, their interests worthy of consideration. By the time New York enacted women's suffrage in 1917, it gave the cause of women's suffrage a sense of inevitability. As Catt explained, we "used the political dynamite in the victories gained in the States as a means of blasting through to success at Washington."[36]

Alice Paul's Congressional Union, which in 1916 became the National Woman's Party, was smaller than NAWSA, numbering perhaps sixty thousand at its peak.[37] Her protests at the White House, her campaigning ceaselessly against a progressive president, were less pragmatic, more riveting. For Paul, the path to victory lay in a drumbeat of protests, heckling, and picketing that cheered her supporters and shamed Wilson and his party's lawmakers into supporting the cause. If Catt appealed to the wider public, Paul focused on energizing the base.

There was no love lost between the two camps, reflecting the tensions that had complicated the campaign. As chairman of the Empire State Campaign Committee, Catt had urged Paul to stay out of New York during the failed 1915 campaign, charging that Paul's "agents are handicapping the campaign" by telling voters that a federal amendment was the only way to ensure the franchise.[38] Denying that her troops had spread anti-suffrage messages, Paul replied, "I need hardly tell you that we are deeply interested in the success of the New York campaign."[39]

Antagonisms between the two groups inflamed memories. Crystal Eastman, a Paul ally, was particularly biting about Vira Whitehouse, Harriet Laidlaw, and others "who had scorned and condemned when the pickets stood for months at the White House gates, when they insisted on going to jail and starved themselves when they got there—all these came now with their wreaths and their flowers and their banners to celebrate victory."[40]

In fact, despite their dislike for one another, Catt and Paul had unwittingly arrived at a one-two punch for women's rights, proving more successful than either would have been alone.[41] Paul's tactics "endowed woman suffrage with high drama," said one scholar, while Catt's plan piled up pressure from state victories.[42] Both approaches proved critical to the outcome, as they have been in many movements for social change in American history. In the 1960s, civil rights leaders protested amid much national indifference until young African American college students marched in the streets of Selma, Alabama. When southern sheriffs turned their hoses on the protesters, the sight was broadcast on nationwide television, turning the nation's conscience and forcing President Johnson to pursue congressional recourse in Washington. LGBT leaders pressing for reform, beginning in the 1990s, benefitted both from those who ran for office to change the political system from within, and those who demonstrated at Stonewall or in Queer Nation die-ins to pry open its doors from without. In state after state, first in the campaign for women's suffrage and a century later in the fight for marriage equality, ballot initiatives fell like dominos before a national consensus that emerged to welcome or at least accept these reforms. The long incubation period of debate, the slow drive to turn a once controversial idea into a familiar notion, the humanizing of advocates from radicals to relatives—all played a role.

Like any effort to reclaim the "upstairs long missing from women's history," this book seeks to return New York's elite women, as gilded suffragists, to the history of the twentieth-century women's suffrage movement, and to the memory of readers interested in the cause.[43] The darlings of a celebrity-crazed media, they embraced a cause that had seemed to be in the doldrums, conferring the first celebrity endorsement on a political movement for social change in the twentieth century. To credit their contributions would also be to concede a role in activism for the spectacles of the public square—the parades, the advertisements, the stunts, the publicity that can turn the wheel of public opinion. Those tactics mattered a great deal to the trajectory of the cause, not least in rescuing it from the intellectual fringes where it had begun.

The involvement of society suffragists in civic reforms occurred against a backdrop of great social change in American political life. As immigrants swarmed into harbors and the working class added a new texture to urban life, the United States underwent a cultural shift. In what might be called a transition from male oligarchy to egalitarian democracy, the rules of class and gender that had guided the country for a century gave way to a modernist instinct. For the men of the gilded class, the period brought new dangers, as they were roiled by a federal income tax that slashed their wealth, the diminution of fortunes distributed among children and ex-wives, and the rise of a government more interventionist in curbing business excesses. For the women, there was but one opportunity: to become engaged in the issues of their day or to succumb to irrelevancy. For all of them, a revolution in gender norms upended the society of their parents, as men left the exclusivity of their clubs and sports for a life of work in business, and women went to college, pursued professional interests, experimented with new models of marriage—and joined suffrage.

The exuberant parades where women of all professions and income levels marched to claim their rights of citizenship, the insistence of working-class women on having a voice of their own to combat the twin evils of drunken husbands and intolerable workplace conditions, the grievances of society women about the class power denied them because of their gender—all these currents hurtled suffrage toward victory, silencing its chief opponents, the liquor lobby on Main Street and the political bosses in Tammany Hall.[44]

The financial donations made by gilded suffragists were substantial, and consequential. Olivia Sage made so many financial contributions to the National American Woman Suffrage Association that as the NAWSA contingent passed Sage's window on Fifth Avenue from which she watched the 1912 parade, each Assembly district leader dipped her flag in appreciation.[45] Phoebe Hearst, wife of Senator George Hearst of California and mother of *New York Journal* publisher William Randolph Hearst, contributed so frequently to Alice Paul's Congressional Union that when one letter came in requesting more, Hearst wrote in the margin, "No, impossible, can't consider it."[46] On her death in 1914, Miriam Leslie, widow of Frank Leslie and inheritor of his publishing empire, left nearly $1 million (nearly $26 million in today's dollars) to the National American Woman Suffrage Association, putting that organization "on firm financial footing for the first time in its history."[47]

Not content to limit their funding to their own resources, they proved particularly adept at corralling contributions from others. Vira White-house muscled Wall Street brokers to contribute to the New York State Woman Suffrage Party during the First World War, chiding one reluctant financier with, "How dare you refuse to give to the most important cause in your lifetime?"[48] It was the kind of appeal—from power to power, money to money—that would not have been possible without her and her equally well-connected lieutenants—Harriet Burton Laidlaw, Gertrude Foster Brown, Helen Rogers Reid, and Narcissa Cox Vanderlip. "They were well-married, were rich and they were stylish, . . . people who were well placed and could batter their way into anybody's office or anybody's living room," recalled Frances Perkins, who described Whitehouse and Laidlaw as "really great beauties."[49]

But their overriding contribution was cultural. When victory came to the women's suffrage movement in New York in 1917, by one estimate some 250,000 suffragists had joined the fight.[50] Some were men, and they too have been largely omitted from the story, dismissed as victims of what one scholar called a "lifelong romantic attraction to unpopular causes."[51] Even in the moment, male suffragists or sympathizers were easy to miss. A few days after the victory, a reporter asked Governor Charles Whitman who had won women's suffrage. "I rather thought that it was the men of New York who carried that amendment," Whitman noted drily. "But what matter who wins the praise as long as the work is done?"[52]

George Creel, director of Woodrow Wilson's wartime propaganda agency, the Committee on Public Information, was so impressed by the final campaign in New York that he appointed Vira Whitehouse to serve as an envoy for the agency. "Mrs. Whitehouse's job was to put America across in Switzerland just as she had put equal suffrage across in New York," he explained.[53] The appointment drew protests from suffragists who resented her tactics and antis who thought that her work for suffrage during the war was unpatriotic. Barbara Wendell, an anti-suffragist who headed the Massachusetts Special Aid Society for American Preparedness, enlisted a friend to stop the appointment. "I cannot imagine a person into whose hands I would less wish to put the affairs of the United States," she wrote.[54] Mary Garrett Hay, perhaps still smarting over the credit showered on Whitehouse for the victory, later sought to block Whitehouse's appointment to a postwar Peace Commission. "It would be a disgrace for such a woman to represent the United States," she wrote a friend. "We would prefer to have no woman."[55]

Whitehouse readily accepted Creel's diplomatic challenge. Here was a chance to practice citizenship—a newly enfranchised woman, serving her country. Roadblocks were profound. No woman had ever served abroad for the U.S. government, and reaction from the striped-pants set at the State Department was blatantly hostile. Secretary of State Robert Lansing, whose wife was a fervent anti-suffragist, declined to issue her a diplomatic passport. Legation officials, including a young Second Secretary Allen Dulles, a nephew of Lansing who would later head the Central Intelligence Agency, crippled her efforts at every turn. Finding it unfathomable that a woman had come to do a man's job, convinced that propaganda was a covert mission, they thwarted her efforts to rent office space or hire staff, concealed CPI news items meant for press distribution through her offices, intercepted her outgoing telegrams, and undercut her credibility with local officials.[56] At war's end, when the Austro-Hungarian Empire crumbled, Wilson used her offices—not those of the legation—to spread a message of restraint. He understood, better than his diplomats, that the conduct of foreign affairs now required appeal to the public. For all their skill at the levers of statecraft, the legation staff, perhaps blinded by misogyny, missed this advent of public diplomacy.[57]

Later, on Whitehouse's return from Europe, at a testimonial dinner at the Hotel Biltmore, five hundred suffragists paid tribute to her suffrage advocacy and her war service, understanding implicitly the sacrifices she had made in both. "Why not the 'Welcome Home' cards like the soldiers have?" asked one guest. "Aren't we welcoming home a woman who fought, in her way, just as valiantly and just as tellingly as any soldier or even as any Marine?"[58]

If Vira Boarman Whitehouse is missing from accounts of how women won the vote, so too Harriet Burton Laidlaw, Whitehouse's lieutenant in the New York campaign and a valued player on the national stage. Daisy Harriman, who introduced the topic of suffrage to members of the exclusive Colony Club, and by extension, welcomed them to the reform politics that motivated her, is rarely mentioned. Katherine Duer Mackay, who electrified interest just at the moment when suffrage was at its lowest ebb, has disappeared from the record, perhaps a victim of her personal life's public collapse. Rita Lydig's couture fashions became the foundation for the Metropolitan Museum of Art's Costume Institute, but her activism for suffrage as Mackay's treasurer and as one of the movement's most fashionable advocates is nowhere on display.[59] Katrina Ely Tiffany was so valued for her suffrage and war relief work that organizers gave her the honor of carrying the flag at the 1917 suffrage parade, but they never mentioned her in any books they wrote or commissioned about the campaign. Even Alva Belmont, who casts such a long shadow on suffrage politics that she could not be ignored, is often derided for her autocratic ways, her contributions belittled as the affectations of a woman avenging the public philandering of a first husband and the sneers that came in its wake. Others are missing at the whim of writers, the snub raising questions of stereotype. Why is Irene Langhorne Gibson remembered only as an icon of white beauty and not as an activist for suffrage? Why are Helen Hay Whitney, a poet, Fanny Villard, a reformer, and Mamie Fish, a socialite, all absent from these histories?

That their involvement gave the cause a sense of vogue was undeniable. "With the two society leaders, Mrs. Mackay and Mrs. Belmont, leading rival camps of suffrage fighters," said the *American* in 1909, "the coming fall campaign will be a lively one."[60] Equally evident is that they attracted new recruits to the campaign. Amid increasing public interest, the voice of celebrity carried. Ida Crouch Hazlett, a grassroots activist in the Socialist Party not inclined to look kindly on the latest stirrings of wealthy society ladies, had no doubt about their ability to attract new converts. Lamenting the movement's "snobbish truckling to the women of influence and social position," she complained that the campaign was seducing young activists toward suffrage and away from the more prosaic work of labor organizing.[61]

Looking back over the history of suffrage, Marie Manning, who in 1898 penned the first newspaper advice column, called "Dear Beatrice Fairfax," credited their fashion. Observing that in the nineteenth century, "the clothes that suffragists wore when they went about petitioning were grim as shrouds," she claimed that those "unbecoming clothes . . . hadn't worked in sixty years." Now, she wrote, with the advent of Alva Belmont, "the smartest drawing rooms in the country echoed with the applause of jeweled hands."[62] She too had expunged faces from the record, so blinded by Belmont's glitter that she did not see Gibson, Laidlaw, Lydig, Mackay, Milholland, Sage, Whitehouse, and all the others.

To trace their footsteps and narrate their story is to underscore the importance of the suffragists' physical appearance in defusing male resistance, the importance of celebrity in exciting mainstream opinion, and the need for public acceptance of any social change. In the end, their legacy is simply this: For a brief moment in early twentieth-century America, when change was in the air, they helped push women's suffrage over the finish line. Familiarity is the ballast of social change. Wives and daughters of the most powerful men in Gotham were well-known figures on the public stage, reassuring in their very presence. As hostesses of extravagant parties and managers of massive estates, they had learned the skills of managing a press corps hungry for controversy. This dexterity they now exported to the suffrage movement, harnessing their own social influence to attract new believers to the cause. If they did not win suffrage outright, they did something very critical to the success of those who did. They gave the movement currency, making it less threatening to men and more appealing to women, more acceptable to a mainstream public.

One year after suffragists had won the right to vote in New York, former president Theodore Roosevelt set off for the polls, as he had done for more than forty years. As he got in his car, the great spokesman for male vigor, who preached against feminization of the public square, was surprised to see his wife, Edith, already waiting in the car. "Why Ee-die, why are you coming?" he asked. "I'm going to vote of course, Theodore," she replied. To Roosevelt, as others of his time and gender, the abstract concept of equal rights was one thing but, as his longtime friend Owen Wister explained, "the sight of his own wife casting a ballot took his breath away." Theodore Roosevelt, who had overseen so much progressive legislation as the presidential master of the bully pulpit, who had first ignored women's suffrage and then embraced it as part of his attempted political comeback, now confronted personally the result of this social change. And in Wister's words, he simply "sat back in the car, silent for a time."[63]

Acknowledgments

A s a journalist, I wrote for story, eager to spin a narrative that would compel even as it informed. As a historian, I learned to look for meaning beneath layers of documents. Throughout my late-in-life doctoral education, I nursed an aspiration to combine these two threads into a single fabric, convinced that historians were at heart readers, and readers in essence historians. I offer this book as a first test of that ambition.

Many are owed many thanks. Colleagues at American University, including Alan Kraut, Pamela Nadell, and Max Paul Friedman, offered guidance, critiques, and wisdom. Kate Haulman was insightful about how the project could contribute to the field of women's suffrage, and Katarina Vester was instrumental in introducing me to important landmarks in nineteenth-century cultural history. An informal circle of confidants, including Lisa Leff, a scholar of Jews in Europe, and Victoria Brown, biographer of Jane Addams, offered guidance and reassurance. From England, Eric Homberger, whose *Mrs. Astor's New York* served in some sense as the prequel for this book, offered timely insights that made a difference. Robyn Muncy, a historian of the period, playfully reminded me, a former political correspondent, not to forget politics amid the abundant cultural and social material I had gathered. Marc Pachter, a former director of the Smithsonian's National Portrait Gallery and American History Museum and a student of biography, asked questions that made me think deeper. And Patrick Sammon, former president of the Log Cabin Republicans, helped me think through themes of social change amid resistance.

I owe a special debt to Sven Beckert of Harvard University. An informal adviser, this scholar of New York wealth and the father of the history of capitalism as a new discipline changed the contours of this project. Over coffee in Cambridge, Beckert urged me to bolster my argument by building a database of information about these gilded suffragists, learning everything I could—what church they attended, whether their money was old or new, what clubs and parties they belonged to. His suggestion gave me the statistical authority to make claims not just about individuals but about the group, greatly enriching the result.

Institutions contributed funding, for which I am grateful and honored, including the Sophia Smith Collection at Smith College in Northampton, Massachusetts, and the American University's Office of Graduate Studies and College of Arts and Sciences. I am grateful too for fellowships awarded. The American University History Department's Patrick Clendenen Fellowship and the New York Historical Society's Klingenstein Fellowship offered not just funding but affirmation to a scholar just learning the craft. The *Journal of the Gilded Age and Progressive Era* and the *Women's History Review* graciously granted permission to publish portions of articles I wrote for them on topics stemming from this research.

Librarians and archivists at various institutions were unfailingly helpful, none more so than Teresa Barnett of the Charles E. Young Research Library at the University of California, Los Angeles, who scoured the library for an oral history interview, critical to my work, which had gone missing likely for decades. Special thanks to Elspeth Kursh, the archivist at what is now the Belmont-Paul Women's Equality National Monument, who welcomed me to research (albeit in a refrigerated room) the phenomenal archive of fifty scrapbooks kept by Alva Belmont; to

Coline Jenkins, great-great-granddaughter of Elizabeth Cady Stanton, who opened her home and private collection to me on a fall day in Greenwich, Connecticut; and to Dean Rogers at Vassar, whose requirements to preorder specific folders from finding aids made me a better researcher. In Washington, thanks go the staffs of the Library of Congress Manuscripts Department and the Rare Books Collection; George Washington University's Special Collections; the Smithsonian American Art Archives; the Women's National Democratic Club, where a crew had to break the lock on a file drawer so I could gain access to Florence Harriman's papers; and at American University to Andrea Paredes-Herrera and Clement Ho, who went beyond duty to acquire collections instrumental for my research. In New York, Ted O'Reilly, Tammy Kiter, and Valerie Paley at the New York Historical Society, Richard Berenson at the Museum of American Illustration, and the staffs of Columbia University, New York Public Library, the Tamiment Library at New York University, and the Morgan Library all were helpful.

From the Schlesinger Library at Harvard to the Huntington Library in Pasadena, everyone was kind. Everywhere the rules for handling these sensitive archival records were different—some required washing of the hands while others offered gloves; most encouraged quiet while others thrived on conversation—and everywhere I learned more about the rigor needed for the task. These librarians are teachers. I thank them all.

A great note of thanks to the team at New York University Press—Ellen Chodosh, Mary Beth Jarrad, Betsy Steve, Dorothea Stillman Halliday, and Amy Klopfenstein, who steered the project to completion with encouragement and intelligence. As for my editor at New York University Press, Clara Platter was the advocate every author dreams of, fighting to win the book, and then to preserve its integrity and promote its unique contributions as a piece of both narrative and scholarly writing.

One of the reaffirming lessons of returning to the university after a long career is the camaraderie of students who, despite the divide in years, offered friendship, chief among them Susan Perlman, Loren Miller, and Rebecca DeWolf. To my own friends who cheered and listened—Mel

Antonen, Ben Bycel, Valerie and Ian Calder, McCall Credle-Rosenthal, Mary Curtius, Luigi De Luca, Kendra Blackett-Dibinga and Omekongo Dibinga, Norine Fuller, Sloane Hagenstad, Angela and Rea Hederman, Leslie Hoffecker, Joy Howell, Nina Pino-Marina Hughey, Susan Lebrun, Angela and Terry McCullagh, Caron McGinley, Alison McIntyre, Penny Oranburg, Gay Pirozzi, and Miriam Polan—thank you beyond words.

To my family—my sister and brother-in-law, Hildie and Bill Lyddan, my California clan of Roz and Warren Steinhauser, Dorothy Leeb, and so many cousins, my grandsons Stephen and Phillip Nessen, my nieces and nephews and their families—Clarie and Steve Garnett, Nicole and Mark Johnson, Robert Lyddan and Courtney Dimling, Colin Lyddan and Julie Hansard Lyddan—and to Bari Leigh and Jay Glazer, I thank you all for your cheers from afar. Finally, to my husband-without-title, Jeffrey Glazer, so intuitive that he kept silent for hours that I might think, I express the kind of sweeping gratitude that can only be understood between those who are in love.

Notes

INTRODUCTION

1 "The clothes that suffragists wore when they went out petitioning were grim as shrouds," wrote the *New York Evening Journal*'s Marie Manning. "Unbecoming clothes . . . hadn't worked in 60 years." See Marie Manning, *Ladies Now and Then* (New York: Dutton, 1944), 101.

2 Joseph D. Straubhaar and Robert LaRose, *Media Now: Understanding Media, Culture, and Technology* (Boston: Cengage Learning, 2008), 94.

3 "400 to Be at National Meet of Suffragists," *New York Journal*, February 14, 1910, Mackay Family Scrapbooks, reel 7, Bryant Library, Roslyn, New York.

4 "Our Suffrage Movement Is Flirtation on a Big Scale," *New York Times*, May 25, 1913. See also letters to the editor about the comment, including "Smiles Mrs. Dodge Noticed Must Be Due to Odd Claims They Make," *New York Times*, May 27, 1913, 10; and "Suffragists' Appeal," *New York Times*, May 27, 1913, 10.

5 William L. O'Neill, *Everyone Was Brave: The Rise and Fall of Feminism in America* (Chicago: Quadrangle, 1969).

6 Ellen Carol DuBois, *Harriot Stanton Blatch and the Winning of Woman Suffrage* (New Haven: Yale University Press, 1997), 109.

7 The three-volume *History of Woman Suffrage* written by Elizabeth Cady Stanton, Susan B. Anthony, and Matilda Joslyn Gage (1881–1886), as well as the later three volumes overseen by Anthony and Ida Husted Harper, guided scholarship for more than a century. Lisa Tetrault, *The Myth of Seneca Falls: Memory and the Women's Suffrage Movement, 1848–1898* (Chapel Hill: University of North Carolina Press, 2014) has questioned their selective memory. Much recent historiography has come in the form of biographies, including Grace Farrell, *Lillie Devereux Blake: Retracing a Life Erased* (Amherst: University of Massachusetts Press, 2002); Ruth Crocker, *Mrs. Russell Sage: Women's Activism and Philanthropy in Gilded Age and Progressive Era America* (Bloomington: Indiana University Press, 2006); Sylvia D. Hoffert, *Alva Vanderbilt*

Belmont: Unlikely Champion of Women's Rights (Bloomington: Indiana University Press, 2012); Linda Lumsden, *Inez: The Life and Times of Inez Milholland* (Bloomington: Indiana University Press); Robert P. J. Cooney Jr., *Remembering Inez: The Last Campaign of Inez Milholland, Suffrage Martyr* (Half Moon Bay, CA: American Graphic Press, 2015); Armond Fields, *Katharine Dexter McCormick: Pioneer for Women's Rights* (Westport, CT: Praeger, 2003); Leila R. Brammer, *Excluded from Suffrage History: Matilda Joslyn Gage, Nineteenth-Century American Feminist* (Westport, CT: Greenwood, 2000); and Peter Geidel, "Alva E. Belmont: A Forgotten Feminist" (Ph.D. diss., Columbia University, 1993).

8 Christine Stansell, *American Moderns: Bohemian New York and the Creation of a New Century* (New York: Macmillan, 2001).

9 A. Scott Berg, *Kate Remembered* (New York: Putnam, 2003), 44.

10 Letter from Inez Haynes Gillmore to Maud Wood Park, March 29, 1910, NAWSA Papers, reel 11, Manuscripts Division, Library of Congress.

CHAPTER 1. A CLUB OF THEIR OWN

1 Henry Cabot Lodge, *Early Memories* (New York: Scribner's, 1913), cited in Cleveland Amory, *Who Killed Society?* (New York: Harper, 1960), 23.

2 Elizabeth Wharton Drexel Lehr, *"King Lehr" and the Gilded Age* (Philadelphia: Lippincott, 1935), 14.

3 Maureen E. Montgomery, *Displaying Women: Spectacles of Leisure in Edith Wharton's New York* (New York: Routledge, 1998), 25.

4 Lehr, *"King Lehr" and the Gilded Age*, 14.

5 Deborah Davis, *Gilded: How Newport Became America's Richest Resort* (Hoboken, NJ: Wiley, 2009), 69.

6 Eric Homberger, *Mrs. Astor's New York: Money and Social Power in a Gilded Age* (New Haven: Yale University Press, 2002), 170.

7 Jerry E Patterson, *The First Four Hundred: Mrs. Astor's New York in the Gilded Age* (New York: Rizzoli, 2000), 187.

8 Letter from Harold Seton to Lucius Beebe, January 15, 1935, Harold Seton Papers, New York Historical Society.

9 Florence Jaffray Harriman, *From Pinafores to Politics* (New York: Henry Holt, 1923), 74. There is some dispute over the timing and venue of the meeting. In her memoirs and her papers, Harriman cites Newport but does not mention Bailey's Beach. In the Colony Club's official history, published in 1984, author Anne F. Cox wrote that the idea for the club was first discussed among five women at Bailey's Beach, although this is not supported by contemporaneous newspaper accounts. Though Cox suggests that this meeting took place in 1900, all other sources—including biographies of Stanford White and Elsie de Wolfe, the Harriman papers at the Library of Congress, and newspaper and magazine coverage at the time of the club's debut in 1907—suggest that the meeting took place in 1902. There is a great variety in these and other sources about the identity of the five women who attended this first brainstorming session. I have tended to adhere to Harriman's version, as I see no reason for her to exaggerate. The Colony Club refused my request to use its archives, perhaps out of fear that the original documents would rebut the official Cox version, which has been widely cited by other writers.

10 Harriman, *From Pinafores to Politics*, 73.

11 Harriman, *From Pinafores to Politics*, 72.

12 Amory, *Who Killed Society?*, 198–206.

13 Jean Strouse, *Morgan: American Financier* (New York: Random House, 1999), 521.

14 Alfred Allan Lewis, *Ladies and Not-so-Gentle Women* (New York: Viking, 2000), 208.

15 Stansell, *American Moderns*, 1.

16 Anne Morgan diary, January 16, 1909, Anne Morgan Papers, box 41, item 6, Morgan Library, New York; Fanny Villard diary, January 26, 1909, Fanny Villard Papers, series 901, Houghton Library, Harvard University.

17 Eric Homberger, *The Historical Atlas of New York City: A Visual Celebration of 400 Years of New York City's History* (New York: Macmillan, 2005), 117; Paula J. Giddings, *Ida: A Sword among Lions* (New York: HarperCollins, 2009), 231.

18 Clarice Stasz, *The Vanderbilt Women: Dynasty of Wealth, Glamour, and Tragedy* (New York: St. Martin's, 2000), 201.

19 Ron Chernow, *The House of Morgan: An American Banking Dynasty and the Rise of Modern Finance* (New York: Simon and Schuster, 1990), 46; see also Harriman, *From Pinafores to Politics*, 16–17.

20 Judith A. Leavitt, *American Women Managers and Administrators: A Selective Biographical Dictionary of Twentieth-Century Leaders in Business, Education, and Government* (Westport, CT: Greenwood, 1985), 103.

21 "Mrs. J. Borden Harriman, Ex-Envoy, Dies at 97," *New York Times*, September 1, 1967.

22 "The Wedding of Miss Hurst and Mr. Harriman at St. Thomas's," *New York Times*, November 14, 1889.

23 Harriman, *From Pinafores to Politics*, 44.

24 "'Daisy' Harriman Outruns Bombs," *Life Magazine*, May 13, 1940, 32–35.

25 "News of Newport," *New York Times*, July 2, 1902.

26 Laura Claridge, *Emily Post: Daughter of the Gilded Age, Mistress of American Manners* (New York: Random House, 2009), 104.

27 "A Bank for Women All to Themselves," *New York Times*, September 23, 1906. "Depositing or taking out money is an inspiration with women," reported an employee in explaining the bank's decision to open a female branch. "They are afraid of changing their minds after they have decided. Delay in the line unnerves them."

28 Harriman, *From Pinafores to Politics*, 73. Three residential clubs were flourishing in Manhattan at the time—the Town and Country Club, the Woman's University Club, and the Woman's Club, but they catered to a more middle-class clientele. Cited in Montgomery, *Displaying Women*, 95.

29 Patterson, *The First Four Hundred*, 166. Wharton saw him as a Renaissance man whose talents were wasted on society, saying, "He lived his life in dilettantish leisure."

30 "September Days at Newport," *New York Times*, September 7, 1902, 9.

31 Harriman, *From Pinafores to Politics*, 74.

32 Edward James, Janet Wilson James, and Paul Boyer, eds., *Notable American Women, 1607–1950: A Biographical Dictionary*, vol. 3 (Cambridge: Belknap, 1971), 208.

33 Harriman, *From Pinafores to Politics*, 74–75.

34 "Lady into Dynamo," *New Yorker*, October 22, 1927, 22.

35 Strouse, *Morgan: American Financier*, 468, 521.

36 Lewis, *Ladies and Not-so-Gentle Women*, xiv.

37 Cherie Fehrman and Kenneth Fehrman, *Interior Design Innovators, 1910–1960* (San Francisco: Fehrman Books, 2009), 5.
38 James Trager, *Park Avenue: Street of Dreams* (New York: Atheneum, 1990), 160.
39 Harriman Papers, box 10, folder 1, Library of Congress.
40 "A. S. Alexander Weds Miss Helen Barney," *New York Times*, April 9, 1905, 9.
41 Harriman, *From Pinafores to Politics*, 56. For discussion of Smith and his literary merits, see letters to the editor, *New York Times*, March 18, 1905.
42 Historical note, "Ladies Four-in-Hand Driving Club Scrapbook, 1904–1910," National Sporting Library, Middleburg, VA.
43 "A Notable Wedding," *New York Tribune*, April 29, 1900, 23.
44 R. Stephen Sennott, ed., *Encyclopedia of Twentieth-Century Architecture* (New York: Taylor and Francis, 2004), 219.
45 Mosette Broderick, *Triumvirate: McKim, Mead & White: Art, Architecture, Scandal, and Class in America's Gilded Age* (New York: Knopf Doubleday, 2010), 368.
46 Harriman, *From Pinafores to Politics*, 75.
47 Anne F. Cox, *The History of the Colony Club, 1903–1984* (New York: Colony Club, 1984), 28. Calculations of current dollar value are from www.measuringworth.com; throughout the book, I use this site for currency conversions, using the Consumer Price Index.
48 Harriman Papers, box 10, folder 1; Cox, *The History of the Colony Club*, 33.
49 Cox, *The History of the Colony Club*, 29–36.
50 Claridge, *Emily Post*, 185.
51 Elsie de Wolfe, *After All* (London: Heinemann, 1935), 57.
52 Lindy Woodhead, *War Paint: Madame Helena Rubinstein and Miss Elizabeth Arden: Their Lives, Their Times, Their Rivalry* (Hoboken, NJ: Wiley, 2003), 67.
53 Jane S. Smith, *Elsie de Wolfe: A Life in the High Style* (New York: Atheneum, 1982), xi.
54 Fehrman and Fehrman, *Interior Design Innovators*, 7; "Colony Club, House Rules, Revised June 1920," Main Collection, New York Historical Society.
55 Harriman, *From Pinafores to Politics*, 73–74.
56 Harriman Papers, box 23, folder 2.
57 Cox, *The History of the Colony Club*, 9–10.
58 John McCain, "A Cause Greater Than Self," *Time Magazine*, June 25, 2008.
59 Imogen Oakley, "The Women's Club Movement," *American City*, vol. 6 (June 1912), 805, cited in *Gender, Class, Race, and Reform in the Progressive Era*, ed. Nancy Schrom Dye and Noralee Frankel (Lexington: University Press of Kentucky, 1991), 1.
60 Claridge, *Emily Post*, 131.
61 "A Wonderful Building," *New York Tribune*, June 29, 1902, 33.
62 "Westinghouse Celebrates Fiftieth Anniversary," *Commercial America*, vol. 32 (1936), 14; David McCullough, *The Great Bridge: The Epic Story of the Building of the Brooklyn Bridge* (New York: Simon and Schuster, 2007); Brian J. Cudahy, *Rails under the Mighty Hudson: The Story of the Hudson Tubes, the Pennsy Tunnels, and Manhattan Transfer* (Bronx: Fordham University Press, 2002).
63 Hermione Lee, *Edith Wharton* (New York: Knopf Doubleday, 2008), 48.
64 Catherine Gourley, *Society's Sisters: Stories of Women Who Fought for Social Justice in America* (Brookfield, CT: Twenty-First Century Books, 2003), 11–12.
65 Henry Whittemore, *The Heroes of the American Revolution and Their Descendants: Battle of Long Island* (New York: Heroes of the Revolution Publishing Company, 1897), 5.

66 National Association of Colored Women's Clubs, "Who Are We?," www.nacwc. org.

67 Charlotte Perkins Gilman and Larry Ceplair, *Charlotte Perkins Gilman: A Nonfiction Reader* (New York: Columbia University Press, 1991), 39.

68 "Miss Tarbell Talks to the Suffragists," *New York Times*, January 20, 1911.

69 "Says Suffragettes Lean to Socialism," *New York Times*, April 1, 1908, 7.

70 Beth Marie Waggenspack, *The Search for Self-Sovereignty* (Westport, CT: Greenwood, 1989), 14.

71 "Colony Club Debate," *New York Tribune*, April 1, 1908, 5.

72 "Special Notice," Catherine Palmer Abbe Scrapbooks, reel 1, National American Woman Suffrage Association records, New York Public Library.

73 Harriman, *From Pinafores to Politics*, 92–93.

74 "Woman Suffrage Upheld by Prominent Speakers," *Brooklyn Daily Eagle*, December 5, 1908, 8.

75 Harriman, *From Pinafores to Politics*, 93.

76 Adaline Wheelock Sterling, "The Street Meeting," *Woman Voter*, August 1913, 17–18.

77 Susan E. Marshall, *Splintered Sisterhood: Gender and Class in the Campaign against Woman Suffrage* (Madison: University of Wisconsin Press, 1997), 103.

78 "Suffragists Hold a Street Meeting," *New York Times*, May 14, 1909.

79 Joseph O. Baylen, "Stead, William Thomas (1849–1912)," *Oxford Dictionary of National Biography* (New York: Oxford University Press, 2004).

80 "Stead Addresses Suffrage League," *New York Times*, April 18, 1907.

81 "Nature Will Down the Suffragists," *New York Times*, February 11, 1910, 7.

82 USGA, "Historical Notes," http://usga.usopen.com.

83 Lissa Smith, ed., *Nike Is a Goddess: The History of Women in Sports* (New York: Atlantic Monthly Press, 1999), 130.

84 *Club Fellow*, October 19, 1910, Mackay Family Scrapbooks, reel 7.

85 "Mrs. Mackay's Cards Bring a Fashionable Throng to the Colony Club," *New York American*, April 9, 1909, Mackay Family Scrapbooks, reel 6.

86 "The Suffrage Question at the Colony Club," *Town & Country*, April 17, 1909, Mackay Family Scrapbooks, reel 6.

87 "Audacities," *Club Fellow*, April 14, 1909, Mackay Family Scrapbooks, reel 6.

88 *New York Herald*, Alva Belmont Scrapbooks, vol. 3, Florence Bayard Hilles Feminist Library, Belmont-Paul Women's Equality National Monument, Washington, D.C.; "Equal Franchise Society Holds Brilliant Meeting," *Club Woman's Weekly*, April 17, 1909, Mackay Family Scrapbooks, reel 6.

89 Homberger, *Mrs. Astor's New York*, 235.

90 Louis Auchincloss, *The Vanderbilt Era: Profiles of a Gilded Age* (New York: Scribner's, 1989), 46–47.

91 Gayle V. Fischer, *Pantaloons and Power: Nineteenth-Century Dress Reform in the United States* (Kent: Kent State University Press, 2001).

92 "Mrs. Fish Gone Over to the Suffragists," *New York Times*, January 16, 1910, 7.

CHAPTER 2. THE CELEBRITY ENDORSEMENT

1 Rebecca H. Insley, "An Interview with Mrs. Astor," *Delineator*, vol. 72 (October 1908), 550.

2 Donald Albrecht and Jeannine J. Falino, *Gilded New York: Design, Fashion, and Society* (New York: Monacelli, 2013), 90; Alva Belmont Memoir, 110–17, Mathilda Young Papers, Duke University; Homberger, *Mrs. Astor's New York*, 14.

3 Claridge, *Emily Post*, 38; Sven Beckert, "Bourgeois Institution Builders: New York in the Nineteenth Century," in *The American Bourgeoisie: Distinction and Identity in the Nineteenth Century*, ed. Sven Beckert and Julia B. Rosenbaum (New York: Palgrave Macmillan, 2010), 108. Many accounts suggest that Alva Vanderbilt used the costume ball to maneuver Caroline Schermerhorn Astor into accepting the Vanderbilts into her circle. Some historians view the story as unlikely, since both women had met before. They served together on the executive board of the Bartholdi Pedestal Fund, which raised money for the pedestal underneath the Statue of Liberty, and attended balls hosted by the Patriarchs, a club even more select than Mrs. Astor's Four Hundred, this one capped at the twenty-five most influential families in the city. A number of historians consider this an apocryphal story, an anecdote with traction (and longevity) because it fits the narrative of Alva as socially ambitious. See Homberger, *Mrs. Astor's New York*, 270–71.

4 Susannah Broyles, "Vanderbilt Ball," Museum of the City of New York blog, August 6, 2013, mcnyblog.org.

5 Albrecht and Falino, *Gilded New York*, 90–93; Henry Clews, *Fifty Years in Wall Street* (Hoboken, NJ: Wiley, 2006), ix.

6 Charles Anderson Dana, who as managing editor of Horace Greeley's *New York Tribune* had turned that paper into a robust center of abolitionist journalism, purchased the *New York Sun* in 1868. By 1880, he had added a new feature, the society reporter. The *Tribune* followed suit, as did the *World*, whose new owner, Joseph Pulitzer, "made an ostentatious display of Society's activities in the Sunday edition of the paper." Pulitzer's "In Millionaire Society" reported "everything that had occurred during the past week . . . with a schedule of events to come." See Frank M. O'Brien, *The Story of the Sun* (New York: Doran, 1918), 199; and Charles L. Ponce de Leon, *Self-Exposure: Human-Interest Journalism and the Emergence of Celebrity in America, 1890–1940* (Chapel Hill: University of North Carolina Press, 2002), 52.

7 "Balshazzar's Feast," *St. Louis Post-Dispatch*, March 24, 1883, 4, cited in Hoffert, *Alva Vanderbilt Belmont*, 30.

8 Some scholars have since argued that Horatio Alger's main message was that the poor could achieve middle-class status, rather than the unparalleled wealth implied in the phrase "rags to riches." See Harlon Dalton, "Horatio Alger," in *Rereading America: Cultural Contexts for Critical Thinking and Writing*, 9th ed., ed. Gary Colombo, Robert Cullen, and Bonnie Lisle (Boston: Bedford/St. Martin's, 2013), 303–9. Also see John D. Stevens, *Sensationalism and the New York Press* (New York: Columbia University Press, 1991), 53, U.S. Census, 1890.

9 George Wotherspoon, "I Hunt in the Attic," part 3, unpublished memoir, New York Historical Society.

10 Ponce de Leon, *Self-Exposure*, 52.

11 Wotherspoon, "I Hunt in the Attic," part 4.

12 Robert Love, "Shakedown!," *Columbia Journalism Review*, July–August 2006, 48–49.

13 Homberger, *Mrs. Astor's New York*, 207.

14 Reporters gave the title of the "Trial of the Century" to the case trying millionaire Harry Kendall Thaw for murdering society architect Stanford White the following year.

15 "Mann Tells How He Borrowed $184,500," *New York Times*, January 23, 1906, 1.

16 Andy Logan, *The Man Who Robbed the Robber Barons* (New York: Norton, 1965), 64, 175, 152.

17 Logan, *The Man Who Robbed the Robber Barons*, 192–93.

18 Love, "Shakedown!"

19 Logan, *The Man Who Robbed the Robber Barons*, 164–67.

20 Letter from Harold Seton to Lucius Beebe, July 15, 1935.

21 Wotherspoon, "I Hunt in the Attic," part 3, 6.

22 Hoffert, *Alva Vanderbilt Belmont*, 27–28.

23 Wotherspoon, "I Hunt in the Attic," part 3.

24 Consuelo Vanderbilt Balsan, *The Glitter and the Gold* (New York: Harper, 1952), 46.

25 Amanda Mackenzie Stuart, *Consuelo and Alva Vanderbilt: The Story of a Mother and a Daughter in the "Gilded Age"* (New York: HarperCollins, 2012), 141–44.

26 Balsan, *The Glitter and the Gold*, 45.

27 Homberger, *Mts. Astor's New York*, 10–13.

28 Henry James, *The Notebooks of Henry James*, ed. F. O. Matthiessen and Kenneth Murdock (Chicago: University of Chicago Press, 1981), entry for November 17, 1887, 82, cited in Homberger, *Mrs. Astor's New York*, 11.

29 "Fashionable Moments in Suffrage History," *Woman Citizen*, vol. 3 (March 22, 1919), 900–901.

30 See Farrell, *Lillie Devereux Blake*, 148; Ellen Carol DuBois, "Working Women, Class Relations and Suffrage Militance: Harriot Stanton Blatch and the New York Woman Suffrage Movement, 1894–1909," in *One Woman, One Vote: Rediscovering the Woman Suffrage Movement*, ed. Marjorie Spruill Wheeler (Troutdale, OR: NewSage Press, 1995), 225; and Katherine Devereux Blake and Margaret Louise Wallace, *Champion of Women: The Life of Lillie Devereux Blake* (New York: Fleming H. Revell, 1943), 181.

31 Ira Rosenwaike, *Population History of New York City* (Syracuse: Syracuse University Press, 1972), 110.

32 Richard B. Stark, "Robert Abbe and His Contributions to Plastic Surgery," *Plastic and Reconstructive Surgery*, vol. 12, no. 1 (July 1953), 55, in Abbe Scrapbooks.

33 "The City History Club," *New York Times*, March 23, 1902, 24; Abbe kept scrapbooks of newspaper clippings about suffrage activities in New York from 1894 to 1920, an important resource for this and other books on the subject.

34 Ruth J. Abram, ed., *Send Us a Lady Physician: Women Doctors in America, 1835–1920* (New York: Norton, 1985), 97–101.

35 Joan Waugh, *Unsentimental Reformer: The Life of Josephine Shaw Lowell* (Cambridge: Harvard University Press, 1997), 113.

36 "Troy Female Seminary," December 9, 1999, *Encyclopedia Britannica*, http://www.britannica.com.

37 Mrs. Russell Sage, "Opportunities and Responsibilities of Leisure Women" (1905), in "The Woman Question, 1849–1987," special heritage issue, *North American Review*, vol. 2, no. 3 (September 1987), 78–81.

38 "Working for Woman Suffrage," *New York Times*, March 25, 1894, 11.

39 "Society Women Want Votes," *New York Times*, April 11, 1894, 1.

40 Lillie Devereux Blake, "Our New York Letter," *Woman's Journal*, March 10, 1894; "Society Women Want Votes"; Susan Goodier, *No Votes for Women: The New York State Anti-Suffrage Movement* (Urbana: University of Illinois Press, 2013), 33.

41 "Society Women Would Vote," *New York Evening World*, March 26, 1894, 5.

42 "Woman and the Suffrage," *New York Sun*, March 31, 1894, Abbe Scrapbooks, reel 1.

43 DuBois, "Working Women, Class Relations and Suffrage Militance," 225.

44 See "The City History Club," 24.

45 "Society Women Want Votes."

46 "Not Room for All Who Came," *New York Times*, May 4, 1894, 8, Abbe Scrapbooks, reel 1.

47 "Miss Curtis on Equal Suffrage," *New York Times*, April 20, 1894, 2.

48 "The Lady and the Female," *New York Evening World*, April 14, 1894, cited in Crocker, *Mrs. Russell Sage*, 157.

49 "A Meeting at Mrs. Sage's," *New York Sun*, April 15, 1894, Abbe Scrapbooks, reel 2.

50 "In the World of Fashion," *New York Sun*, April 5, 1894, 7.

51 Crocker, *Mrs. Russell Sage*, 30.

52 "Friends Pay Tribute to Theodore Sutro," *New York Times*, August 31, 1927, 21.

53 "Society Women Want Votes."

54 "Society Women Want Votes."

55 "Why She Should Have the Ballot," *New York World*, February 27, 1894, 14.

56 "Why They Demand a Vote," *New York Times*, April 17, 1894, 8.

57 John Drake Townsend, *New York in Bondage* (New York: Issues for Subscribers, 1901).

58 "Equal Suffrage for Women," *New York Times*, April 18, 1894, 8.

59 "Suffragists on the Warpath," *New York Times*, May 3, 1894, 9.

60 "Their Enthusiasm Growing," *New York Times*, April 19, 1894, 5.

61 "Seeking the Right to Vote," *New York Times*, April 13, 1894, 1.

62 *New York Herald*, April 8, 1894.

63 Society Supplement, *Vogue*, May 3, 1894, C3.

64 "Following Brooklyn's Lead," *New York Times*, April 27, 1894, 9.

65 James, James, and Boyer, *Notable American Women, 1607–1950*, vol. 2, 492–93.

66 Thomas J. Jablonsky, *The Home, Heaven, and Mother Party: Female Anti-Suffragists in the United States, 1868–1920* (Brooklyn: Carlson, 1994), 17.

67 Manuela Thurner, "'Better Citizens without the Ballot': American Anti-Suffrage Women and Their Rationale during the Progressive Era," *Journal of Women's History*, vol. 5, no. 1 (March 1, 1993), 33–60.

68 "Anti-Suffragists Protest," *New York Times*, May 2, 1894, 5.

69 Crystal Eastman, *Crystal Eastman on Women and Revolution* (New York: Oxford University Press, 1978), 65.

70 Goodier, *No Votes for Women*, 16–17; Aileen S. Kraditor, *The Ideas of the Women's Suffrage Movement, 1890–1920* (New York: Norton, 1965).

71 "Society Women Would Vote."

72 "The Lady and the Female."

73 Joseph Hodges Choate and Edward Sandford Martin, *The Life of Joseph Hodges Choate as Gathered Chiefly from His Letters* (New York: Scribner's, 1921), vol. 1, 222.

74 Choate and Martin, *The Life of Joseph Hodges Choate*, vol. 1, 131.

75 "Equal Suffrage Their Aim," *New York Times*, April 12, 1894, 5.

76 Anne Myra Goodman Benjamin, *Women against Equality: A History of the Anti-Suffrage Movement in the United States from 1895 to 1920* (Lewiston, NY: Edwin Mellen Press, 1991), 28.

77 Elizabeth Cady Stanton, Susan B. Anthony, and Matilda Joslyn Gage, *History of Woman Suffrage*, vol. 4, *1883–1900* (Indianapolis: Hollenbeck, 1902), 850–52.

78 *Brooklyn Life*, February 9, 1895, 20.

79 "The League for Political Education," *New York Times*, November 8, 1902, 8.

80 James S. Fishkin, *The Voice of the People: Public Opinion and Democracy* (New Haven: Yale University Press, 1997), 135.

81 Andrew Dolkart, *Guide to New York City Landmarks* (New York: Wiley, 2008), 78.

82 Town Hall, "History," thetownhall.org.

83 Sarah Hunter Graham, "The Suffrage Renaissance: A New Image for a New Century, 1896–1910," in Wheeler, *One Woman, One Vote*, 162.

84 Beverly Beeton, *Women Vote in the West: The Woman Suffrage Movement, 1869–1896* (New York: Garland, 1986), 111–13.

85 For more on the Colorado campaign, see Jeanne E. Abrams, *Jewish Women Pioneering the Frontier Trail: A History in the American West* (New York: New York University Press, 2007). Other works about early suffrage victories in the West include Rebecca J. Mead, *How the Vote Was Won: Woman Suffrage in the Western United States, 1868–1914* (New York: New York University Press, 2006); and Holly J. McCammon and Karen E. Campbell, "Winning the Vote in the West: The Political Successes of the Women's Suffrage Movements, 1866–1919," *Gender and Society*, vol. 15, no. 1 (February 1, 2001), 55–82.

86 "Crusade for the Vote," National Women's History Museum, www.crusadeforthevote.org.

87 *New York American*, February 25, 1910, Mackay Family Scrapbooks, reel 6.

CHAPTER 3. THE BIRTH OF A RIVALRY

1 Mabel Potter Daggett, "Suffrage Enters the Drawing Room," *Delineator*, January 1910, Alva Belmont Scrapbooks, vol. 3.

2 Katherine Duer Mackay, American Historical Manuscripts Collection, New York Historical Society.

3 Richard Guy Wilson, *Harbor Hill: Portrait of a House* (New York: Norton, 2008), 40.

4 "Well-Known Daughters of Famous Men: Mrs. Clarence H. Mackay," *Pittsburgh Sun*, October 14, 1910, Mackay Family Scrapbooks, reel 7; Wilson, *Harbor Hill*, 42.

5 *Pittsburgh Sun*, October 14, 1910, Mackay Family Scrapbooks, reel 7.

6 Wilson, *Harbor Hill*, 42.

7 Ellin Berlin, *Silver Platter* (New York: Doubleday, 1957), 408.

8 Wilson, *Harbor Hill*, 1, 58, 107–10.

9 Wilson, *Harbor Hill*, 66.

10 Mackay's first two children were girls, Katherine (1899) and Ellin (1903). A third child, John, was born in 1907, after her election; see Wilson, *Harbor Hill*, 69; Elizabeth Frost-Knappman and Kathryn Cullen-DuPont, *Women's Suffrage in America* (New York: Infobase, 2009), 241.

11 "An Interview with Mrs. Clarence Mackay on Woman Suffrage," *Munsey's*, April 1909, Sophia Smith Collection, box 37, folder 7, Smith College.

12 *Nation*, August 10, 1905, 110.

13 Wilson, *Harbor Hill*, 129–30.

14 "Woman's World," *New York Irish American*, October 10, 1908, Mackay Family Scrapbooks, reel 5.

15 "Mrs. Clarence Mackay," *New Idea Magazine*, January 1911, Mackay Family Scrapbooks, reel 7.

16 Mary Chapman and Angela Mills, eds., *Treacherous Texts: U.S. Suffrage Literature* (New Brunswick: Rutgers University Press, 2011), 170.

17 Harriot Stanton Blatch and Alma Lutz, *Challenging Years: The Memoirs of Harriot Stanton Blatch* (New York: Putnam's, 1940), 91–93.

18 Sandra Adickes, *To Be Young Was Very Heaven: Women in New York before the First World War* (New York: St. Martin's, 1997), 84.

19 Ellen Carol DuBois, "Harriot Stanton Blatch and the Transformation of Class Relations among Woman Suffragists," in Dye and Frankel, *Gender, Class, Race, and Reform*, 162–79; see also Mari Jo Buhle, *Women and American Socialism, 1780–1920*, The Working Class in American History (Urbana: University of Illinois Press, 1981), 225–26.

20 DuBois, *Harriot Stanton Blatch*, 110.

21 Blatch and Lutz, *Challenging Years*, 119.

22 Stephen Samuel Wise, *Challenging Years: The Autobiography of Stephen Wise* (New York: Putnam's, 1949), 110.

23 Blatch and Lutz, *Challenging Years*, 117–19.

24 Alice Northrop Snow, *The Story of Helen Gould: Daughter of Jay Gould, Great American* (New York: Revell, 1943), 162.

25 Tim McNeese, *The Robber Barons and the Sherman Antitrust Act: Reshaping American Business* (New York: Infobase, 2009), 49.

26 Earle G. Shettleworth Jr., *Bar Harbor* (Charleston, SC: Arcadia, 2011), 81; Biographical Directory of the U.S. Congress, "Pratt, Ruth Sears Baker," bioguide.congress.gov; *American Gymnasia and Athletic Record*, vol. 2 (1905), 171; "Mrs. Charles Iselin, Turf Figure and Social Leader, Dies at 102," *New York Times*, April 6, 1970; W. A. Swanberg, *Whitney Father, Whitney Heiress* (New York: Scribner's, 1980), 407.

27 "Society for Suffrage," *Baltimore Sun*, November 20, 1908.

28 Alice Blackwell, "State Correspondence," *Woman's Journal*, January 28, 1909.

29 Andrea Moore Kerr, *Lucy Stone: Speaking Out for Equality* (New Brunswick: Rutgers University Press, 1992), 52–55.

30 Blackwell, "State Correspondence."

31 "Mrs. Mackay Pleads for Equal Suffrage," *New York Times*, January 16, 1909, 18.

32 "Society and Woman Suffrage," *New York Times*, January 17, 1909, 10.

33 William Hemmingway, "Campaigning for Equal Franchise," *Harper's Weekly*, March 13, 1909, 15–16.

34 Grace R. Clarke, "Beauty and Fashion Aid Suffrage," *Woman Beautiful*, April 1909, Mackay Family Scrapbooks, reel 6.

35 Hemmingway, "Campaigning for Equal Franchise," 15–16.

36 "Woman Suffrage Made Fashionable," newspaper n/a, December 23, 1908, Abbe Scrapbooks, reel 4.

37 Maud Wood Park, "How I Came to Start in the Business of Being a Reformer," n.d., Edna Lamprey Stantial Papers, MC 733, box 10, folder 20, Schlesinger Library, Radcliffe Institute for Advanced Study, Cambridge, MA.

38 Gillmore to Park, March 29, 1910.

39 "Her Plan to Meet All Suffragettes," *New York Herald*, December 7, 1909, Alva Belmont Scrapbooks, vol. 2.

40 "The Modern Way," *Club Fellow*, November 16, 1910, Mackay Family Scrapbooks, reel 7.

41 "Suffrage Merry War," *Vogue*, September 18, 1909.

42 "Grateful to 'Antis,' Suffrage Cause Indebted to Them, Says Mrs. Mackay," *New York Tribune*, March 12, 1909, Mackay Family Scrapbooks, reel 6.

43 "Mrs. Mackay and Her Suffragettes Told They Must Be Unbearable," *American*, March 12, 1909, Mackay Family Scrapbooks, reel 6.

44 Priyanka Aggarwai, "Fighting for Respect: The Untold Story of Underdogs," *Wharton Journal*, November 27, 2013, http://whartonjournal.com.

45 Hoffert, *Alva Vanderbilt Belmont*, 1–9.

46 Stuart, *Consuelo and Alva Vanderbilt*, 27.

47 Hoffert, *Alva Vanderbilt Belmont*, 10–11; Homberger, *Mrs. Astor's New York*, 270.

48 Belmont Memoir, chap. 4, pp. 5–7, chap. 3, pp. 8–9, Sara Bard Field Papers, in Charles Erskine Scott Wood Papers, mssWD 101 (1), Huntington Library, San Marino, CA.

49 Stuart, *Consuelo and Alva Vanderbilt*, 92.

50 Stephen Birmingham, *America's Secret Aristocracy* (Boston: Little, Brown, 1987), 215.

51 Wayne Craven, *Gilded Mansions: Grand Architecture and High Society* (New York: Norton, 2009), 45.

52 During the 1905 libel trial by *Town Topics* editors against *Colliers*, Belmont testified that in 1899 Mann offered him shares of *Town Topics* stock for $5,000. After Belmont refused, some fifty abusive items about him appeared in the magazine's pages. See Logan, *The Man Who Robbed the Robber Barons*, 164–67.

53 Stuart, *Consuelo and Alva Vanderbilt*, 93–94.

54 Auchincloss, *The Vanderbilt Era*, 49.

55 Amelia Fry, oral history interview with Sara Bard Field, 1959–1963, 291, University of California Suffragist Oral History Project, http://content.cdlib.org; "Colby Comes Out for Suffragettes," *New York Times*, December 17, 1909, 6.

56 Sara Bard Field Papers, mssWD 101 (1).

57 Eleanor Flexner, *Century of Struggle: The Woman's Rights Movement in the United States* (Cambridge: Harvard University Press, 1996), 250; Robert Booth Fowler and Spencer Jones, "Carrie Chapman Catt and the Last Years of the Struggle for Woman Suffrage," in *Votes for Women: The Struggle for Suffrage Revisited*, ed. Jean H. Baker (Oxford: Oxford University Press, 2002), 130–42.

58 Hoffert, *Alva Vanderbilt Belmont*, 73.

59 Preservation Society of Newport County, "Marble House," www.newportmansions.org.

60 Craven, *Gilded Mansions*, 161–63.

61 "Glories of Marble House Attract Many," *New York Times*, August 20, 1909, 7.

62 *New York American*, August 29, 1909, Alva Belmont Scrapbooks, vol. 1.

63 "Sentiment in the cottage colony on the woman suffrage meeting is not altogether favorable, as some of the prominent members are of the opinion the meeting has given Newport altogether too much of the publicity which they do not desire." See "Newport Divides on Suffrage Gathering," *New York Times*, August 24, 1909.

64 "Busy Week for Newport," *Philadelphia Public Ledger*, August 23, 1909, Alva Belmont Scrapbooks, vol. 1.

65 Homberger, *Mrs. Astor's New York*, xiv.

66 "Women of the Four Hundred Are Suffrage Converts," *New York American*, August 30, 1909, Alva Belmont Scrapbooks, vol. 1; *New York World*, September 5, 1909, Alva Belmont Scrapbooks, vol. 1.

67 Daggett, "Suffrage Enters the Drawing Room."

68 Daggett, "Suffrage Enters the Drawing Room."

69 Daggett, "Suffrage Enters the Drawing Room."

70 "Society Meets Suffrage at Mrs. Belmont's Marble House in Newport," *New York World*, August 25, 1909, Alva Belmont Scrapbooks, vol. 1.

71 *Chicago Inter Ocean*, August 26, 1909, 1, Alva Belmont Scrapbooks, vol. 1.

72 Mildred Adams, "Rampant Women," in National American Woman Suffrage Association, *Victory, How Women Won It: A Centennial Symposium, 1840–1940* (New York: Wilson, 1940), 33.

73 *Town Topics*, August 19, 1909, Mackay Family Scrapbooks, reel 6.

74 "Woman's Cause Gives Public Entrance to Marble House Wonderland of Art," *New York Herald*, August 22, 1909, Alva Belmont Scrapbooks, vol. 1.

75 Editorial, *New York Herald*, August 27, 1909.

76 Geidel, "Alva E. Belmont," 116.

77 Hoffert, *Alva Vanderbilt Belmont*, 73.

78 Richard Barry, "A Political Promise from Women," *Pearson's Magazine*, vol. 23, no. 2 (February 1910), 156.

79 Geidel, "Alva E. Belmont," 87.

80 *New York World*, October 25, 1909, Alva Belmont Scrapbooks, vol. 1.

81 "The Green-Eyed Monster," *Washington Times*, December 19, 1909, Alva Belmont Scrapbooks, vol. 2.

82 Alva Belmont Scrapbooks, box 13, Political Equality Association, 1909–1917.

83 Hildegard Hoeller, "Invisible Blackness in Edith Wharton 's Old New York," *African American Review*, vol. 44, nos. 1–2 (Spring–Summer 2011), 49–66.

84 "Negro Women Join in Suffrage Movement," *New York Times*, February 7, 1910, 4.

85 Rosalyn Terborg-Penn, *African American Women in the Struggle for the Vote, 1850–1920* (Bloomington: Indiana University Press, 1998).

86 "Negroes at Suffrage Ball," *New York Times*, April 7, 1911.

87 "Won't Break Color Line," *New York Tribune*, August 21, 1911, Alva Belmont Scrapbooks, vol. 3.

88 "Forbid Suffrage Rally in Apartment," *New York Times*, February 25, 1911, 5, Alva Belmont Scrapbooks, vol. 3.

89 "Negroes Show Little Interest," *New York Tribune*, November 24, 1911, Alva Belmont Scrapbooks, vol. 3.

90 *Louisville Times*, October 14, 1911, Alva Belmont Scrapbooks, vol. 4; "Suffrage Merger," *New York Sun*, November 7, 1911, Alva Belmont Scrapbooks, vol. 4.

CHAPTER 4. A RIVALRY COLLAPSES

1 Laurence Housman quote, Program, Votes for Women Grand Ball and Vaudeville at Patchogue, Long Island, July 30, 1913, Portia Willis Fitzgerald Papers, box 1, folder 22, Sophia Smith Collection; Housman was a founder of the Men's League for Woman's Suffrage in Britain.

2 "Mrs. Mackay Joins Third House," *Chicago Tribune*, March 10, 1909, Mackay Family Scrapbooks, reel 6.

3 "Has Mrs. Mackay Hypnotic Eyes?," *Evening Mail*, March 9, 1909, Mackay Family Scrapbooks, reel 6.

4 *Club Fellow*, April 7, 1909, Mackay Family Scrapbooks, reel 6.

5 "The Clamor of the Women," *New York Times*, February 26, 1909, 6.

6 Theodora Bean, "Statement from Mrs. Mackay," *New York Morning Telegraph*, October 14, 1909, Mackay Family Scrapbooks, reel 6.

7 "Mrs. Mackay Says Dignity Is Best," *Chicago Daily Tribune*, October 14, 1909, Mackay Family Scrapbooks, reel 6.

8 *New York World*, June 16, 1909, Alva Belmont Scrapbooks, vol. 1.

9 Blatch and Lutz, *Challenging Years*, 131.

10 Paula Bartley, *Emmeline Pankhurst* (London: Routledge/Taylor and Francis, 2002), 161–62.

11 Steven C. Hause and Anne R. Kenney, *Women's Suffrage and Social Politics in the French Third Republic* (Princeton: Princeton University Press, 1984), 103–9.

12 Hoffert, *Alva Vanderbilt Belmont*, 75.

13 "For Ballots or a Jail," *Washington Post*, June 19, 1909, Alva Belmont Scrapbooks, vol. 1.

14 "Mrs. O.H.P. Belmont among Militants," *New York Times*, September 19, 1913, 9.

15 Sara Bard Field Papers, mssWD 101 (1).

16 *Syracuse Herald*, May 11, 1913, Alva Belmont Scrapbooks, vol. 7.

17 Interview with Coline Jenkins, May 18, 2014, Greenwich, CT.

18 Princeton University, *General Catalogue of Princeton University, 1746–1906* (1908), 291; Steven A. Riess, *The Sport of Kings and the Kings of Crime: Horse Racing, Politics, and Organized Crime in New York, 1865–1913* (Syracuse: Syracuse University Press, 2011), 303.

19 George Bliss Agnew Papers, box 2, folder 3, and box 3, folder 8, New York Public Library.

20 Letter from Katherine Mackay to Mr. Agnew, December 28, 1909, George Bliss Agnew Papers, box 2, folder 12.

21 "Five Stars Are Now in the Suffrage Flag," *New York Morning Telegraph*, November 11, 1910, Mackay Family Scrapbooks, reel 7.

22 *Washington News*, January 8, 1933, Sara Bard Field Papers, box 183, folder 37.

23 "Mrs. Mackay Pleads for Equal Suffrage."

24 "Wins Suffragists by Her Good Looks," *New York Times*, April 9, 1909, 11.

25 Mercedes de Acosta, *Here Lies the Heart* (New York: Reynal, 1960), 320.

26 One man complained to the *Brooklyn Daily Eagle* that Mackay's foppery was a prima facie bar to politics. "When women cease to encourage the massacre of brooking birds, and the extinction of rare and beautiful varieties, for the barbaric pleasure of decking themselves in the spoils, then men will have more confidence in their ability to frame laws and to use the ballot wisely," he wrote. "Roslyn and Suffrage," *Brooklyn Daily Eagle*, March 6, 1909.

27 *The Club Fellow: The Society Journal of New York and Chicago* (New York: Club Fellow Publishing Company, 1905).

28 "Audacities."

29 "Mrs. Mackay's Office," *New York Tribune*, September 23, 1909, Mackay Family Scrapbooks, reel 6.

30 "Clothes and the Ballot: Frocks Vie with Arguments at Colony Club Meeting," *New York Sun*, April 9, 1909, Mackay Family Scrapbooks, reel 6.

31 "The Modern Way."

32 Max Eastman, *Enjoyment of Living* (New York: Harper, 1948), 306.

33 "Women's Rights," *London Traveler*, April 7, 1909, Mackay Family Scrapbooks, reel 6.

34 Ethel Gross Hopkins Conant Oral History, tape 2, Charles E. Young Research Library, UCLA.

35 Ethel Gross Hopkins Conant Oral History, tape 1.

36 Craven, *Gilded Mansions*, 161–63.

37 Wilson, *Harbor Hill*, 1, 58, ix, 133.

38 *Club Fellow*, March 1, 1911, Mackay Family Scrapbooks, reel 7.

39 "Mrs. Mackay Carries the Olive Branch," *New York World*, September 21, 1909, Mackay Family Scrapbooks, reel 6, and Alva Belmont Scrapbooks, vol. 1.

40 "Mrs. Mackay Silent on Suffrage," *New York Press*, September 21, 1909, Mackay Family Scrapbooks, reel 6.

41 "Gowns Rivals of Suffrage," *New York Globe*, September 16, 1909.

42 "Mrs. Mackay Missed at Suffrage Luncheon," *New York Evening Journal*, September 15, 1909, Mackay Family Scrapbooks, reel 5.

43 "Tiff Rumor Denied," *New York American*, September 20, 1909, Mackay Family Scrapbooks, reel 6.

44 Wilson, *Harbor Hill*, 130.

45 *Club Fellow*, July 20, 1910, Mackay Family Scrapbooks, reel 7.

46 "Mrs. Mackay Quits as Suffragist Head," *Philadelphia Evening Bulletin*, April 13, 1911, Mackay Family Scrapbooks, reel 7.

47 Alva Belmont Scrapbooks, vols. 1–7.

48 Wilson, *Harbor Hill*, 142; see also "$6,000,000 Mackay Home Deeded to Son," *New York Times*, February 21, 1913.

49 "Mrs. Catharine Blake to Visit San Francisco," *Oakland Tribune*, December 20, 1914, 8.

50 "Mackays Are Divorced by Court in Paris," *New York Evening World*, February 18, 1914, 1.

51 Wilson, *Harbor Hill*, 133.

52 Laurence Bergreen, *As Thousands Cheer: The Life of Irving Berlin* (Boston: Da Capo, 1996), 299.

53 "Mrs. Catharine Blake to Visit San Francisco."

54 Theodora Bean, "Unfurl the Flag, On to the Attack," *Morning Telegraph*, June 30, 1909, Mackay Family Scrapbooks, reel 6.

55 "Fashionable Society-Suffragists Fighting among Themselves," *New York American*, April 2, 1911, Mackay Family Scrapbooks, reel 7.

56 "Fight for City Suffrage," *New York Sun*, March 26, 1909, Mackay Family Scrapbooks, reel 6.

57 *Omaha Morning World*, December 31, 1911, Alva Belmont Scrapbooks, vol. 4.

58 *Town Topics*, March 21, 1912, Alva Belmont Scrapbooks, vol. 4.

59 *Milwaukee Wisconsin*, December 20, 1909, Alva Belmont Scrapbooks, vol. 2.

60 "The Lost 1866 Havemeyer House," Daytonian in Manhattan (blog), April 8, 2013, daytoninmanhattan.blogspot.com.

61 "Two Sixteen-Story Buildings Projected in Fifth Avenue's Choice Retail Area," *New York Times*, May 30, 1915.

62 Alan M. Kraut, *Crusaders and Compromisers: Essays on the Relationship of the Antislavery Struggle to the Antebellum Party System* (Westport, CT: Greenwood, 1983), 7; see also David Herbert Donald, "Toward a Reconsideration of Abolitionists," in *Lincoln Reconsidered: Essays on the Civil War Era* (New York: Vintage, 2001), 31–43.

63 Hugh Stevens, *Henry James and Sexuality* (New York: Cambridge University Press, 2008), 27.

64 Preservation Society of Newport County and Tom Gannon, *Newport Mansions* (Newport: Preservation Society of Newport County, 2010), 64.

65 Kerry Segrave, *Women and Smoking in America, 1880–1950* (Jefferson, NC: McFarland, 2005); *Ocala Evening Star*, January 23, 1908, 7.

66 Helen Miller Gould Shepard Papers, box 1, folder 3, New York Historical Society.

67 "Miss Gould to Feed Bowery's Hungry," *New York Times*, January 21, 1913, 6.

68 Kate Chopin, *The Awakening* (Chicago: Stone, 1899), 1.

CHAPTER 5. THE GILDED FACE OF MODERNITY

1 "Society Out Strong for the Suffragettes," *San Francisco Examiner*, February 5, 1910, Mackay Family Scrapbooks, reel 6.

2 Frank W. Hoffman and William G. Bailey, *Fashion and Merchandising Fads* (New York: Psychology Press, 1994), 100.

3 *Chicago Inter Ocean*, August 28, 1895, 8; "The Gibson-Langhorne Wedding," *Staunton (VA) Spectator*, November 6, 1895, 2.

4 James Fox, *Five Sisters: The Langhornes of Virginia* (New York: Simon and Schuster, 2001), 280. Over the next twenty-five years, Irene Gibson would chair the Child Planning and Adoption Committee of New York's State Charities Association, join the Society for Prevention of Cruelty to Children, create a New York branch of the Southern Women's Educational Alliance and, with Anne Vanderbilt and Louisine Havemeyer, help found Big Sisters Inc., which, as one biographer wrote, "worked with the Children's Courts to improve the lives of troubled girls." See Charlie Lawing, "Irene Langhorne Gibson (1873–1956)," *Encyclopedia Virginia*, November 12, 2012, www.encyclopediavirginia.org.

5 Lawing, "Irene Langhorne Gibson."

6 "Society Women Out on Mitchel Carts," *New York Times*, October 23, 1913.

7 Lawing, "Irene Langhorne Gibson."

8 "Suffragists March up 5th Ave. To-Day," *New York Sun*, October 27, 1917, 7.

9 Frances Diodato Bzowski, "Spectacular Suffrage; Or, How Women Came out of the Home and into the Streets and Theaters of New York City to Win the Vote," *New York History* 76, no. 1 (January 1, 1995), 68.

10 Adickes, *To Be Young Was Very Heaven*, 2.

11 Stephen Railton, "At Home around the World," University of Virginia Library, http://twain.lib.virginia.edu.

12 Isadora Duncan, *My Life: Isadora Duncan* (New York: Liveright, 1998), 217.

13 Frederick Jackson Turner, *The Significance of the Frontier in American History* (London: Penguin UK, 2008).

14 Letter to "Dear Mother," October 31, 1915, Minerva Kohlhepp Teichert Papers, Smithsonian Archives of American Art.

15 Rosemary Lévy Zumwalt, *Wealth and Rebellion: Elsie Clews Parsons, Anthropologist and Folklorist* (Urbana: University of Illinois Press, 1992), 17–24.

16 Zumwalt, *Wealth and Rebellion*, 36.

17 Desley Deacon, *Elsie Clews Parsons: Inventing Modern Life* (Chicago: University of Chicago Press, 1997), 17–21.

18 "Dr. Dix on Trial Marriages," *New York Times*, November 18, 1906, 12.

19 Quentin R. Skrabec Jr., *The 100 Most Important American Financial Crises: An Encyclopedia of the Lowest Points in American Economic History* (Santa Barbara, CA: ABC-CLIO, 2014), 106.

20 Henry Wise Miller, *All Our Lives: Alice Duer Miller* (New York: Coward-McCann, 1945), 30.

21 Miller, *All Our Lives*, 8–9; Bergreen, *As Thousands Cheer*, 218; Judith Schwarz, *Radical Feminists of Heterodoxy: Greenwich Village, 1912–1940* (Norwich, VT: New Victoria, 1986), 32–34.

22 Schwarz, *Radical Feminists of Heterodoxy*, 32–34.

23 Bernard Harper Friedman, *Gertrude Vanderbilt Whitney: A Biography* (New York: Doubleday, 1978), 3–5.

24 Kathleen D. McCarthy, *Women's Culture: American Philanthropy and Art, 1830–1930* (Chicago: University of Chicago Press, 1991), 216.

25 Friedman, *Gertrude Vanderbilt Whitney*, 35–38.

26 Clipping, date and newspaper n/a, Edith Shepard Fabbri Papers, folder 6, New York Historical Society.

27 Friedman, *Gertrude Vanderbilt Whitney*, 227.

28 Chopin, *The Awakening*.

29 Eva Ingersoll-Brown, president of the International Child Welfare League, a member of the Society to Prevent Cruelty to Children, and the mother of two, backed a legislative initiative to permit New York physicians and nurses to provide women with birth control information. This burst of outspoken zeal by a member of the *Social Register* set shocked society and prompted the *Herald* to call the idea a "revolt against motherhood." See Helen Todd, "A Revolt against Motherhood," *New York Herald*, March 4, 1917, 4.

30 Edith Wharton, *The House of Mirth*, ed. Jeffrey Meyers (New York: Barnes and Noble, 2004), 1.

31 Edith Wharton, *The House of Mirth* (New York: Charles Scribner's Sons, 1905).

32 E. Digby Baltzell, *The Protestant Establishment: Aristocracy and Caste in America* (New Haven: Yale University Press, 1964), 112–13.

33 Lee, *Edith Wharton*, 172.

34 Deacon, *Elsie Clews Parsons*, 52–56.

35 Deacon, *Elsie Clews Parsons*, 281.

36 Deacon, *Elsie Clews Parsons*, 69; *New York World*, November 22, 1906, 19.

37 "Elsie Clews Parsons," *Encyclopaedia Britannica*, www.britannica.com.

38 Berg, *Kate Remembered*, 44.

39 "Society Roars as Baby Cries in Living Picture," *New York Evening Journal*, January 18, 1911.

40 McCarthy, *Women's Culture*, 216–21.

41 Deacon, *Elsie Clews Parsons*, 13.

42 Friedman, *Gertrude Vanderbilt Whitney*, 5.

43 McCarthy, *Women's Culture*, 217.

44 Oscar Wilde, *A Woman of No Importance: A Play* (London: Methuen, 1908), 111.

45 Frederick Townsend Martin, *The Passing of the Idle Rich* (New York: Doubleday, Page, 1911), 231.

46 Katharina Vester, "Regime Change: Gender, Class and the Invention of Dieting in Post-Bellum America," *Journal of Social History*, Fall 2010, 47.

47 James R. McGovern, "The American Woman's Pre–World War II Freedom in Manners and Morals," *Journal of American History*, vol. 55, no. 2 (September 1968), 327–28.

48 Catherine Gourley, *Gibson Girls and Suffragists: Perceptions of Women from 1900 to 1918* (Minneapolis: Twenty-First Century Books, 2008), 15–17.

49 Lehr, *"King Lehr" and the Gilded Age*, 139.

50 Miller, *All Our Lives*, 23–24.

51 Deacon, *Elsie Clews Parsons*, 20.

52 Marion Elizabeth Rodgers, *Mencken: The American Iconoclast* (New York: Oxford University Press, 2005), 44; Jane Mushabac and Angela Wigan, *A Short and Remarkable History of New York City* (Bronx: Fordham University Press, 1999), 72.

53 Woodhead, *War Paint*, 65–66.

54 Nelly Bly, "Champion of Her Sex: Interview with Susan B. Anthony," *New York World*, February 2, 1896, cited in Jesse J. Gant and Nicholas J. Hoffman, *Wheel Fever: How Wisconsin Became a Great Bicycling State* (Madison: Wisconsin Historical Society, 2013), 210.

55 Montgomery, *Displaying Women*, 2.

56 Hoffert, *Alva Vanderbilt Belmont*, 40–41.

57 "The Persons Interested in the Vanderbilt Case," *New York World*, March 6, 1895, 1.

58 "Mrs. Vanderbilt Free, Granted an Absolute Divorce from Her Husband," *Brooklyn Daily Eagle*, March 6, 1895, 7.

59 Hoffert, *Alva Vanderbilt Belmont*, 42.

60 "Social War at Newport," *New York Times*, July 25, 1908, 1.

61 Davis, *Gilded*, 132.

62 "Newport Women Seek Vote," *Washington Post*, November 19, 1914, 3.

63 "What Is a Shirtwaist?" *The American Experience*, PBS, www.pbs.org.

64 Lumsden, *Inez*, 45.

65 "Miss Morgan Aids Girl Waiststrikers," *New York Times*, December 14, 1909, 1. See also Joseph J. Portanova, "Anne Morgan and the Shirtwaist Strike of 1909–1910," Open Source, 2010.

66 Laura Bufano Edge, *We Stand as One: The International Ladies Garment Workers' Strike, New York 1909* (Minneapolis: Twenty-First Century Books, 2011), 67; Hoffert, *Alva Vanderbilt Belmont*, 79.

67 David von Drehle, *Triangle: The Fire That Changed America* (New York: Atlantic Monthly Press, 2003), 50.

68 "Vassar Girl Is Arrested," *Chicago Daily Tribune*, December 16, 1909.

69 DuBois, "Harriot Stanton Blatch and the Transformation of Class Relations," 173.

70 Von Drehle, *Triangle*, 76; "Mrs. Belmont in Night Court," *Baltimore Sun*, December 20, 1909, 1.

71 *San Francisco Call, Syracuse Post Standard, New York Sun, Brooklyn Daily Eagle, Baltimore Sun*, December 20, 1909.

72 Edge, *We Stand as One*, 69.
73 "Colony Club Purses Open," *New York Sun*, December 16, 1909, 9.
74 Meredith Tax, *The Rising of the Women: Feminist Solidarity and Class Conflict, 1880–1917* (New York: Monthly Review Press, 1980), 216.
75 Von Drehle, *Triangle*, 73.
76 Nancy Schrom Dye, *As Equals and as Sisters: Feminism, the Labor Movement, and the Women's Trade Union League of New York* (Columbia: University of Missouri Press, 1980), 92–93.
77 O'Neill, *Everyone Was Brave*.
78 *Call*, December 16, 1909, cited in von Drehle, *Triangle*, 77.
79 Buhle, *Women and American Socialism*, 225–26.
80 See Diane Kirkby, "Class, Gender and the Perils of Philanthropy: The Story of *Life and Labor* and Labor Reform in the Women's Trade Union League," *Journal of Women's History*, vol. 4, no. 2 (September 1, 1992), 37–51; Annelise Orleck, *Common Sense and a Little Fire: Women and Working-Class Politics in the United States, 1900–1965*, Gender and American Culture (Chapel Hill: University of North Carolina Press, 1995); and Tax, *The Rising of the Women*.
81 "As Seen by Him," *Vogue Magazine*, January 8, 1910.
82 "The Needs of Working Girls," *New York World*, May 4, 1908, Mackay Family Scrapbooks, reel 5.
83 "Banker's Wife Dines Labor Delegates," *New York Times*, August 19, 1909.
84 Smith, *Elsie de Wolfe*, xi.
85 "Woman Suffrage at Marble House 'For the Masses,'" *New York World*, August 24, 1909, Alva Belmont Scrapbooks, vol. 1.
86 Fox, *Five Sisters*, 310.
87 "Mere Men Are Invited," *Brooklyn Daily Eagle*, April 3, 1910.

CHAPTER 6. MERE MEN

1 One [Raymond Brown], "How It Feels to Be the Husband of a Suffragette," *Everybody's Magazine*, vol. 30, no. 1 (January 1914), 63.
2 "Funeral Services Held over Body of Col. Astor," *Atlanta Constitution*, May 5, 1912, 2.
3 "Col. Astor at Rest in Family Vault," *New York Times*, May 5, 1912, 4; "How Col. Astor Died to Let Woman Live," *New York Times*, April 19, 1912, 7.
4 Larry Stanford, *Wicked Newport. Sordid Stories from the City by the Sea* (Charleston, SC: History Press, 2008), 78.
5 Steven Biel, *Down with the Old Canoe: A Cultural History of the Titanic Disaster*, updated ed. (New York: Norton, 2012), 30.
6 "20,000 Women in Suffrage March, 500,000 Look On," *New York Times*, May 5, 1912, 1.
7 Walter Lord, *The Good Years: From 1900 to the First World War* (New York: Harper, 1960), 272.
8 Biel, *Down with the Old Canoe*, 103–5.
9 Blatch and Lutz, *Challenging Years*, 132–33.
10 Denise H. Sutton, *Globalizing Ideal Beauty: How Female Copywriters of the J. Walter Thompson Advertising Agency Redefined Beauty for the Twentieth Century* (Basingstoke, UK: Palgrave Macmillan, 2009), 40–41; Adickes, *To Be Young Was Very Heaven*, 6.

11 Susan A. Glenn, *Female Spectacle: The Theatrical Roots of Modern Feminism* (Cambridge: Harvard University Press, 2000), 147.

12 "Why Suffragists Will Parade on Saturday," *New York Tribune*, May 12, 1912, 1.

13 "Men in Line Braved Jeers," *New York Times*, May 5, 1912.

14 Stephen Wise diary, May 4, 1912, series 1, Special Collections, Gelman Library, George Washington University.

15 Letter to "Dear Mother."

16 Stephen Wise diary, May 4, 1912.

17 George Middleton, *These Things Are Mine: The Autobiography of a Journeyman Playwright* (New York: Macmillan, 1947), 124.

18 One, "How It Feels to Be the Husband of a Suffragette," 63.

19 *New York Tribune*, May 5, 1912, cited in Harriet Burton Laidlaw, *James Lees Laidlaw, 1868–1932* (New York: Private printing, 1932), 93.

20 "Rush to Sign Suffragist Enlistment," newspaper, date n/a, Harriot Stanton Blatch Scrapbooks, reel 1, Library of Congress.

21 Harriet Burton Wright Laidlaw Papers, A65, box 14, Schlesinger Library.

22 Sherna Berger Gluck, *From Parlor to Prison: Five American Suffragists Talk about Their Lives* (New York: Vintage, 1976), 204.

23 Laidlaw, *James Lees Laidlaw*, 11–12.

24 Laidlaw Correspondence, box 8, folder 10, Sophia Smith Collection.

25 Laidlaw, *James Lees Laidlaw*, 20–38.

26 Michael S. Kimmel and Thomas E. Mosmiller, *Against the Tide: "Pro-Feminist Men" in the United States: 1776- 1990, a Documentary History* (Boston: Beacon, 1992); Raymond Matthew Ortiz, "Ladies and *Gentle* Men: The Men's League for Woman Suffrage and Its Liberation of the Male Identity" (Ph.D. diss., California State University, Fullerton, 2014).

27 Kevin F. White, "Men Supporting Women: A Study of Men Associated with the Women's Suffrage Movement in Britain and America, 1909–1920," *Maryland Historian*, vol. 18 (Spring 1987), 45–49.

28 Kimmel and Mosmiller, *Against the Tide*, 28–30.

29 Avivah Wittenberg-Cox, "Gender at Work Is Not a Woman's Issue," *Harvard Business Review*, November 17, 2015.

30 "The Uprising of the Women," *New York Times*, May 5, 1912, 14.

31 "Women Take Front Rank in National Campaign Ranks," *Washington Post*, August 11, 1912, 6.

32 Robert P. J. Cooney Jr., "California Women Suffrage Centennial," California Secretary of State website, http://www.sos.ca.gov; Jo Freeman, "The Rise of Political Woman in the Election of 1912," www.uic.edu.

33 Burton J. Hendrick, "Recall in Seattle," *McClure's Magazine*, October 1911, 647.

34 Hendrick, "Recall in Seattle," 662.

35 "Mrs. Belmont Quit Suffragists? No!," *New York Times*, February 12, 1911, 10.

36 Fanny Villard diary, January 26, 1909, Fanny Villard Papers, series 901.

37 Letter from Villard to Shaw, January 7, 1908, letter from Shaw to Villard, February 6, 1908, Oswald Garrison Villard Papers, Correspondence, 3494, Houghton Library, Harvard University, cited in Ortiz, "Ladies and *Gentle* Men," 32 33.

38 Wise, *Challenging Years*, 86–94.

39 "Churches Thronged for Thanksgiving," *New York Times*, November 26, 1909, 2.

40 "Well-Known Men Advocate It," *New York Times*, February 21, 1909, p. SM2, also in Miller NAWSA Suffrage Scrapbooks, 1897–1911, scrapbook 7, p. 94, Library of Congress.

41 Max Eastman, "Early History of the Men's League," *Woman Voter*, vol. 2 (October 1912), 17–18.

42 Steven Biel and Rozalina Ryvkina, *Independent Intellectuals in the United States, 1910–1945* (New York: New York University Press, 1995), 55; Kimmel and Mosmiller, *Against the Tide*, 37.

43 Max Eastman, "Is Woman Suffrage Important?," *North American Review*, January 1911, 62; see also "Women at Albany, Big Mass Rally," *New York Tribune*, February 17, 1910, 2.

44 Letter from Oswald Garrison Villard to Anna Howard Shaw, January 7, 1908, Oswald Garrison Villard Papers, Correspondence, 3494.

45 "Charles Burlingham Dies at 100," *New York Times*, May 26, 1914.

46 Eastman, "Early History of the Men's League," 17–18.

47 Finding Aid, City Club of New York Papers, New York Public Library.

48 Richard Welling, *As the Twig Is Bent* (New York: Putnam's, 1942), 65.

49 Welling, *As the Twig Is Bent*, 73; Letters of the City Club, 1907–1908, City Club of New York Papers, box 1, folder 1.

50 Kimmel and Mosmiller, *Against the Tide*, 27; Jill Lepore, *The Secret History of Wonder Woman* (New York: Knopf Doubleday, 2014); Robert Cooney, *Winning the Vote: The Triumph of the American Woman Suffrage Movement* (Half Moon Bay, CA: American Graphic Press, 2005), 213.

51 For 1915 letterhead, see letter from James Lees Laidlaw to Henry Kaufman, April 23, 1915, Harriet Burton Wright Laidlaw Papers, folder 124; for the league's constitution, see also Helen Brewster Owens Papers, folder 93, Schlesinger Library.

52 Mary Gray Peck, *Carrie Chapman Catt: A Biography* (New York: Wilson, 1944), 231.

53 Elizabeth Cady Stanton et al., *History of Woman Suffrage*, vol. 5, *1900–1920* (New York: Little and Ives, 1922), 484.

54 Middleton, *These Things Are Mine*, 120.

55 Middleton, *These Things Are Mine*, 125–29.

56 Miller, *All Our Lives*, 30.

57 Miller, *All Our Lives*, 89.

58 George Creel, *Rebel at Large: Recollections of Fifty Crowded Years* (New York: Putnam's, 1947), 144–45.

59 Harriet Burton Wright Laidlaw Papers, box 7, folder 123.

60 "Suffrage Luncheon Wins $50,000 Fund," *New York Times*, May 9, 1915, C3.

61 "Malone Weds, Sails for Europe Today," *New York Times*, December 10, 1921, 4.

62 A. Scott Berg, *Wilson* (New York: Simon and Schuster, 2013), 490.

63 "'Big Bill' Edwards for Malone's Post," *New York Sun*, September 9, 1917, 6.

64 "'Big Bill' Edwards for Malone's Post."

65 "Hardware Dealer Married Malone," *New York Times*, December 11, 1921.

66 Kimmel and Mosmiller, *Against the Tide*, 31.

67 Hoffert, *Alva Vanderbilt Belmont*, 187.

68 Harriet Burton Wright Laidlaw Papers, box 7, folder 134.

69 "These Men Ready to Give Up Seats," *Brooklyn Daily Eagle*, June 10, 1913, 7.

70 "Ostentatious Gallantry," *Brooklyn Life*, July 26, 1913, 9.

71 "Women's Clubs," *Brooklyn Life*, April 12, 1913, 22.

72 "Mere Man of Suffrage," *New York Telegram*, November 8, 1912.

CHAPTER 7. THE TACTICAL TURN

1 Maroula Joannou and June Purvis, eds., *The Women's Suffrage Movement: New Feminist Perspectives* (Manchester, UK: Manchester University Press, 1998), 1.

2 "Suffragettes Hiss Taft, Their Guest," *New York Times*, April 15, 1910, 1.

3 "President Hissed by Woman Suffragists for Attacking Their Claim to the Ballot," *Syracuse Post-Standard*, April 15, 1910, 1.

4 Arnaldo Testi, "The Gender of Reform Politics: Theodore Roosevelt and the Culture of Masculinity," *Journal of American History*, vol. 81, no. 4 (March 1, 1995), 1509–33.

5 Julia Swindells, *The Uses of Autobiography* (New York: Taylor and Francis, 2014), 36–37.

6 Cooney, *Winning the Vote*, 125.

7 "The Sowing of Bad Seed," *Vogue*, vol. 35, no. 14 (May 15, 1910), 13.

8 Emmeline Pankhurst, *My Own Story* (London: Eveleigh Nash, 1914).

9 Alice Stone Blackwell, "The Suffragette Riots," letter to editor, *New York Times*, December 20, 1910, 12.

10 "Mob After Women: English Suffragettes in Peril from Dublin Crowd," *Washington Post*, July 20, 1912, 1; "Suffragettes Ply Torch," *Washington Post*, February 21, 1913, 5; "Suffragette Bomb," *Washington Post*, February 20, 1913, 1.

11 Krista Cowman, *Women of the Right Spirit: Paid Organisers of the Women's Social and Political Union (WSPU), 1904–18* (Manchester, UK: Manchester University Press, 2007), 178.

12 Constance Rover, *Women's Suffrage and Party Politics in Britain, 1866–1914* (London: Routledge and Kegan Paul, 1967), 87.

13 Elizabeth Crawford, *The Women's Suffrage Movement: A Reference Guide, 1866–1928* (London: Routledge, 1999), 452.

14 Laura E. Nym Mayhall, *The Militant Suffrage Movement: Citizenship and Resistance in Britain, 1860–1930* (Oxford, UK: Oxford University Press, 2003).

15 Judith Apter Klinghoffer and Lois Elkis, "'The Petticoat Electors': Women's Suffrage in New Jersey, 1776–1807," *Journal of the Early Republic*, vol. 12, no. 2 (Summer 1992), 159–93.

16 Michael McGerr, "Political Style and Women's Power, 1830–1930," *Journal of American History*, vol. 77, no. 3 (December 1990), 869.

17 Margaret Mary Finnegan, *Selling Suffrage: Consumer Culture and Votes for Women* (New York: Columbia University Press, 1999).

18 In Britain, Millicent Fawcett, president of the National Union of Women's Suffrage Societies, a far larger organization than the Women's Social and Political Union, likewise embraced the new science of advertising. As one scholar noted, British suffrage leaders were the first to "exploit new publicity methods made possible by the rise of national, daily, penny and halfpenny newspapers," the first to turn an advertising poster "into a new political instrument, and the first to develop a pictorial rhetoric which drew on but also challenged the terms of bourgeois Edwardian femininity." See Lisa Tickner, *The Spectacle of Women: Imagery of the Suffrage Campaign, 1907–14* (Chicago: University of Chicago Press, 1988), xii.

19 "Reminiscences of Frances Perkins: Oral History, 1955," 194–95, Columbia Center for Oral History, Columbia University.

20 Belle Fligelman Winestine, "Mother Was Shocked," *Montana: The Magazine of Western History*, vol. 24, no. 3 (Summer 1974), 73.

21 Gluck, *From Parlor to Prison*, 217–19.

22 "Women Press Agents," letter to the editor, *New York Times*, May 3, 1913.

23 "Mere Men Couldn't Stop 500 Women 'Voting,' " *New York Times*, November 7, 1906, 9.

24 David Huyssen, *Progressive Inequality* (Cambridge: Harvard University Press, 2014); Bzowski, "Spectacular Suffrage," 68.

25 Thomas J. Jablonsky, "Female Opposition: The Anti-Suffrage Campaign," in Baker, *Votes for Women*, 121.

26 Letter from Mrs. George Phillips, secretary of the New York State Association Opposed to Woman Suffrage, to Edward Dreier, president of the Brooklyn Woman Suffrage Party, October 29, 1917, Dreier Papers, box 7, folder 9, Sophia Smith Collection.

27 "Suffrage on Parade, Husband Pleads, but Mrs. Richard Stevens Won't March," *New York Tribune*, May 5, 1911, Mackay Family Scrapbooks, reel 7.

28 Blatch and Lutz, *Challenging Years*, 130.

29 "Franchise Society Loses Mrs. R. Stevens," *New York Times*, May 5, 1911, Mackay Family Scrapbooks, reel 7.

30 "With Missing Mr. Theodore Roosevelt, Who Declined with Thanks, the Suffragists Will Have a Great Parade," *New York World*, May 4, 1912.

31 Allen Churchill, *The Upper Crust: An Informal History of New York's Highest Society* (Englewood Cliffs, NJ: Prentice-Hall, 1970), 226.

32 *Town Topics*, May 11, 1911, Mackay Family Scrapbooks, reel 7.

33 Lehr, *"King Lehr" and the Gilded Age*, 222.

34 DuBois, *Harriot Stanton Blatch*, 142.

35 "Suffrage Army Out on Parade," *New York Times*, May 5, 1912, 1.

36 Lehr, *"King Lehr" and the Gilded Age*, 222–23.

37 Manning, *Ladies Now and Then*, 187.

38 "Home Cooking Making Converts to Woman Suffrage," *New York Sun*, January 22, 1911, Alva Belmont Scrapbooks, vol. 3.

39 "Suffragist Enjoyed Prize Fight and Didn't Mind Hooting She Got," *New York World*, July 23, 1915, Abbe Scrapbooks, reel 2.

40 Alice Duer Miller, *Are Women People?* (New York: Doran, 1915); see also the e-book, available at www.gutenberg.org.

41 Carolyn Christensen Nelson, ed., *Literature of the Women's Suffrage Campaign in England* (Toronto: Broadview, 2004), 201.

42 "Hello! Do You Favor Suffrage? 'Yes' Say 75 Per Cent," *New York Sun*, July 30, 1915, Abbe Scrapbooks, reel 2.

43 "Anti-Suffrage President Criticises [*sic*] Phone Stunt," *New York World*, July 31, 1915, Abbe Scrapbooks, reel 2.

44 "Suffs' Home Food Pleases Wall Street; Brokers Listen Attentively to Talks," *New York Sun*, September 16, 1915, Abbe Scrapbooks, reel 2.

45 "Suffrage Leaders Get Their Innings," *New York Times*, May 19, 1915, 5.

46 Heywood Broun, "Suffragists See Cubs Shut Out the Giants," *New York Tribune*, May 19, 1915, 12.

47 De Acosta, *Here Lies the Heart*, 85–86.

48 William Allen Rogers, "The Smooch versus the Harangue," *Van Norden Magazine*, February 1910, reprinted in the *New York Herald*. *Van Norden* was published from 1906 to March 1910; see "Van Norden's Quits after $265,000 Loss," *New York Times*, March 3, 1910, 3.

49 DuBois, *Harriot Stanton Blatch*, 106.

50 Nancy F. Cott, *The Grounding of Modern Feminism* (New Haven: Yale University Press, 1987), 27.

51 James A. Edgerton, "The Advance of Woman Suffrage," *New York Star*, September 6, 1909, Alva Belmont Scrapbooks, vol. 1.

52 Elisabeth Griffith, *In Her Own Right: The Life of Elizabeth Cady Stanton* (London: Oxford University Press, 1984), 145.

53 Agnes E. Ryan, *The Torch Bearer: A Look Forward and Back at the "Woman's Journal," the Organ of the Woman's Movement* (Boston: Woman's Journal and Suffrage News, 1916), 42.

54 Finnegan, *Selling Suffrage*, 111.

55 "Suffragist Has Caused a Row," *Scranton (PA) Truth*, May 26, 1910, 14.

56 "Mrs. Mulliner Draws Some Biting Retorts," newspaper n/a, April 25, 1910, Mackay Family Scrapbooks, reel 7.

57 *Washington Post*, January 16, 1911, 9; see also "Suffragettes Urged to Dress Well," *New York Press*, January 15, 1911, Alva Belmont Scrapbooks, vol. 3.

58 Some accounts suggest that at the 1912 parade, women wore red lipstick, a still-controversial act of middle-class defiance. See Woodhead, *War Paint*, 98; and Madeleine Marsh, *Compacts and Cosmetics: Beauty from Victorian Times to the Present Day* (Barnsley, South Yorkshire: Pen and Sword, 2009), 48. There is no mention of this in the newspapers or magazines available through library databases, the memoirs of Blatch, Alva Belmont's unpublished memoirs, or the scholarship of Cooney, DuBois, Flexner, Montgomery, and others.

59 Alfred Allan Lewis and Constance Woodworth, *Miss Elizabeth Arden* (New York: Coward, McCann and Geoghegan, 1972), 60–61. See also Linda M. Scott, *Fresh Lipstick: Redressing Fashion and Feminism* (New York: Palgrave Macmillan, 2005), 135; and Woodhead, *War Paint*, 97–98.

60 Allison Giffen and June Hopkins, eds., *Jewish First Wife, Divorced: The Correspondence of Ethel Gross and Harry Hopkins* (Lanham, MD: Lexington, 2003), 94.

61 "Our Suffrage Movement Is Flirtation on a Big Scale." See also letters to the editor about the comment, including "Smiles Mrs. Dodge Noticed"; and "Suffragists' Appeal."

62 "De Forest Blames Suffrage," *New York Times*, October 19, 1911, 9.

63 Kristie Miller, *Ruth Hanna McCormick: A Life in Politics, 1880–1944* (Albuquerque: University of New Mexico Press, 1992), 94.

64 "Mrs. M'Cormick to Quit Cause . . . He Puts Foot Down," newspaper n/a, September 24, 1914, Abbe Scrapbooks, reel 3.

65 "Baby Better Than Votes," *New Castle (PA) News*, September 26, 1914, 7; "Her Baby Comes First," *Bismarck (ND) Tribune*, September 26, 1914, 4.

66 Iphigene Ochs Sulzberger and Susan W. Dryfoos, *Iphigene: My Life and the New York Times; The Memoirs of Iphigene Ochs Sulzberger as Written by Her Granddaughter Susan W. Dryfoos* (New York: Times Books, 1981), 72.

67 "Clark Declares for Suffrage," *New York Times*, June 28, 1914.

68 Resa Willis, *Mark and Livy: The Love Story of Mark Twain and the Woman Who Almost Tamed Him* (New York: Routledge, 2013), 74–75.

69 Melvin I. Urofsky, *A Voice That Spoke for Justice: The Life and Times of Stephen S. Wise* (Albany: State University of New York Press, 1982), 77.

70 Joyce Antler, *The Journey Home* (New York: Simon and Schuster, 2010), 66.

71 "Woman Routs Man in Suffrage Debate," *New York American*, January 29, 1909, Nathan Papers, reel 1, Schlesinger Library.

72 Antler, *The Journey Home*, 55.

73 John Taliaferro, *All the Great Prizes: The Life of John Hay, from Lincoln to Roosevelt* (New York: Simon and Schuster, 2013), 13.

74 "Women Begin Tour of Land for Hughes," *New York Times*, October 3, 1916, 10.

75 Benjamin, *A History of the Anti-Suffrage Movement*, 199.

76 "Letters," *New York Times*, March 16, 1918, 14.

77 Anne Marie Nicolosi, "'The Most Beautiful Suffragette': Inez Milholland and the Political Currency of Beauty," *Journal of the Gilded Age and Progressive Era*, vol. 6, no. 3 (July 2007), 286–309.

78 Nicolosi, "'The Most Beautiful Suffragette,'" 298.

79 Eastman, *Enjoyment of Living*, 320; Cooney, *Remembering Inez*, 14.

80 "Reminiscences of Frances Perkins," 191.

81 Letter from Curtis Campaigne to My Dear Miss Milholland, March 24, 1912, Inez Milholland Papers, reel 2, folder 27, Schlesinger Library.

82 *New York Telegraph*, October 25, 1910, Alva Belmont Scrapbooks, vol. 3.

83 Finnegan, *Selling Suffrage*, 100.

CHAPTER 8. THE GREAT WARS

1 "Men of New York, Cast Your Vote for Women!," advertisement, *New York World*, October 31, 1917, 10.

2 "What a Woman Marcher Saw in the Big Suff Parade," *Brooklyn Daily Eagle*, October 28, 1917, 5.

3 Katrina Ely (Tiffany) Alumna File (12H), Special Collections Department, Bryn Mawr College Library.

4 Scrapbook "Suffrage Education," Woman Suffrage and Women's Rights Collection, folder 8.40, vol. 1, Vassar Library; Memorabilia Collection, 105.1.6, carton 1, tray 1, Property of Miss Elsie W. Coolidge, Class of 1895, Schlesinger Library.

5 One of the Marchers, "How It Seemed to March in the Suffrage Parade," *Outlook*, vol. 111 (1915), 553–54.

6 Marjorie Dorman, "Suffragists Traitors to Democracy," *Woman's Protest*, vol. 8, no. 2 (December 1915), 6.

7 "Suffrage Banners Torn to Threads," *Chillicothe (MO) Constitution-Tribune*, June 21, 1917, 2.

8 Joyce Blackwell, *No Peace without Freedom: Race and the Women's International League for Peace and Freedom, 1915–1975* (Carbondale: Southern Illinois University Press, 2004), 39.

9 James M. Volo, *A History of War Resistance in America* (Westport, CT: ABC-CLIO/ Greenwood, 2010), 321.

10 "The Woman's Parade," *Woman Citizen*, September 29, 1917.

11 Gertrude Foster Brown, "Suffrage and Music—My First Eighty Years," unpublished memoir, Gertrude Foster Brown Papers, 1v, 171, Schlesinger Library.

12 "The Woman's Parade," *Woman Citizen*, November 3, 1917.

13 "20,000 March in Suffrage Line," *New York Times*, October 28, 1917, 1.

14 John C. Broad, "The Lady from Montana," *Montana: The Magazine of Western History*, vol. 17, no. 3 (Summer 1967), 125.

15 Norma Smith, *Jeannette Rankin, America's Conscience* (Helena: Montana Historical Society, 2002), 84.

16 Smith, *Jeannette Rankin*, 105–6.

17 James J. Lopach and Jean A. Luckowski, *Jeannette Rankin: A Political Woman* (Boulder: University Press of Colorado, 2005), 6.

18 Cynthia A. Julian, "Visuality in Woman Suffrage Discourse and the Construction of Jeannette Rankin as National Symbol of Enfranchised American Womanhood" (M.A. thesis, Empire State College, State University of New York, 2011), 119.

19 Woodrow Wilson, War Messages, 65th Cong., 1st Sess., Senate doc. no. 5, serial no. 7264, Washington, D.C., 1917; pp. 3–8, passim.

20 Hannah Josephson, *Jeannette Rankin: First Lady in Congress* (Indianapolis: Bobbs-Merrill, 1974), 76; see also Smith, *Jeannette Rankin*, 127.

21 Winestine, "Mother Was Shocked," 75.

22 Lopach and Luckowski, *Jeannette Rankin*, 148–49.

23 "Miss Rankin Votes 'No' on War Resolution: Only Woman in Congress in Collapse as She Decides," *Chicago Daily Tribune*, April 6, 1917, 1.

24 Ronald Schaffer, "Jeannette Rankin, Progressive-Isolationist" (Ph.D. diss., Princeton University, May 1959), 85.

25 Schaffer, "Jeannette Rankin," 86.

26 Smith, *Jeannette Rankin*, 112.

27 "Suffrage Leaders Pardon Miss Rankin," *New York Times*, April 7, 1917.

28 Donna Hightower-Langston, *A to Z of American Women Leaders and Activists* (New York: Infobase, 2002), 181.

29 Belinda A. Stillion Southard, *Militant Citizenship: Rhetorical Strategies of the National Woman's Party, 1913–1920* (College Station: Texas A&M University Press, 2011), 145, discloses that Edith Galt Wilson called the picketers "disgusting creatures" and "detestable." See also Phyllis Lee Levin, *Edith and Woodrow: The Wilson White House* (New York: Simon and Schuster, 2002), 181; Levin reports that both Wilsons were repelled by the picketers, and that Edith chose not to vote in 1920.

30 "'Silent Sentinels' Picketed Near White House," *Chanute (KS) Daily Tribune*, January 10, 1917, 1; Inez Haynes Irwin, *The Story of Alice Paul and the National Women's Party* (Fairfax, VA: Denlingers', 1977), 203.

31 Doris Stevens, *Jailed for Freedom* (New York: Boni and Liveright, 1920), 67.

32 Linda J. Lumsden, *Rampant Women: Suffragists and the Right of Assembly* (Knoxville: University of Tennessee Press, 1997), 125.

33 Kathlyn Gay, *American Dissidents: An Encyclopedia of Activists, Subversives, and Prisoners of Conscience* (Santa Barbara, CA: ABC-CLIO, 2012), 479.

34 Stevens, *Jailed for Freedom*, v.

35 "Pickets Are Praised," *New York Times*, December 10, 1917, 13.

36 "Call Prison Special Democracy Limited," *New York Times*, January 27, 1919, 13; "In re: National Women's Party Organization—The 'Prison Special,'" report, Los Angeles, March 5, 1919, FBI File OG 8000–25035, RG 65, Investigative Case Files of the Bureau of Investigation, 1908–1922, roll 364, National Archives and Records Administration.

37 Stevens, *Jailed for Freedom*, 200, quotes "a successful young Harvard engineer as telling her, 'I don't believe you realize how much men objected to your picketing the White House.'"

38 "Women Who Injure Their Own Case," *Baltimore Sun*, February 12, 1917, 6.

39 "Wrong Method of Pleading Their Cause," *Boston Daily Globe*, June 21, 1917.

40 Beth Behn, "Woodrow Wilson's Conversion Experience: The President and the Federal Woman Suffrage Amendment" (Ph.D. diss., University of Massachusetts, Amherst, 2012), 166.

41 Linda Ford, *Iron-Jawed Angels: The Suffrage Militancy of the National Woman's Party, 1912–1920* (Lanham, MD: University Press of America, 1991), 114, fn 3.

42 Ford, *Iron-Jawed Angels*, 127.

43 Katherine H. Adams and Michael L. Keene, *Alice Paul and the American Suffrage Campaign* (Urbana: University of Illinois Press, 2007), 171.

44 "Resent Pickets 'Disloyalty,'" *New York Times*, June 23, 1917.

45 Ford, *Iron-Jawed Angels*, 157.

46 Blatch and Lutz, *Challenging Years*, 260.

47 Aline B. Saarinen, *The Proud Possessors: The Lives, Times, and Tastes of Some Adventurous American Art Collectors* (New York: Random House, 1958), 152.

48 Ford, *Iron-Jawed Angels*, 97.

49 Katherine H. Adams and Michael L. Keene, *After the Vote Was Won: The Later Achievements of Fifteen Suffragists* (New York: McFarland, 2010), 40–41.

50 Louisine Havemeyer, "The Suffrage Torch: Memories of a Militant," *Scribner's Magazine*, vol. 71 (May 1922), 529.

51 Saarinen, *The Proud Possessors*, 167.

52 Frank Arthur Vanderlip, *From Farm Boy to Financier* (New York: Appleton-Century, 1935), 154.

53 Adams and Keene, *After the Vote Was Won*, 39–40.

54 Marilynn Johnson and Michael John Burlingham, *Louis Comfort Tiffany: Artist for the Ages* (New York: Scala, 2005), 34; letter from Aileen Tone to Dorothy Warren, February 27, 1957, Ruth Draper Papers, box 7, New York Historical Society.

55 Saarinen, *The Proud Possessors*, 149–56.

56 Frances Weitzenhoffer, *The Havemeyers: Impressionism Comes to America* (New York: Abrams, 1993), 195.

57 Louisine Waldron Elder Havemeyer, *Sixteen to Sixty: Memoirs of a Collector* (New York: Metropolitan Museum of Art, 1961), 279.

58 Havemeyer, "The Suffrage Torch," 530–34.

59 Louisine Havemeyer, "The Prison Special: Memories of a Militant," *Scribner's*, vol. 71 (June 1922), 663–70.

60 Maud Wood Park, *Front Door Lobby* (Boston: Beacon, 1960), 233.

61 Havemeyer, "The Prison Special," 672–76.

62 "Armory Too Small for Suffrage Ball," *New York Tribune*, January 12, 1913, 2; "Freed Women Pickets Suing District for $400,000," *Pittsburgh Daily Post*, December 3, 1917, 5.

63 Stevens, *Jailed for Freedom*, 205.

64 "Move Militants from Workhouse," *New York Times*, November 25, 1917, 6.

65 "Mrs. J. W. Brannan Dead Here at 82," *New York Times*, November 15, 1936, 9.

66 Stevens, *Jailed for Freedom*, 365.

67 Ford, *Iron-Jawed Angels*, 97; Stevens, *Jailed for Freedom*, 367.

68 "Suffrage and Sedition," *Masses* 9 (August 1917), 42.

69 "20,000 March in Suffrage Line," *New York Times*, October 28, 1917, 1.

70 "25,000 Suffs Win Cheers in Parade," *Brooklyn Daily Eagle*, October 28, 1917, 5.

71 "Mrs. Blatch Pours Out Wrath on Root," *New York Times*, November 3, 1915.

72 DuBois, *Harriot Stanton Blatch*, 180; Harriot Stanton Blatch, *Mobilizing Woman-Power* (New York: Woman's Press, 1918), 34.

73 National American Woman Suffrage Association, *Victory, How Women Won It*, 115.

74 Brown, "Suffrage and Music," 165.

75 Blatch and Lutz, *Challenging Years*, 217.

76 "State Suffragists Plan 1917 Fight," *New York Times,* November 22, 1916, cited in Kathryn M. Brown, "The Education of the Woman Citizen, 1917–1918" (master's thesis, Bowling Green State University, 2010), 25.

77 Adickes, *To Be Young Was Very Heaven*, 91.

78 Brown, "Suffrage and Music," 168.

79 Jacqueline Van Voris, *Carrie Chapman Catt: A Public Life* (New York: Feminist Press, 1996), 143.

80 Brown, "Suffrage and Music," 168.

81 "Pilgrims for Peace to Visit Congress," *New York Times*, February 9, 1917.

82 "To the Voters," Scrapbook, Susan B. Anthony Ephemera Collection, Huntington Library.

83 Peter H. Hare, *A Woman's Quest for Science: Portrait of Anthropologist Elsie Clews Parsons* (Amherst, NY: Prometheus, 1985), 108–17.

84 Schwarz, *Radical Feminists of Heterodoxy*, 43.

85 Goodier, *No Votes for Women*, 93.

86 Susan Goodier, "Anti-Suffragists," *New York State Archives*, Fall 2007, 24.

87 Goodier, *No Votes for Women*, 75.

88 Alice Hill Chittenden, "Woman's Service or Woman Suffrage," *Woman's Protest*, vol. 11, no. 1 (May 1917).

89 Goodier, *No Votes for Women*, 93–94.

90 Christine A. Lunardini and Thomas J. Knock, "Woodrow Wilson and Woman Suffrage: A New Look," *Political Science Quarterly*, vol. 95, no. 4 (Winter 1980–81), 663.

91 Vira Whitehouse Papers, 15f, Schlesinger Library

92 "The Woman Suffrage Amendment," *New York Times*, November 3, 1917, 14.

93 "Man Suffrage for War," *New York Times*, November 2, 1917, 14.

94 Brown, "Suffrage and Music," 174.

CHAPTER 9. WHO WON SUFFRAGE?

1 John Lukacs, *Historical Consciousness: The Remembered Past* (Piscataway, NJ: Transaction, 1968), 33.

2 The measure passed by a margin of 102,344 votes. See Brown, "Suffrage and Music," 173.

3 *New Republic*, vol. 12, no. 158 (November 10, 1917).

4 S. Josephine Baker, *Fighting for Life* (New York: New York Review of Books, 2013), 200; "Reminiscences of Frances Perkins," 199.

5 "Roosevelt Helps Suffs Celebrate," *New York Sun*, November 21, 1917, 5.

6 "Will Accept Wreath," *Brooklyn Daily Eagle*, December 2, 1917, 36; "Mrs. Whitehouse to Accept Wreath from Suffragists," *New York Tribune*, December 1, 1917.

7 Carrie Chapman Catt and Nettie Rogers Shuler, *Woman Suffrage and Politics: The Inner Story of the Suffrage Movement* (Seattle: University of Washington Press, 1969).

8 Peck, *Carrie Chapman Catt*, 280.

9 Peck, *Carrie Chapman Catt*, 437; Leila Rupp, "Sexuality and Politics in the Early Twentieth Century: The Case of the International Women's Movement," *Feminist Studies*, vol. 23, no. 3 (Autumn 1997), 585.

10 Stanton et al., *History of Woman Suffrage*, vol. 5, *1900–1920*, 276–77, 678.

11 Ford, *Iron-Jawed Angels*, 33.

12 Patricia Greenwood Harrison, *Connecting Links: The British and American Woman Suffrage Movements, 1900–1914* (Westport, CT: Greenwood, 2000), 185.

13 Kris Ann Cappelluti, "The Confines of Class: Alva Belmont and the Politics of Woman Suffrage" (master's thesis, Sarah Lawrence College, 1995), 33.

14 Peck, *Carrie Chapman Catt*, 170.

15 Cappelluti, "The Confines of Class," 28–29.

16 Rose Schneiderman and Lucy Goldthwaite, *All for One* (New York: Eriksson, 1967), 91–92.

17 Ford, *Iron-Jawed Angels*, 107; see also Cott, *The Grounding of Modern Feminism*, 56.

18 "Why Women Want to Vote," Tamiment Library and Robert F. Wagner Labor Archives, Printed Ephemera, boxes 18 and 21, New York University.

19 Adickes, *To Be Young Was Very Heaven*, 95.

20 Cappelluti, "The Confines of Class," 29–30.

21 Edge, *We Stand as One*, 83–84.

22 Berg, *Kate Remembered*, 44.

23 Letter from Katharine Houghton Hepburn to Alice Paul, January 15, 1914, National Woman's Party Papers, reel 6, frame 1301, Belmont-Paul Women's Equality National Monument, Washington, D.C.

24 Hoffert, *Alva Vanderbilt Belmont*, 226, fn 131.

25 Hoffert, *Alva Vanderbilt Belmont*, 141–43.

26 Stuart, *Consuelo and Alva Vanderbilt*, 445.

27 Geidel, "Alva E. Belmont," 732. Her children requested that the funeral take place at St. Thomas Episcopal Church, where there were no female clergy.

28 Hoffert, *Alva Vanderbilt Belmont*, 181.

29 Douglas Keister, *Stories in Stone New York: A Field Guide to New York City Area Cemeteries and Their Residents* (Layton, UT: Gibbs Smith, 2011), 54–55.

30 Stanford, *Wicked Newport*, 56.

31 Keister, *Stories in Stone New York*, 54–55.

32 Tetrault, *The Myth of Seneca Falls*, 4–5; Kerr, *Lucy Stone*, 52–55.

33 Letter from Abigail Adams to John Adams, March 31, 1776, available at Hanover College History Department website, history.hanover.edu.

34 Elizabeth Cady Stanton, Susan B. Anthony, and Matilda Joslyn Gage, *History of Woman Suffrage, 1861–1876* (New York: Susan B. Anthony, 1881), 94–95.

35 DuBois, *Harriot Stanton Blatch*, 260.

36 Catt and Shuler, *Woman Suffrage and Politics*, 280.

37 Leila J. Rupp and Verta A. Taylor, *Survival in the Doldrums: The American Women's Rights Movement, 1945 to the 1960s* (Oxford: Oxford University Press, 1987), 26.

38 Letter from Carrie Chapman Catt to Alice Paul, April 12, 1915, Alice Paul Papers, box 16, folder 230, Schlesinger Library.

39 Letter from Alice Paul to Carrie Chapman Catt, April 15, 1915, Alice Paul Papers, box 16, folder 230.

40 Crystal Eastman, "Alice Paul's Convention," *Liberator*, April 1921, 9.

41 Correspondence between Carrie Chapman Catt and Alice Paul, April–June 1915, Alice Paul Papers, box 16, folder 230.

42 Nancy F. Cott, "Feminist Politics in the 1920s: The National Woman's Party," *Journal of American History*, vol. 71, no. 1 (June 1984), 46.

43 Crocker, *Mrs. Russell Sage*, ix.

44 Because of the Women's Trade Union League's activism, and the clever ploy of suffrage leaders in putting the wives of Tammany Hall officials on their boards, New York's machine politicians, longtime foes of expanding the electorate to include women, were now "shrewd enough to read the political winds." As one suffragist said after the victory, "We owe a great debt to Tammany Hall." The cross-class coalition of working class and gilded class had convinced the political establishment that suffrage was inevitable, that change was coming, and some, such as Tammany boss Charlie Murphy, even rushed to join the bandwagon. See Van Voris, *Carrie Chapman Catt*, 147; and Alexander Keyssar, *The Right to Vote: The Contested History of Democracy in the United States* (New York: Basic Books, 2009), 173.

45 Mary Alden Hopkins, "Women March" (1912), in Chapman and Mills, *Treacherous Texts*, 197.

46 Letter from Alice Paul to Phoebe Hearst, January 27, 1917, Phoebe Apperson Hearst Papers, reel 73, box 47, folder 5–6, University of California at Berkeley.

47 Fowler and Jones, "Carrie Chapman Catt and the Last Years of the Struggle for Woman Suffrage," 139.

48 Van Voris, *Carrie Chapman Catt*, 143.

49 "Reminiscences of Frances Perkins," 190.

50 Holly J. McCammon et al., "How Movements Win: Gendered Opportunity Structures and U.S. Women's Suffrage Movements, 1866 to 1919," *American Sociological Review*, vol. 66, no. 1 (February 1, 2001), 49.

51 Kevin Francis White, "The Flapper's Boyfriend: The Revolution in Morals and the Emergence of Modern American Male Sexuality, 1910–1930" (Ph.D. diss., Ohio State University, 1990), 242.

52 "Suffragists Dine, Put Men in Gallery," *New York Times*, November 22, 1917, 15.

53 George Creel, *How We Advertised America: The First Telling of the Amazing Story of the Committee on Public Information That Carried the Gospel of Americanism to Every Corner of the Globe* (New York: Harper and Brothers, 1920), 317.

54 Gregg Wolper, *The Origins of Public Diplomacy: Woodrow Wilson, George Creel, and the Committee on Public Information* (Chicago: University of Chicago, Department of History, 1991), 228.

55 Letter from Mary Garrett Hay to Maud Wood Park, November 23, 1918, Mary Garrett Hay Folder, Woman's Rights Collection, folder 79, Schlesinger Library.

56 Vira Boarman Whitehouse, *A Year as a Government Agent* (New York: Harper and Brothers, 1920), 30–35.

57 Wolper, *The Origins of Public Diplomacy*, 230–34.

58 "Women Pay Tribute to Mrs. Whitehouse," *New York Times*, February 9, 1919.

59 Robert A. Schanke, "Mercedes de Acosta," www.robertschanke.com; see also Robert A. Schanke, *That Furious Lesbian: The Story of Mercedes de Acosta* (Carbondale: Southern Illinois University Press, 2004).

60 "Rich Rivals Plan for Suffrage Fight," *New York American*, August 18, 1909, Mackay Family Scrapbooks, reel 6.

61 Buhle, *Women and American Socialism*, 225.

62 Manning, *Ladies Now and Then*, 101.

63 Owen Wister, *Roosevelt: The Story of a Friendship* (New York: Macmillan, 1930), 202.

Index

About the Author

JOHANNA NEUMAN is an author, historian, and Scholar in Residence at American University in Washington, D.C. A former journalist for the *Los Angeles Times* and *USA Today*, she covered the White House, the State Department, Congress, and the Smithsonian Institution. A former Nieman Fellow at Harvard University, she also served as president of the White House Correspondents Association in 1989–1990. Now a full-time writer and lecturer, she lives with Jeff Glazer in Delray Beach, Florida.